SLACKER, MBA

A Business Memoir

By

Michael Pollard

Table of Contents

Introduction	1
Slacker Beginnings	4
Prepping for Espionage	10
All's Well in Chernobyl	15
Welcome to the Real World	33
Beginning a Career in Finance	42
Eyes on the Prize	48
Hit the Beach	52
MBA Year Two	67
Lightning Strikes	87
King of Queens	98
The Power of Coffee	109
The Great New York City Job Search	110
The Big Cheese	125
Russia is… Casino	140
Back in the CIS	148
Leaving Moscow	160
Big Bob	166
It's the Pits	178
Rags to Riches	184
Things Get Ugly	189
Muddling Through	194
Downward Spiral	200
Hyper Capitalism	203
Out West	205
Another Crash	211
Back East	214
Procuring a New Job	218
No More Debt	227
The Big Box Grind	230
7 Nights a Week	235
Hot for Teaching	240
Back to Big Box	247
Girls Against Boys	249
Hey Mike, Get a Life	253
Best Wedding Ever	257
The Best Years Ever	260
The End of the Book?	263

Introduction

I was sitting there in the lounge of the Jiffy Lube in Washington, DC. Or was it Precision Tune? It could have been either one, because the car was going to get a check up in a jiffy, and it would cost precisely $19.99. That is if I wanted the mechanics to just look at it, tell me what was wrong with it, and then not fix anything. A friendly service representative would poke his head out every few minutes, and give me a good look at a sample of one of the defective fluids of the defective, old family car that was mine now.

"Here's your brake fluid, it looks terrible, want us to replace it? It will cost more if we do," he asked. "Ok, replace it," I replied. He went back to the car, and I wondered, does anybody actually just pay $19.99? If I thought everything was going to check out fine, I probably would not be here, would I? I knew what to do. When all the work was finished I would drive straight to another Jiffy Tune location, or a Precision Lube location, whatever, and get another $19.99 check up.

"Here's your brake fluid, it's beautiful! Looks brand new. Want us to replace it? It will cost more if we do," he would ask. "No, leave it as it is. Thanks for asking though!" Excellent. Precisely $19.99.

My auto repair fantasy was interrupted by a special report on the lounge TV. Special reports can give you a chill down your spine in that brief interval when you know the report is coming, but you have no idea what it is about. I got a chill and then some when I saw the expression on the news anchor's face. He looked worried. I was scared just looking at him.

It was Monday, October 19, 1987. Black Monday. Today we think of it as the day of the record drop in the stock market. Now we know that the market stopped dropping, and eventually recovered. But not that day. Nobody knew what was going to happen, especially not this news anchor, and his face showed it. The break fluid did not seem so important anymore.

I suppose a lot of people heard about the crash after the fact, summed up nicely in articles and news stories, and it was just more bad news in the paper. To me though, Black Monday was one of those days I will always remember, like people remember where they were and what they were doing when John F. Kennedy was shot. But I will not go on and on about it, because bad things happen from time to time, and one should expect that. For me, though, Black Monday was the symbolic beginning of our time, the "Slackers" or "Generation X." The economy did not suddenly enter a recession, unemployment did not double overnight, and most people's lives were not changed radically that day. The crash was something that happened up there on Wall Street. But somewhere around that time things did begin to change, slowly but steadily. Bright young people of my generation stopped expecting to get everything they wanted, and started taking whatever they could get.

Thinking back on all that has happened to me in my career, it is hard for me to believe. But this is no sob story. I am in good health, I have enough to eat, and I have a good education behind me. Most importantly I have a family I can count on. I realize countless Americans have had it much worse; my story is just a bit more incredible than most. When I was in college in the mid-1980's I could not have imagined all of the surprises life had in store for me.

I brought a lot of what happened to me upon myself by taking many risks early in my career during an economic period when risk taking was dangerous. But, like they used to say in the old beer commercial, you only go around once, right? So why not go for the gusto? What does gusto mean anyway? Ok, the dictionary says, "hearty enjoyment." Not just enjoyment, *hearty* enjoyment. The first thing that springs to my mind when I hear "hearty enjoyment" is a six pack of Guinness. Anyway, the risk taking actually came from the high expectations many of us had who came of age in the 1980's, watching yuppies and their fast track careers. This was an affliction of my age group. Most young people today do not have this and you can see the hopelessness in their faces. They expect nothing more than to move back in with mom and dad and make whatever they can, which usually is not much. At least I had some hope. For the *gusto* that is.

In addition to my search for the gusto, or maybe as a part of it, I am a big music fan. I thought a lot about David Grohl lately, who is a drummer. I like the way he plays, and so do a lot of other people; he was a member of the famous Seattle "grunge" band Nirvana and went on to front the band Foo Fighters. During my college years I played drums as well, for a punk band out of Baltimore. David is a few years younger than I am, but like me, he is from the Washington, DC area. The difference between David and me is that although I loved the drums, I was smart enough to give them up when I finished college. He dropped out of high school to play drums full time. I became serious, pursued a career in business, acquired work experience in finance, and eventually went on to receive an MBA from an internationally respected university. Oh, one other difference between David and me. He has a huge bank account. It makes me laugh to think that I might be better off today if I had just stayed in Baltimore, kept playing those drums, and taken any job I could get on the side.

Slacker Beginnings

All my years growing up, at school, at home, and even on Saturday morning TV public service ads, one idea was drilled into my head... do well in school, then you will do well in life. And I bought into this myth, studying hard and getting good grades through junior high and high school. This is not to discount the value of a good education, if I had it to do all over again I would work just as hard in school. But being knowledgeable about a lot of subjects, while terrific for cocktail parties and for one's self esteem, does not mean a whole lot in terms of a career.

Getting those good grades in high school was more of an achievement for me than for most of the overachievers with whom I went to college. This was because my high school, located a few miles east of Washington, DC in Maryland, was a sacred holy place in the religion of underachievement. A's were for atheists in this religion and the trick for potential problem cases like myself was to not care during the day, then study like my life depended on it at night to make sure I was prepared for the exams and quizzes. There was a program to protect non-believers in underachievement, it was called TAG (Talented and Gifted). TAG only classes were created to shield hard working students from fundamentalist oppression in the religion of underachievement, the "we're going down and we're going to drag everyone down with us" mentality of most public school students.

The thing was, I carried some of the underachiever mentality with me during the day too, and with one or two others became infiltrators in these advanced placement classes. Many of my classes consisted of a few dozen well groomed and attentive students and two or three scrappy looking, flannel shirt and rock t-shirt wearing students who sat in the back corner of the room; students who, even though they also received good grades, pretended that they did not care. I was one of these. You see, I started playing drums at age twelve and I was such a cool dude, or wanted to be, that while racking up straight A's toward the end of junior high I mocked all the trappings of scholastic achievement. I was voted "Most Intelligent" in my ninth grade class but I dissed the National Junior Honor Society by never attending the meetings. When the time came for an entrance exam into a "technical" high school (school with advanced math and science classes for above average students) I did not bother to take it. I made a deliberate choice to go to the screw up school because it was "cool," even though I still intended on doing well academically.

To me, my high school was a beautiful place. There was little or no enforcement of the rules. The first time I was absent I brought a note in the next day and got one of those yellow slips for my teacher to sign. When I presented this slip to my music teacher he chuckled a bit. "We don't bother with those things here," he said, and that was fine with me. He was right, you could skip classes, ignore your teachers, abuse your teachers, as long as your body was at school reasonably often and you stayed enrolled until graduation the administration was happy. I was happy too.

Each morning upon arriving at school one was treated to a crowd of white students in the parking lot, smoking cigarettes next to their tricked out cars straight out of "World of Wheels." Once inside the building you were in the black students' territory. They ruled the hallways in groups of ten or so with boom boxes blasting out homegrown DC funk called "go-go music" or, if they did not have a boom box, making their own music. They would chant, "Do it one time for the Maryland crew y'all…" as hands, pens, and pencils banged out wicked percussive beats onto the walls, metal beams, and windows of our school. It was one big playground and I loved it.

My favorite high school activity was not an afterschool hobby club, or an academic society, or even a sports team. It was simply hanging around doing nothing with a friend or two, making profound statements like "that's cool" or "shit man." The official uniform for this activity was a flannel shirt, long hair in my face, and a few days' growth on my chin.

I was a good soccer player in high school, but I was anything but a jock in attitude. In fact, I was very anti-jock, and thankfully so were most of the people in our school relative to other schools. The ultimate achievement on our soccer team was to be cool, to be good without practicing, and to win without trying.

My first taste of the real world came through soccer. With the encouragement of my high school coach I contacted a good number of college coaches my junior year. I wrote of my interest in each coach's school and its soccer team, and mentioned that I was a goalkeeper who had received recognition on my team and in the DC area for my play that year. The idea was to perk their interest so that they might watch my progress in my senior year. Hopefully then they would offer me a scholarship or at least recruit me to attend their school and to play on their team. I received responses from almost all the coaches with brochures and press guides to their teams, and one coach from an Ivy League school also sent me a brochure for a summer soccer camp in which he was involved. He noted in his letter that this camp would be of great benefit to me, and that I could meet him in person there.

So, good old mom was nice enough to send me to New England for a week to hone my soccer skills and to do my first bit of networking. On the first full day of camp I was guarding the goal during a scrimmage, and marveling at the ball handling skills of some of the people in the game. There was definitely a choice group of soccer players at the camp. Soon the coach from the Ivy League school appeared, came over to the goal where I was stationed and introduced himself. When I mentioned my name and where I was from he said, "Oh yeah, you're from that good soccer area in Maryland, you wrote me, right?" This conversation seemed to be going well, unfortunately I was also involved in a game at the moment and my performance in this game would no doubt stick in his mind. I strained to keep the conversation going with one eye on the coach and one eye on the flow of the game.

The situation became more nerve racking as the other team advanced the ball into our half of the field and methodically worked their way toward our goal. I made one easy save, but a minute later they were on the attack again. A dive this time, but not too difficult, ok another save, then cleared the ball, all the while discussing my soccer background with this coach. As the other team made a third foray into our half, the coach mentioned that his school had been lucky enough to recruit a player who was rated as one of the top goalkeepers in the nation. So, I was told, if I were to come to his school to play I could expect to spend most of my time viewing from the sidelines. Just then an attacker broke through our defense. I went out to cut off the angle but too late, a nice fake and SWOOOOSH, that evil sound of the ball connecting with the back of the net. As I picked myself up off the ground the coach said, "Well it was nice meeting you, thanks for coming up to the camp (and thanks for your money, sucker)."

Of course he did not say "thanks for your money, sucker" but the point was moot anyway. The next fall in a preseason scrimmage my collarbone snapped and that was that. Out for the season. One college coach from my area still tried to recruit me with the line, "Apply to the school, then once you're in and practicing with the team we'll work on getting you a scholarship." I did not really want to go to that school anyway and I was not falling for that line. If I needed any confirmation of my suspicions, I got it when I met privately with a few of his freshmen players. They could not say enough nice things about their beloved coach… "Coach is a jerk, man," "Yeah, he told me I might get a scholarship, then I sat on the bench all year and didn't get anything."

As I said earlier, I loved the loose atmosphere of my school but I was only really a part of that atmosphere between classes. For the academic subjects like English, math, history, and science the advanced students were kept apart in an atmosphere very different from the rest of school. We were lucky enough to have some very good teachers as well so I did not really miss much by not attending the technical school. I was not interested in even the most standard high school activities like homecoming dances, which was just as well because there were not a lot of girls at the school interested in going with me to those dances as far as I could see. I admit though that I did become a member of the National Honor Society (NHS) but only because the faculty sponsor was cool. She was an advanced placement English teacher and a good one.

At the first meeting of the NHS all the Muffy Teppermans started to discuss how often the society should meet (to talk about how intelligent all of its members were I suppose). If you never watched the television show *Square Pegs* which ran while I was in high school in the early 1980's, Muffy Tepperman was the ultimate preppy who got top grades and had to participate in every student government activity and extracurricular club. Anyway, the NHS faculty sponsor broke into the conversation and said, "All you have to do is meet once more, at the end of the school year to pick up your gold tassels for the graduation ceremony." Ha ha, sweet! I never saw so many disappointed faces in my life.

It was not always easy trying to be an honor roll student and a screw up drummer at the same time. In my junior year I got straight A's one quarter and made the mistake of letting someone else see the report card. One of my underachiever wannabe friends from my advanced English class abused me, following me down the hallway to my next class. He pointed his finger at my head the whole way announcing very loudly, "hey, this guy got straight A's, he got straight A's, this guy got straight A's." Another time I was home on a Friday night and I had the achievement tests the next day (similar to SAT's but they test one's knowledge of particular subject areas like math, history, and science). There is not much you can do to prepare for these the night before except get a good night's rest, but I could not even do that. Around 9pm that night the guitar player from my band showed up at my house unannounced with his van and easily talked me into going out for a little while. About five hours and some underage beers later I was home, and I needed to be up around 6am for the exam. Amazingly I still bagged an impressive 770 out of 800 on the US History achievement test, a great slacker achievement, excelling without caring.

On the last day of high school I had one more final exam. The first class of my day was a joke elective called "Basic Guitar," and even less learning than usual was taking place in "Basic Guitar" on that last day of the year. So, I got out my history text and started reviewing for the exam next period. The singer for my band caught sight of me and burst out laughing. He said, "Christ, Pollard, it's the *last* day of school, don't you ever stop? Give it a rest man!"

I started laughing too, it *was* the last day of school, I was already accepted into Johns Hopkins University, what the hell was I doing? There was just something inside me, a certain competitiveness I guess, that drove me to do well on exams. I liked to screw around in high school but when push came to shove I usually did the "right" thing, the "smart" thing. I was constantly torn between hanging out with the underage drinking, class skipping rockers and the always studying academic overachievers. I did things with people from both groups, I had friends in both groups, but I never was completely a part of either group. I was the "brain" of the screw up group, the "rebel" (if there can be such a thing) of the advanced placement group.

Prepping for Espionage

So, I had the grades, the SAT scores, the Advanced Placement (AP) credits, and the Muffy Tepperman gold tassels for graduation day. Now it was payoff time. I was accepted into Johns Hopkins University, placed out of two years of history requirements with my AP exam scores, and I would begin my bachelors degree in international relations. The international relations degree was probably Hopkins' most demanding non-science degree, with stiff requirements of languages, economics, history, and political science. With two years of history out of the way before I started, I was able to double up on the languages, four years each of Russian and French. I was on the road to big success.

Basically my plan was to have a career like Jack Ryan of Tom Clancy's novels (*The Hunt for the Red October*, *Patriot Games*). I would be a superstar spy, government foreign policy expert, published college professor, with a beautiful wife who is a top eye surgeon at Johns Hopkins Hospital. She drives a cool European sports car, has a few kids with me, does not mind that I disappear for months at a time to go spying, and even finishes surgery in time to come home and make dinner for me and the kids in our big house overlooking the Chesapeake Bay. I figured this all would happen by my late twenties.

The first day of orientation at Johns Hopkins we listened to a speech by our slick, well dressed, and well-tanned president. He was renowned for his fundraising abilities, which helped support the construction of many beautiful new buildings during my four years at Hopkins. He was also renowned for his skill with the tanning oil, so much so that Hopkins students called him the "Tan Man." Our president was the only person at Johns Hopkins with a tan in January.

The thrust of Tan Man's speech to us was that regardless of what we thought at the time, most of us would not end up having the career we planned on having. We should take great pains to learn all that we could, practical skills that would help us in many areas, and intellectual subjects simply for our own personal enrichment. To emphasize this last point he brought up the example of those who study subjects like art history, the classics, or anthropology, which did not prepare students for fast track, high paying careers. "I think that's great, the woman who works as a cashier at the grocery store who did her degree in art history for the love of the subject." A nice sentiment, but what the Tan Man did not mention was that it takes a lot of double shifts at the grocery store to pay for a Hopkins education. This did not concern me anyway, I was too smart for all this silly talk. I was destined for great success, I was sure of that.

    I studied hard just like everyone at Johns Hopkins. I mean I had plenty of fun times, parties, and beer, but Hopkins was no party school. The atmosphere was like night and day from my high school. More often than not I was ready to party and everyone else was studying, so I would break down and study some more. In high school there was peer pressure not to study, but at Johns Hopkins it was the opposite. You made sure you studied so you would not look like a moron in class and when the grades came out.

    There were many nicknames at Hopkins for people who studied all the time… "geek," "dweeb," "throat" (short for cutthroat). Nowhere was this competitive attitude more evident than in what the pre meds called the "Zeke 500." This was a race of sorts, but slightly different from the Indy 500. Two of the more important pre med classes were scheduled one after the other, and in the ten minute interval between the two there was a sprint from one building to the next. Pre med students from the first class were racing each other across campus, the prize for the winners being the best seats in the second lecture, closest to the board. But to laugh too hard at the pre med sprinters was only to delude oneself. As a friend of mine put it, "everyone at Hopkins is a dweeb, if you weren't you wouldn't be here."

Ever the rebel, I did not go in for the fraternity thing at Johns Hopkins. Although I had plenty of college friends who were in frats, I spent a lot of my free time involved in the local punk rock scene. Toward the end of high school I caught on to punk rock, as well as the early rap music, trashed my stadium rock t-shirts and cut my hair short. Washington, DC was a city on the forefront of hardcore punk rock in the early 1980's. Much of the DC punk was very positive, encouraging young people to think for themselves and to be themselves. Many punks followed a set of ideas called "straightedge" which typically meant no alcohol and no drugs, but the core of the philosophy was using your head and taking responsibility for you own actions. As a smaller version of the DC punk scene developed in Baltimore I got involved, playing drums for a band, skateboarding around town, and even giving up beer. After a year or so I decided to drink beer socially again.

Oftentimes these punk shows in Washington and Baltimore were located in halls or warehouses in predominately black areas, and this would cause some entertaining culture clashes. One night I was outside a punk show at the Wilson Center (actually in the basement of a church in Northwest DC) when two black men from the neighborhood turned the corner and were amazed to see a crowd of about one hundred white kids there, all dressed in black, Doc Marten boots, flipping around on skateboards. The two men just stood there for a minute taking it all in, then one began a speech, a sarcastic call to arms to the punks. "Damn boy, would you look at that!" he shouted. "Serious punk rock, aww shit. Naw, that's alright though, that's alright, y'all bad though, serious. Y'all gotta get yourselves organized though. I don't know, do something, make a movie or something. Yeah, that's it, make a movie. You can call it 'How the Punks Took Reagan!' Yeah, that's it, that's what y'all need to do!"

Things have not changed much in DC over the years, styles are different but disparate groups of people are still struggling to coexist. Years after the Wilson Center show I mentioned, I saw an underground "death metal" show in Washington with a friend. The band names were "Morbius" and "Corpse Grinder" and they played heavy metal where the guitars rage at triple speed, band members have hair in their faces, and the singers scream in deep evil voices. The show took place in a tiny club on the second floor of the building. On the first floor was an Ethiopian restaurant. Best of all, the only way to get to the club was to walk through the Ethiopian restaurant and up the stairs to the second floor. Probably not a great night out for the Ethiopian clientele. First they have their appetizers interrupted by groups of black clad, long haired metalheads stomping between their tables. Then when it is time for the main course, they have to hold their vibrating tables still while shouting dinner conversation to each other over the soothing sounds of Corpse Grinder.

For two summers during my college years I had a job as an intern at the Pentagon. Every Friday I would leave my job at the Pentagon and take a train up to Baltimore to practice, perform, and hang out with my punk rock band. The military officers with whom I worked at the Pentagon were all great guys, most in their 30's and 40's. These were sharp guys stuck at desk jobs as there were no major military operations taking place at the time. One officer named Navy Commander Smith and I used to talk fairly often. He was a baseball expert and knew more about sports in general than almost anyone I have ever met. He could recite batting averages to you on a daily basis, "let's see, George Brett went 2 for 4 last night, that should put him at about .298 for the season, with a .678 slugging percentage."

The week after the Live Aid Concert, the benefit which included all the major stars in pop music to raise money for Ethiopian famine relief, I asked Commander Smith if he had seen the concert. Did he like it at all? He replied, "it was the biggest collection of misfits and rejects ever assembled in one place." I did not exactly agree, but I thought that was a pretty cool thing to say. I watched Live Aid in the Baltimore rowhouse where my band's singer and bass player lived and where we practiced. The house doubled as a crash pad for punk bands on tour when they played a show in Baltimore. On Live Aid weekend a punk band called DOA was staying at the rowhouse, and I watched Live Aid with a few members of my band and some of the DOA guys. None of the punks seemed very impressed by the concert and hurled abuse at every band that came on stage. I bet Navy Commander Smith never realized he had the same taste in music as DOA, they both hated Live Aid!

All's Well In Chernobyl

After the first few years of college my Russian professor announced to the class that a half dozen of us, as a result of our superior performance in our Russian classes, had qualified as candidates for a co-op program with the NSA as Russian translator/analysts. This only reinforced my belief that with a lot of hard work, determination, and good grades you can do anything you want. Everything was going according to plan with my career. Now all I had to do was find the cute eye surgeon and start scoping out property on the Chesapeake Bay.

Remember what I said in the introduction about taking risks and going for the gusto? For a month at the end of my junior year in college I went on a Russian language immersion program to Moscow, USSR. And? What's so gusto about that? Well, it was the summer immediately after the disaster at the nuclear reactor in Chernobyl; this in fact was how I managed to get a place on the trip at the last minute. A few students dropped out of the program because they were concerned about the possible health risks of going to the Soviet Union at the time. But not me.

While it was an amazing trip and I learned a lot, it amounted to the first major blunder of my career. I was a book smart young man but a bit clueless about the working world and classified government work in particular. In the middle of a lengthy background investigation by the NSA to verify that I could be trusted to translate and analyze Soviet communications, I went on a study trip to the Soviet Union. And I did not think to tell the NSA that I was going! Oops. NSA employees work under strict travel guidelines for good reason, an employee basically needs to get special permission to go anywhere, and never would a junior NSA Russian analyst be allowed to travel to the USSR, ever. Too risky for the US government.

I had to go for the gusto, didn't I? When I got back from the trip there was another in a series of many interviews I had with the NSA. They asked me casually, "So, how was your summer, what did you do?" "Oh, I studied Russian in the Soviet Union," I said nonchalantly, expecting them to be impressed at my initiative in improving my Russian. My two interviewers flipped! "You did what?!" one said. I had just destroyed their day. They did not immediately tell me I was out of the running for the position, the process continued of course, but I had ruined everything. The two men spent hours questioning me about everything I did and everyone with whom I spoke in Moscow for a report they would have to write about my Russian immersion trip to the USSR. Regardless of my Russian language skills and my patriotism, I was not getting that job.

Anyway, let me tell you about the costly trip, relatively inexpensive in dollars but quite costly for my career. Chernobyl coverage dominated the news on the whopping selection of four television channels in Moscow. No ESPN, no MTV, no Comedy Channel. Some of the Soviet shows I saw were better than the Comedy Channel. The words I heard over and over were "fsyo normalno, fsyo normalno" (everything's fine, everything's back to normal). I guess that depends on your definition of "normalno." A nuclear reactor in flames, radiation everywhere, hmmm. Another useful Russian phrase I learned watching Soviet news was "menshe i menshe"(fewer and fewer). Reporters assured TV viewers that menshe i menshe people were coming to hospitals and clinics in the Chernobyl area every day. Sure, because the rest were dead now. What next? Menshe i menshe cows born with five legs on Chernobyl area farms? Menshe i menshe Soviet morons in the Kremlin? One could only hope.

I remember one news story in particular meant to assuage our fears showing a Russian man with a remote control device in his hands. It was kind of like the ones that go with those

Radio Shack remote control cars that make great Christmas gifts. He was using it to control a driverless bulldozer; the plan was to clear radioactive debris from the Chernobyl site, without endangering the lives of those involved in the cleanup operation. Problem was, this bulldozer was only as big as I am, and it was about as well constructed as most things Soviet. The man with the remote seemed so proud of the machine as it chugged along at a few miles per hour, struggling to move small piles of dirt and pebbles. I doubt it could have moved a molehill, let alone tons of radioactive debris. The bulldozer was a failure in every way, too small to clean up Chernobyl and too big to sell at Radio Shack.

The Soviet tour guide for our group in Moscow was a nice middle aged Russian mother and housewife named Natasha. Natasha helped us check into our hotel where we were introduced to the good life, Soviet style. The bathroom in my hotel room was so small that you had to back in, then close the door. The sink in the bathroom came in handy for washing my clothes as there was no laundry service available. And, the sleeping accommodations were meant for guests much shorter than I am. At 6'3" my feet, ankles, and calves dangled off the edge of the bed as I slept each night.

Meals at the hotel's restaurant were never dull; some nights the food was surprisingly good while other times it was pretty harsh. One day we were served nice hot bowls of chicken soup for lunch (yes! a good day I thought). That's it, dig in! I took my first big spoonful of soup, making sure to get plenty of chicken with the broth, mmmm. The chicken was a bit chewy though. Wait, it was really chewy. Oh man, it was like gum. Brand new from the Colonel, it's Chernobyl Fried Chicken. It actually was not chicken at all, it was fat. Finely cut, tasty chunks of fat in a delicate fat broth.

Another day our group rose early for breakfast, and soft Russian music was playing in the hotel restaurant. We settled down with some tea and bread, then it happened. Mood change. Out of nowhere, those first few chords of AC/DC's metal hit "You Shook Me All Night Long" rang out. Beautiful. I do not know who, or why, but it was 8:30am. I suspected that a few members of the restaurant staff name Yuri and Oleg were responsible. These guys were always up to something.

A few other students in the group and I drank vodka with Yuri and Oleg one afternoon when the restaurant was empty. I made a deal, a couple of my blank cassette tapes for a bottle of Stolichnaya from the restaurant. I think our Soviet tour guide Natasha got wise to the Stoli party because a day or two later our group was informed, "We are not able to eat in that restaurant now, there is problem with pipes, we must eat in other restaurant in hotel." Later a few of us happened to stroll by that restaurant with the faulty pipes… gee, it was packed with hotel guests enjoying more fat soup. Quick repair job there. There were two restaurants in the hotel but our group never ate in the restaurant where Yuri and Oleg worked for the remainder of our stay.

Later in the same week Natasha gave us some strange advice at the lunch table. As she left us for the day she said, "Now all of you, just keep healthy, do whatever you want, enjoy yourself, but don't do anything you will regret later. Goodbye for now." Ok? One of my friends in our group whispered, "She's KGB man, you know she is!"

The Soviets did not play around when it came to education; most of the crew from my high school would not have lasted a day in a Soviet classroom. Our young Russian language teacher Tatiana could speak English very well but she never uttered a word to us in any language but Russian. Classes were six days a week, from the early morning until the middle of the afternoon, and not a minute of class time was wasted. Tatiana was a pretty brunette, and a very nice person overall, but very strict and serious when it came to teaching. It was sad to watch her lead our lessons, Tatiana was obviously very bright but she was forced to tow the Soviet party line in classroom discussions. The subject of cold war politics would inevitably rear its ugly head, and Tatiana made statements like, "Soviets know the USSR is not a rich country like the United States, but that is because the American military buildup has forced us to spend everything on our defense."

I liked Tatiana, she had a good heart, so I rarely argued with her over her many dubious comparisons of the United States and the Soviet Union. For example, "Soviet newspapers are better than American newspapers. You see, Soviet papers such as *Pravda* cover the entire USSR, while in America you only have newspapers for each city such as the *Washington Post* and the *New York Times*." The saddest day in class was a discussion we had about an article in *Pravda* (the word "pravda" means truth in Russian). The article described a peace demonstration in the United States and it was accompanied by a photo that obviously had been tampered with. The protesters carried signs, one said "Peace to the Nations of the World!" and another said in Russian (!) "Mir Miru!" (Peace to the World!)

These slogans were mainstays in the list of top Soviet clichés, but generally unheard of outside of the USSR. And as for one slogan being in the Russian language at an American peace demonstration, well, no comment. I just cringed when I saw the picture (no, please Tatiana, skip to the next page, ok?!). Some people in our class liked to argue more than I did, and I could not bear to watch. The debate was about as one sided as a basketball game between the Chicago Bulls (American students) and the Johns Hopkins basketball team (Tatiana). Unfortunately, there was no way for Tatiana to know the picture was a fake, she never had the opportunity to visit the United States, nor had she ever read newspapers such as the *Washington Post* and the

New York Times. Memories of the Soviet Union such as these made me ecstatic when the hardline Soviet coup failed in 1991 and democratic reforms began in earnest (short lived of course).

Tatiana's wardrobe was enough to make an American feel like a spoiled brat. She had two teaching outfits, and she wore one of the two every day, sometimes the same one for several days at a stretch. The standard of living was obviously much lower in the Soviet Union than in the United States, and many services in the USSR left a lot to be desired. Dental care was a good example. Russians have a habit of putting about ten sugar cubes in each cup of tea and Soviet dentistry just could not stem the tide of tooth decay. Many older Soviets had mouths full of black teeth and metal fillings. One day Tatiana appeared in class with a kerchief wrapped around her head, moaning about her toothache. Although I did feel bad for her, she definitely played her misfortune for all it was worth. Russians that I met tended to wallow in misery, and they were very pessimistic about things.

Russians also seemed to have a talent for being brutally honest and to the point. They did not mean to be rude or insulting, but sometimes it could sound that way to an American ear. Conversations often lacked the superfluous pleasantries you might find in the English language, as evidenced by the way Tatiana would answer the phone in our classroom. Where in English one might say, "Hello, who's calling please?" Tatiana's telephone etiquette amounted to "Slushayu" (I'm listening). In class once Tatiana gave us a heart warming compliment on our progress in learning her native language. She said, "This is a good class, better than the others I have had except one, that one was much better than you." Thanks loads, Tatiana!

Our only respite from the classes were tea breaks several times a day which were signaled by Tatiana giving a tired sigh, smiling, and saying, "Pora otdikhat, da?" (Time to relax, yes?) While we were in the lounge area enjoying our Russian tea Tatiana would often pass us walking down the corridor. Her serious demeanor left behind in the classroom, she would always grin and ask, "Otdikhaitye, da? (You are relaxing, yes?) Sure, Tatiana, who needs Club Med when you can otdikhat in the Evil Empire?

These tea breaks were quite a welcome breather from the rigors of class. Every second was utilized to drill us in Russian grammar, vocabulary, literature, and some Soviet politics as well. There is an expression Russians and Americans share, "Povtoreniye mat ucheniya" (Repetition is the mother of learning), and we lived this in class every day. If a student's answer did not match the answer we had been taught word for word, the student's answer was wrong. After being informed of the correct word for word answer, the student was required to repeat it. One morning we were covering the Soviet role in the Second World War. Tatiana asked, "Who were the first into Berlin?" "Russkiye soldati," (Russian soldiers) I droned. "Not correct... the Soviets... the Soviet people," my teacher replied. "Sovietskii narod," (the Soviet people) I repeated like a trained monkey. We jumped through hoops like this all day long.

A favorite technique for teaching Russian was to have us learn and sing a song in the language. Of course, one of the first songs we learned was the Russian classic "Katyusha," a must for any Soviet record collection. It was the story of a woman who waits faithfully for her soldier to return from the war. It was funny though, every time we finished singing "Katyusha" our teacher would say, "Of course, this is a song of wartime, now we have peace, so is this an appropriate way for a man and a woman to talk with each other?" "Nyet, Tatiana," we would answer in unison.

"Of course it is not," Tatiana would say, seemingly satisfied. So satisfied that I often wondered if some young Russian soldier had promised to return to her and then left her high and dry. Later on in the program a class member mentioned that one of the other Russian instructors was about to get married. Tatiana said, "Yes, that is correct, soon she will be married. I however, have not been able to marry," her voice trailing off at the end. Poor Tatiana, too much sugar, not enough Crest to fight the Cavity Creeps. Poor Tatiana, dissed by a soldier, old maid still in her twenties, her life was full of sadness. Hey Tatiana… otdikhaitye (chill out) baby.

After class on most days the group went on guided tours, "excursions" as they liked to call them. These included art museums, history museums, historical sights, the circus, and the Moscow Zoo. The zoo was the most incredible, but for all the wrong reasons. One of Ronald Reagan's famous soundbites of the 1980's was that "there is no word for 'freedom' in the Russian language." Well here is another word they do not have in Russian… SPCA. If you do not believe me you should have seen the Moscow Zoo back in 1986. Those of us with a sick sense of humor had a field day there. First was the elephant area, which was surrounded not with a fence but huge metal spikes (!) in the ground. That ought to keep the elephants where they belong. And then there were the giant eagles, confined in areas smaller than their wingspan. Why didn't they just put a straightjacket on the things? There were animals with dirty, disheveled fur everywhere limping around, chests like xylophones, in areas about as removed from their natural habitat as one could imagine. What a treat for the kids!

Finally there was the polar bear area. Here is something the Soviets should have been able to get right. If anybody knows polar bears, it is the men who conquered Siberia. It turned out that most of the polar bears were not white, they were a light brown color. This might have been caused by the fact that it was the middle of the summer and they were kept in a hot, dirty, dusty area without much vegetation. One of the bears looked delirious, pacing back and forth, unsuccessfully trying to get at some fish that had been left out for him. Unfortunately a swarm of birds, that were not even a part of the zoo, were chowing down on what should have been his dinner that afternoon. One had to wonder how many days in a row this had gone on.

My memories of the trip to the Soviet Union were also chock full of encounters with many gracious Russian people. One sweet old woman, a "babushka" as they are called, slugged me in the arm as we boarded a train together. Another time I stood on the street with our group leader, a Russian language professor from the university back in the States. We stopped by a deserted phone booth and she was fishing through her pocketbook for some change to make a call. Out of nowhere came a young Russian woman in a flat out sprint towards us. "Gee, where is she running?" I wondered. The answer… straight into that deserted phone booth before our group leader could get her change out. FACE!

On the surface, Moscow was the capital of the world's largest socialist state. However, below the surface capitalism and competition were alive and well. Believe it or not, there is a word for business in the Russian language. The word is "biznes." I must have heard this word a million times in the month I was there. In the USSR westerners stuck out like a sore thumb. Go out for a walk in the city and in no time the traders were upon you, most speaking perfect English… "change money?" "your watch, how much?" "here, lacquer box, lacquer box, very popular." After just a few days this oversized flea market became tiresome. I wanted to practice some Russian outside of class but Russians would always speak English. One black market trader came up to me in GUM (short for Gosudarstvennii Universalnii Magazin, the large state run department store) and we got to talking. I complained to him in English, "All you Russians, all you ever want to do is trade things." He replied in a very concerned voice, "Yes… it is a problem." Then he left me and headed straight for the next American would be customer.

Next to our hotel on the outskirts of the city was an inactive construction site. One day my roommate watched out of the window as a group of young Russian biznesmen took the initiative to help themselves to a large pile of lumber there. He said a truck pulled up, then several entrepreneurs got out quickly, hopped the fence, and began shoving pieces of wood under the fence to another entrepreneur who loaded the wood into a truck. This went on for five minutes or so, my roommate said, then the biznesmen quickly hopped back over the fence, the truck doors slammed, and they drove away in a flash. He knew that these were not actual construction workers because no Soviet construction workers alive worked that quickly or efficiently. From the French, entrepreneur is literally "preneur" = taker and "entre" = between; in the true spirit of the entrepreneur, these gentlemen were taking the wood between a construction site where it was not currently in use, and their own place to use it themselves!

I had the opportunity to meet and become friendly with a few young Russians myself. One Russian a few years older than me named Viktor said he was on "vacation" in Moscow from Kiev (meaning he left Kiev temporarily because it was near the Chernobyl site). Viktor was staying with relatives in the city for a while, and he invited a few of us Americans over one day to watch the World Cup soccer match between the Soviet Union and France on the small TV he had in the apartment. After the game he told us about his experiences in Afghanistan as a Soviet paratrooper, where he was wounded in an ambush on a mountain road. Viktor showed us some of his military papers but he said he was no longer obliged to serve after returning from the front in Afghanistan.

Once Viktor and I were walking down a Moscow street when this young Russian woman spotted him. "Hey Viktor, you bastard, what are you doing here? How are you doing?" she asked him in English and then gave him a big hug. They talked for about ten minutes or so, then she left. So I asked, "Hey Viktor, who was that? She was pretty cute." He turned to me and said, "Oh, you want her? She is not very expensive." Never mind.

Viktor was one of the first Russian friends I made in Moscow, but later I became friends with two Russians about my age who were well dressed in western shirts, jeans, and sneakers. One had a shirt he was particularly proud of, it was a red t-shirt that said "Wisconsin" and had a picture of the university's mascot, a muscle bound cartoon badger. The Russian wore this shirt almost every time I saw him. Talk about school spirit! So, I'll call him BMOC (Big Man On Campus) because there seemed to be a lot of young Russian women around who were impressed by his good looks, his midwestern charm, and his university education. His friend I am going to call Jerry Seinfeld. Like Jerry, he was thin and had blond hair, and like Jerry, he was a regular comedian.

This Russian Jerry Seinfeld knew only one joke in English. He insisted on telling this joke to everyone he met who spoke English, and it went something like this…"There is man from Finland, and he is with Russian woman, but she does not know where he is from. They are making love, and when they are making love she asks him, 'Are you Russian?' Then he stops making love, and says, 'No, I am finished.'" (Or Finnish! Get it!) Well, maybe it was better in Russian. Believe me, it got funnier every time Jerry told it.

BMOC and Jerry always had plenty of money. Jerry even bragged to me once, "I have seen American thousand dollar bill before, I have." That made one of us. Even though they could speak English, often we spoke Russian so I could practice. During one of these sessions I made some nice, simple Russian conversation asking them, "So, what do you do in your life? Are you students?" "Nyet" they answered. "Oh, so you work then?" I asked. "Nyet" they replied again. "Umm…" I searched for what to say next in Russian, "uh… that's a good life."

"Da" (or duh?) they said as they both broke into huge smiles and nodded (and thought "you American moron").

I went on a rampage with these guys around Moscow. They always had large wads of money and they would take me various places. We went to eat one day at a Russian cafeteria and they bought just about everything on the menu for me. Another time we were down on the platform of an underground metro station. Sometimes Soviet militiamen were posted down there and became suspicious of anyone just hanging around as we were doing, not boarding trains in either direction. I noticed a militiaman on the other side of the station staring at us, then he began to walk toward us. I turned to BMOC and Jerry and said, "Guys, guys, militiaman's coming!" After a second they looked up but it was too late, the militiaman was right in front of us.

As I watched with amazement, BMOC looked the militiaman straight in the eye and laughed at him. Then he turned to me and said, "Who, him? Ha ha ha. Don't worry about him. Let's go." So we walked away and the militiaman just stood there, dissed and speechless. A lesson learned… these Soviet militiamen must have been the equivalent of private security rent-a-cops in the United States. I did notice that BMOC and Jerry were not as cocky when it came to the KGB men around town. Some KGB wore military uniforms while others went "undercover" in dress clothes, but my two pals could still recognize KGB men from their clothes and the way these men acted.

Even more entertaining than our brush with the Soviet militiamen was the time BMOC and Jerry were approached by two Asian men, probably natives of Kazakhstan or the Soviet Far East. These characters looked like they were straight out of a bad kung fu movie and struck their best gangster poses while talking to BMOC and Jerry in Russian. I looked at BMOC and asked,

"You know these guys?" (brilliant question, I know) He responded, "Oh… yes," in a very matter of fact way and continued on with the Russian conversation. Just then I noticed one of the Asians had brass knuckles on. Nice. Suddenly the conversation ended and BMOC said, "Mike, come with us." "What, where are you going?" I asked. "Just down here," he replied. They were headed into a large underpass beneath the street. Hmm, interesting. Of course I stayed right where I was.

"It's ok, Mike, it's just biznes, we owe them money." (Oh, that's ok then, just biznes, why didn't you say so? I felt better already) "That's all right fellas, go on without me, thanks anyway. I'll be right here when you come out," I said. I waited for a good ten minutes wondering exactly what sort of underground biznes was taking place in that underpass. I listened intently for those high pitched whipping noises that Bruce Lee used to make in the movies, or the sound of brass knuckles connecting with the strong jaw of the fine young student from Wisconsin. But no, a smooth transaction I guessed, no need for me to make a hasty sprint from the area.

Soon BMOC and Jerry made their way back up the steps, and the Kazakh gangsters were nowhere in sight. BMOC smiled and said, "No problem." So, the three of us continued down the street and I did not ask any questions. Had BMOC refinanced at a more favorable rate of interest? Or were there two dead Kazakhs lying in that underpass, killed by the lethal wit of the Russian Jerry Seinfeld? Maybe his joke was funnier in Russian!

If anyone ever tells you the Soviets did not understand business, well maybe they are right. The Soviet economy fell to pieces, the Soviet empire collapsed, and the Soviet leadership fell. But the Soviet guy on the street, he knew his "biznes" as well as anyone.

Although there was a considerable amount of free time for me to roam the city of Moscow with the likes of BMOC and Jerry Seinfeld, I spent most of the trip in class and on various excursions with members of the student group. This group, which consisted of about fifteen smart ass American college students, was as tactful and polite as most groups of American students are in foreign countries. One night, while out a Russian restaurant with some of my classmates, I heard this pearl of wisdom. "Look, I'm an American, I can buy a hamburger, eat half of it, throw it out, then go up and buy another." Beautiful. Another time, sightseeing on a hot Russian summer day, "There are two things this country needs… air conditioning and water fountains."

Our Soviet guide Natasha (the middle aged mother, housewife, tourist guide, and part time KGB agent, remember?) brought our group to a place after classes one day called "Dom Druzhbi" (House of Friendship). It was a place where westerners were brought to meet with Soviets, so that both peoples could get to know each other better. In theory, Dom Druzhbi's relaxed atmosphere would lead to rational discussions, common ground could be found, and the tensions of the cold war could be diffused on a grassroots level. In theory.

At Dom Druzhbi we listened to a talk about the misunderstandings between Americans and Soviets given in fluent English by a Soviet woman. This woman had lived in the United States for a while as the child of a diplomat. After her speech she asked if anyone in our group had a question. Someone did. "If this is a House of Friendship, why were our hotel rooms bugged?" Somebody had been watching too many 007 movies. Hmm, do you suppose the KGB might have had more pressing matters than to spy on a bunch of 20 year old Americans?

The Russian woman, smooth as they come and a walking talking brochure for the Soviet Union, tried to reason with our group very diplomatically. All the while, she dropped little plugs for the Soviet system and little digs at the American system. Finally our time was up, but we were in luck. The woman had no other activities scheduled that day and she invited us to be guests at her house, a rare event we were assured. Rare or not, communist propaganda or not, it could have been interesting to see this woman's house. The only other chance to visit a Soviet home for one of us was if we were able to strike up friendships with Russians on our own outside of the structured program. It was not always easy to meet Russians, ones who were not black market biznesmen that is. So, our group leader asked us, "Isn't that nice of her? Would you like to go visit her home?" A few girls in our group let out a moan and replied, "Can't we just go shopping?"

God bless America. So much for Dom Druzhbi... we like Dom Nordstrom better. Russian women would come around to this way of thinking by the 1990's. The girls in our group got their wish, and we headed for the hard currency store for some serious shopping action. The Dom Druzhbi woman could have talked until she was blue in the face that day about the merits of the Soviet system, but our student group knew better. It is a fact of human nature for Americans, for Russians, and for everyone else. Shopping is king, capitalism is king, and ideology just cannot compete.

Our time in Moscow was drawing to an end. After a farewell party for our Soviet teachers and some warm goodbyes, we were off to Leningrad for a few days as tourists only before returning to the United States. Our flight was on Rodney Dangerfield Airlines, better known as Aeroflot, the one and only Soviet airline. I loved the advertisement on the outside of my plane ticket envelope. Below the Aeroflot logo and its sickle and hammer, the inscription read, "Viy sdelaniy khoroshii viybor" (You have made a good choice). That is for sure, flying Aeroflot was better than walking to Leningrad. Aeroflot specialized in making its customers feel uncomfortable, and why not? What else were you going to do, take Southwest Airlines from Moscow to Leningrad?

Food was served during the flight, but it was on the lower end of the scale of selections we enjoyed at the hotel restaurant. Nothing terrible, no fat soup, but no one was very hungry anyway, most of our attention was diverted to holding on to our seats. For a time the pilot in the cockpit was banking and diving and climbing again like he was still on a mission in Afghanistan. When the bombing run was finally over, and our Aeroflot attack plane eluded the Mujahedeen radar, we settled in for a relatively stable flight the rest of the way. Stable enough for our flight attendant, who could have taken any of us in two out of three falls, to push her cart down the aisle with some reading material. Let's see, what have we got here? *Pravda, Pravda, Pravda* in English, *Pravda, Literaturnaya Gazeta* (the *Literary Newspaper*, for all you artsy flakes not down with the Communist Party program), *Pravda, Komsomolskaya Pravda* (for the teenie boppers), and a stack of pamphlets on policies laid down in the latest meeting of the Central Committee of the Communist Party of the Soviet Union (luckily in English as well as Russian). Dig in! Once you picked them up, you could not put them down.

An interesting sideline to all of this was the rumored KGB-Aeroflot connection. It was said in many quarters that it was Aeroflot policy to have one or more KGB men undercover on every flight, as a deterrent to hijackers. The rumor was that the hijackings in the Soviet Union were less drawn out and dramatic affairs than in the United States. Usually they ended soon after they began, with a KGB agent wasting a would be hijacker before the terrorist knew what hit him. Truth or fiction, this certainly made the flight more exciting. It was fun to play "spot the KGB man" as each passenger moved around the cabin.

After a few nice, uneventful days of sightseeing in Leningrad our student group boarded another Aeroflot plane bound for Sweden. It was our last day in the USSR. My final and strongest memory of the Soviet Union is from this last day in the country as I sat in the cabin waiting for our Aeroflot jet to taxi down to the appropriate runway. I was sitting next to one of my friends who had the window seat. He pointed out the window and said, "Hey Mike, look at that!"

My friend was gesturing toward some sort of radar device on the grass next to our runway, but it was not one of those super, high tech looking ones you might see at an American airport or military base. It looked more like something Wile E. Coyote just pulled out of a wooden crate stamped "Acme." It had all sorts of strange looking rods and dishes sticking out of it, and the rods and dishes of the device were bobbing up and down in different directions, as if it had gone into convulsions. My friend and I were in a stupid, silly mood anyway, and we started laughing so hard that our stomach and jaw muscles began to ache. After I recovered from this extended bout of laughter, I realized that as long as the cold war stayed cold, we had to win eventually. How could we lose? It was McDonnell Douglas, Northrop Grumman, and Lockheed Martin vs. Wile E. Coyote and Acme.

Jokes aside, the trip to the Soviet Union had a much different effect on me from what I expected. I assumed I would learn more about the Russian language, Russian culture, and Soviet politics, and I did. But the trip really taught me the benefits of a free enterprise system. I plowed through the two year economics requirement of my major at Johns Hopkins but I had not cared for the subject much. Economics seemed like a bunch of nonsense to me, which the professors were making up as they went along. At that time I assumed if I did not like economics, then I did not like business either.

After my trip to the Soviet Union I came to realize that business (and "biznes") was a world away from the fantasy land of "let's assume all of these factors are constant for the sake of our model" economics. Many of my friends, particularly my punk rock friends, were anti-business and anti-money. These were the same people who could not live without their "Super Big Gulp" and "Beef and Bean Burritos" from 7-11. Well, you could not get Super Big Gulps and Beef and Bean Burritos in the USSR, where there was no free market, and no incentive for innovation. Well, no incentive for the kind of innovation it took to create the concepts that are the Super Big Gulp and the Beef and Bean Burrito anyway.

Welcome to the Real World

I missed out on the great opportunity to be an NSA Russian analyst, and nothing else panned out for me before graduation. With hindsight of course, this also has me regretting another decision I made in college. I applied for and was offered an Army ROTC scholarship during my freshman year at Hopkins. It was not free of course, years of military service would have been required, but school would have been paid for and I would have had a job waiting for me after graduation.

This did not seem like a big deal at the time, and there was the danger inherent in military service, but now I think I would have liked it and it would have been good for me. Odds are my job would have been as a military intelligence Russian language analyst in West Germany. I could have seen Europe on the Army's dime. My mother advised me against the scholarship at the time saying, "You're a grown man and it's your decision, but I wouldn't do it if I were you, once you sign that paper they can send you anywhere they want." In the end I took my mother's advice, but I'll never know if it would have been a good thing to do.

These poor decisions begat another poor decision. My mother passed away during my junior year in college and I received part of the money from the sale of the house in which our family grew up. I saved some money of course, but used entirely too much on traveling to and attending a French language school in Paris during the summer after college graduation. At the time I thought it would be good to improve my French and add another credential to my resume. In hindsight I should have saved the money and got going on looking for a job without delay after finishing college.

I had a friend from Johns Hopkins named Jeff who was also an international relations major, but instead of Russian he specialized in Arabic language and the Middle East. The two of us decided we would move from Baltimore to Washington, DC and share an apartment while job hunting there as Washington, DC was the center of government and foreign policy work. It was also a center of low paying internships and high rents. We struggled for years when we had both expected a smooth transition to the work world. Oh well, this happens to most people I suppose.

Once we settled into DC the first matter at hand was to secure any type of flexible job. We needed to work while we looked for jobs in our field, which we expected might take a while. Jeff found something first, working as a bicycle courier with a walkie talkie. It turned out to be quite a dangerous profession. He had several close calls and one major wipeout, a woman in a parked car opened her door just as Jeff was sailing by. Smack!!! Jeff went flying and wiped out on the street. The woman looked down on him, as he lay there bruised and cut and she said, "Don't you have a horn on that thing?"

My first idea was to work at a record store, with its flexible late hours, and try to do interviews during the day. When I talked to the manager of a big record store location in the city it turned out to be serious business. Two separate interviews on different days with two different managers. On quizzed me for a few minutes on my musical knowledge. I was most proud when he asked me, "Who plays bass and sings for Motorhead?" (the infamous British metal band) I smiled, "That would be Lemmy Kilmister (a personal hero of mine)." The store manager was fairly impressed because I did well on most of the questions, but not well enough apparently.

After a week of fruitless calls trying to locate him, I finally got the manager on the phone. "You just finished Hopkins, I can tell you're not going to stay here long enough to contribute." I hit a number of restaurants but that was futile because I had no experience waiting tables at that point. I tried a telemarketing job for four days before leaving without making one sale and had nothing to show for it but a very sore throat. Finally I interviewed for an evening job waiting tables at National Airport. At the interview I sat down with a small round guy who had a crew cut. He looked like a retired drill sergeant, and said, "So, you wanna wait tables? Well you've got to have experience for that, I can't let you wait tables." I told him I would be glad to bus tables then. "Yeah, but even then you need experience, you gotta know how to carry lots of dishes over your head and all that, and how to set tables, I can't let you do that," he said.

"I tell you what," said the drill sergeant, "I have something you could do, come along with me." He brought me down to a cafeteria and showed me my new workplace. I would be behind a counter, scooping out plates of food for people. Fine, I did not give a damn, I just needed a job ASAP, so I took it. And there it was. I managed to get myself a job in an international field. Do not be fooled by the name Washington "National" Airport, there is a very international flavor to the place. Everyone who worked there was pretty nice to me. Most of my coworkers were Chinese and Vietnamese who had pretty weak English skills, which did not matter much in this job. The remainder of the staff were blacks from DC.

In a strange sort of way I was excited about this job. You see, the cafeteria was my favorite place at Johns Hopkins. I was a serious eater in college and the Hopkins cafeteria was all you can eat, so I would hang out with my friends and eat plate after plate of food. Most students used to complain about the food there, but I could never understand that. I was what they called a "cafeteria varsity four year letterman." Many nights in college I would arrive at 4:45pm to be the first in line for the 5pm opening, get that first freshly cooked entrée, hit that immaculate untouched salad bar, and settle down for a long, pleasurable evening. By the close at 7:15pm I would have six or seven empty plates stacked on my tray, I would have shared dinner conversation with two or three entirely different groups of friends, and sometimes would have chatted up some of Hopkins' most babe-o-licious women. For years I kept an issue of the cafeteria newsletter with a picture of me waiting in line for an entrée. That was a proud moment. So, when I got the job at the airport cafeteria I was quick to call my college friends and brag.

One perk of the job was that on break I could take any food I wanted for dinner. These poor people did not know what a mistake they made in hiring me. I would munch out there. A few times my supervisor, who was Indian, noticed me on break with my tray stacked to heaven and got really nervous. "You eating all that?" he asked. "Well, yeah," I replied. "Uh, ok, just hurry up and finish," he would say, fearing the arrival of the drill sergeant who made periodic spot checks. In fact the Indian supervisor was always nervous, he would walk by our stations and say, "Please, take rag please, clean again, so looks nice."

My Asian coworkers were fairly quiet, and with the language barrier I only had the most basic of friendships with them. My black coworkers on the other hand were wise guys who always had something smart to say. This made work fun. The insults would go flying day in and day out. The cook Teddy and the janitor Keith always completed their work but at the same time they liked to put one over on the managers in the same way junior high students like to fool their teachers. On the day of the Redskins-Dallas football game Keith brought in his portable TV. We spent that day trying to work and watch the game without letting the boss know the TV was there. Keith had a quick wit as well. Another day a female cafeteria worker ate during her break on a table Keith had just cleaned. He walked over and asked very politely, "Excuse me, do you want this rag?" She answered, "No… why?" Keith snapped back "Cause you gonna need it when you cleanin' up that table you just ate on."

One of the "Skycap" baggage handlers became my friend. His name was Antoine and he was always friendly when he came to eat. One night we got to talking and I asked, "So Antoine, what was the best tip you ever got here?" "Oh, that was Charlie Daniels Band, Charlie Daniels and his band, he gave me $100 for moving his band's gear. He was real nice, not like that Rolling Stones son of a bitch." "What," I said, "what about the Rolling Stones? What happened with them?" "You know that, what's his name, Keith Richard or something? Bitch didn't give me but a few dollars, and you know he got money!" Antoine complained.

One day the drill sergeant had a problem. The guy who washed the pans quit and he needed a replacement. Well, why not that new sucker, he must have thought, so he had another manager named Len talk to me. Len said, "Well just try it out Mike, you'll like it, all you have to do is wash bowls and pans, and when you finish you can do whatever you want until more pans come." I agreed to fill in for one night only and it was harsh. Hot as hell in there, my hands and arms looked like raisins by the end of the night, there was no one to talk to, and the pans never stopped piling up so I never got a break.

I came out and said to Keith, "Shit, I'm not doing that again." Keith replied, "Yeah, they was trying to make it sound sweet for you Mike." I went in and talked to Len, and told him thanks but no thanks, I wanted to keep my old job. Len said ok. The next day I was scheduled at my regular job for the night shift, but I got a call from the drill sergeant in the morning. "Why aren't you in here washing pans? You're supposed to be in this morning!" he said. I replied, "I told Len last night, I tried it once like we agreed and I don't want to do it. I'm going to keep my old job." The drill sergeant was having none of it, "Your regular job isn't open anymore, get in here and wash pans or you don't have a job!"

Shaken a bit, I said, "Ok then, I guess I don't have a job anymore, goodbye." Great. I even got screwed out of a job scooping international foods. What next? An hour or so later, as I was pondering another search for temporary work, the phone rang. It was Len, who spoke in a very humble tone. "Mike, why don't you come in for your regular job today, ok?" he asked. "Fine, no problem," I said.

I figured I'd be working in a dynamic environment when I finished Hopkins, but this was really exciting! Jobs would close, then open again within an hour at the fast paced National Airport Cafeteria. When I arrived at work that day I was king. Apparently all my coworkers had learned of the morning's events, and the start of my shift resembled the scene in the movie *Bad Boys* after Sean Penn beats up the two "barn bosses" of the juvenile prison. I came to my post with shouts of "Yo, Miiiiiike!" "Awlriiiight" "Mike is bad, he don't take shit from nobody!" As one would say in business school, it was a stunning triumph for labor in its age old power struggle with management. All I wanted was a nice little white collar job when I finished Johns Hopkins, but suddenly I had become a blue collar labor leader!

Working as the only white person on the cafeteria staff other than management was an amazing experience. Some of the reactions I received when people came for food were hysterical. There was one white woman in her fifties who worked for an airline and came in every night for food. She would talk to me very slowly and deliberately as one would talk to a child. When she found out I was a Hopkins graduate she said, "That's awful, is there anything I can do?" It was not that awful, you would have thought I told her I had cancer or something. I mean, imagine having to work in a cafeteria as a white person!

There was also a white guy who was a few years older than me and he worked as a baggage handler for one of the big airlines. He used to come in often and was instantly friendly to me. One day about a week after I started the job, he came in, looked around to make sure none of my bosses were listening, then said, "Mike, I can get you an application if you want, and help you get a job with my airline. You don't have to work here." I said, "Thanks, but it's ok, I like this job because I can work evenings and then interview during the day." I can tell you, it's great being white, people sure do look out for you! He was a nice guy and meant well, but I did not see him get any applications for my black coworkers.

Weeks and months were flying by, but finally I was offered a good job. It was an internship in a Senator's office, and best of all the pay was good... $0 per hour. No, that's not a typo, I did not leave off a "1" that is just a plain zero. It was an unpaid internship, one of those "get your foot in the door" opportunities that seem to be especially numerous in Washington, DC. In fact some people have made a good point that this keeps lower income people from working on Capitol Hill and in other similar internships. Who can afford to work a job that pays nothing? Only people like me who had some savings stashed or who had help from their parents.

My goal was to make it through a few months there for free, because the office said it would be hiring an entry level person for a full time paying position shortly. I would have a better chance at the paid position if they already knew and liked me. The next question was how to make money at night. The cafeteria job started early in the afternoon so I could not keep it. After some effort I was able to get a job as an usher at a movie theater in town. This was brilliant! I actually had experience doing this. It was a job I did at a nearby mall while I was a high school student. I knew my ticket stubs, I knew how to organize lines of people for six different shows, and I even knew how to hook and unhook the felt cushion rope things to the metal pole divider things!

Things did not go smoothly the first night however. I arrived ready to rip the hell out of some ticket stubs, but the manager with whom I interviewed was not there. When I walked in I got strange looks from everyone, and the manager on duty said, "Sir, you can't come in yet, it will be a while until the movies start." After a long argument over what my name was and who hired me, he finally relented. "Look, ok, you can get yourself a black vest in there and we'll find somewhere to post you tonight, but I'm going to talk to the manager about this when he comes back tomorrow!"

Later on at home that night I reflected on my first night at work. It is funny how things change when you hit the real world. A year or so earlier at Johns Hopkins I was debating in my mind which career I would feel most comfortable with. Ha! Now I found myself embroiled in a fight to the death for a job I did not like much in high school. Wake up and smell the coffee. Welcome to the jungle. A cold slap in the face. A heaping teaspoon full of reality. A swift kick in the pants. Ok, enough metaphors.

The Senate job went well and it was interesting to watch the inner workings of the office. Watch was about all I did because as an intern your responsibilities are twofold: you have to open envelopes, and you have to date stamp the letters in those envelopes. Senate offices are mini post offices, they receive an incredible amount of mail every single day. I am sure you have heard that expression "write to your congressman." Well, that is no screwing around, people do it, and there are no restrictions such as "one may only write meaningful letters to the Senate" or "one may not write to the Senate if one is whacko." Sorting through this mess creates a demand for $0 per hour interns who outnumber the chairs in the mail sorting areas of Senate offices. We interns would take turns sitting down while working.

Once I did more than open mail. Not because I showed any special potential, but because I was the only expendable person in the office with a driver's license. I was asked to drive the Administrative Assistant (AA), who is the number one person on the Senator's staff, to the train station. I was pretty excited about this, but as I went down to pick up the AA and the car it dawned on me. The train station? Union Station? It could not be, but what other train station?

Union Station was across the street from the Senator's office building. It was a longer walk down to the parking garage than it was to Union Station. I think this person was enjoying the perks of her position a bit too much, having me pick her up like she was a VIP when she could easily have walked across the street. That is Washington, DC for you.

Predictably the plans to hire a new paid entry level person dragged on, and I continued to send out resumes just in case. That was a good idea because a 19 year old college girl interning on her school break was making me look lazy. She would have made anyone look lazy. Around five o'clock each day we were told to go home. The girl would become upset and start begging, "Do we have to leave, can't we stay later and learn more?" I had a little problem called the need to earn money after the internship hours – I needed to work nights at the movie theater.

Luckily impressing members of the Senator's office became a moot point. I found a job with an unbeatable combination… everyone wore suits to work and they actually paid you for your work! I was not sure that was possible in DC, but I did it. The pay was not fantastic of course as it was an entry level job with a foreign currency brokerage. But, it was a good foot in the door to the financial world and it was enough to live on and pay the bills.

Beginning a Career in Finance

I began my career in finance, but initially it was a career in travelers checks (TC's). Our firm offered travelers checks in US Dollars and in many of the major foreign currencies. This was my first job. It was my responsibility to organize and reconcile TC sales, purchases, and shipments. I soon became the firm's resident expert on the checks and I took great pride in my work. Therefore I proclaimed myself the "TC King" because I could answer any and all queries in this area. For example, what are the denominations of Spanish Peseta TC's? That would be 5,000... 10,000... and 20,000 Peseta notes. I truly was the TC King.

Eventually the sad day came when I was forced to relinquish the crown. I trained a young lady to handle TC's and soon enough she was in charge. No longer was I on the cutting edge of the TC business – one day I made the statement, "Yes, they have checks in the denomination of 50." Then I heard a cocky and confident female voice from behind me, "No, Mike, those have been discontinued by the travelers check company." I fell silent, turned, and bowed. The king is dead, long live the new TC Queen.

I loved number crunching, especially when the numbers stood for money. And of course I loved the Reuters screen, an electronic monitor which showed the ups and downs, the highs and lows of the markets. Even before I did much with foreign currency and precious metals I looked forward to days when major economic news was reported. At around 8:30am there would be a sudden beep, and then a highlighted message would flash across the bottom of the monitor, "Fourth Quarter Growth Projected at 1.2%." Suddenly it was fireworks on the screen with the major currency rates such as the Deutsche Mark, French Franc, Japanese Yen, and the British Pound popping and flashing in reaction to the news.

There was a coworker who enjoyed the screen almost as much as I did. He had other hobbies, his main one was amateur bicycle racing, so I'll call him Greg LeMond after the only American to have won the Tour de France at that time. Only some of the screens on the Reuters monitor were relevant to our everyday work, but Greg and I took great pleasure in exploring the meaningless (to us) information available on our Reuters monitor. Our favorite was a screen that listed prices for some obscure precious metals, I guess they were precious to someone. To Greg and me they were simply objects of derision. There was "Wolframite," "Cadmium, Sticks and Bars," "Ferrotungsten," and "Quicksilver 76 lb/dlrs flask." What the hell was this stuff, we wondered? Wolf-ra-mite? Was it vegemite sandwich food, but for wolves instead of people? Unlike the more common precious metals gold, silver, and platinum, the prices almost never changed.

Greg and I worked mainly with currency banknotes, and we also liked to make fun of the most obscure and bizarre notes. There was Papua Kina from the jungles of the Pacific. The Kina banknotes looked like someone left them in the jungle too long, and they required extra care. One had to be gentle with the sacred Kina of Papua, the notes could fall apart in one's hands. Then there was Yugoslavia and its runaway inflation, the Yugoslav Dinar depreciating in value by the second – a whole stack could be worth five US Dollars. Finally there was the infamous 1000 Singapore Dollar note, so damn big that you had to fold it about ten times to fit it in your wallet. When unfolded it was suitable for framing and hanging on the wall, with an enormous picture of ships and docks on one side and a caption that read "Shipbuilding." I thought that Singapore needed to spend less time building ships and concentrate on making its money small enough to fit in a wallet.

Our firm's specialty in obscure currencies was the CFA Franc. CFA stands for Communite Financiere Africaine, a group of West African countries that were once French colonies. These countries used the same currency which was pegged 50 to 1 with the French Franc, so for example if the exchange rate was 6 French Francs to 1 US Dollar then the CFA rate would be 300 CFA to the dollar. Men would show up in our offices with flowing African robes like Eddie Murphy in the movie *Trading Places*… "I'm Nanja Ibeko, exchange student from Cameroon, ha ha ha!"

Our regular CFA customers were characters, very friendly guys. Suddenly I would hear that there was a visitor in the lobby, and then I would hear a loud voice saying, "Bonjour comment ca va Mike! I have some CFA for you today!" One man from Burkina Faso told us that his country's name meant "land of proud men." If you asked me it was more like "land of the proud bargain hunters." Time after time the CFA crew would insist on bargaining on the exchange rate and we would have to remind them that we were not a village market in Dakar.

We had one banknote trader at our firm for a while who was from the Caribbean. This man's main hobby was acquiring duty free goods from his buddies at the embassies until our firm let him go. When he found out that I liked Guinness he whispered to me, "Guinness… I can get it for you cheap mon, duty free mon duty free, I got friends at the embassies!" Some days with the CFA crew and Mr. Duty Free I felt like I worked at a third world bazaar rather than a financial firm.

In general though, I liked the fast pace of the work. Sometimes Greg LeMond and I would work furiously through the day and then realize it was 3pm and we had not eaten lunch yet. One of us would run over to Jerry's Subs to pick up sandwiches, and then the two of us would begin wolfing them down at the same pace we were working. After a minute or so, we would glance at each other with large subs stuffed halfway down our throats, barely slowing down to chew, and double over laughing.

Having grown up in the 1970's, TV had an enormous impact on my life. It is incredible to look back and realize that many of my personal interests and career interests had their origins in a stupid television show from the 1960's. When I was a kid the first women I liked were foreign women, and this interest came from my favorite show the World War II prisoner of war comedy *Hogan's Heroes*. American Colonel Hogan was my idol, and he would cap off each successful mission by getting together with "Tiger" the super cool female French resistance fighter, or the crafty female Russian spy Marya. And which languages did I end up studying in college… French and Russian of course. Where did I go to study abroad after junior year in college… Moscow, Russia. Where did I go to get my MBA? French speaking Montreal, Quebec. I swear I did not go there just to meet French women, of course not!

So, as I became hooked on the financial markets at work, my viewing habits changed accordingly. I became a financial news junkie. I was sure to catch *Nightly Business Report* each evening, and *Wall Street Week With Louis Rukeyser* once a week. It was a good thing I did not have cable. While at my sister's place on vacation I discovered *FNN*, the *Financial News Network*, and sat for hours staring at up to the minute stock charts, averages, and news briefs.

The program *Wall Street Week* was a big event for me each week. Whether or not I had plans on a given Friday night I would try to figure out a way to catch the show. The opening theme song was magic, you switched on PBS and there was that teasing silence. After this the bells ring out in descending pitch "ding dong dong dong" then comes the loud, pre-computer era stock ticker sound "tickatickatickaticka." Finally the song starts with the "dom dom da da, dom

dom da da and horns join in with the melody. All the while cool but dated scenes of the stock market floor action flash across the screen.

Louis Rukeyser had guest analysts on the show from various financial firms and industries. My favorite was a man named Marty Zweig who published his own newsletter on the markets. Not only was Marty a sharp guy who knew the markets, Marty Zweig was a bad ass. The coolest guest on the show by far. He would show up with the freshest suits and hair slicked back like Gordon Gekko from the movie *Wall Street*. Marty had a mean, raspy voice, which sounded like he had permanent strep throat. His evil voice would whip off lethal doses of market reality like, "Louis I can't see anything positive in this market for the next few quarters," in a way that would have made him a standout singer for a death metal band. He could call it "Marty Zweig and the Doomsayers of Black Monday" with hits like "Satanic Corporate Raiders of the Sabbath" and "Index Arbitrage Apocalypse."

Two television broadcasts in particular had a major influence on me. The first was a report on the news magazine *20/20* showing a day in the life of a Salomon Brothers foreign exchange trader. The trader brought his telephone with him everywhere, and he would wake himself up periodically during the night to check the markets. At the time it looked very cool to me. He was doing something that seemed like a nonstop exciting game and making a heap of money in the process. I wanted to be this guy. I was learning about currency markets at work, and I worked hard, but I was earning a typical Washington, DC salary. I felt like I was missing something by not working in the markets up in New York instead. It seemed like a dream to make lots of money just for following the markets, so I knew what I had to do... get an MBA and get a job with a Wall Street investment firm.

Soon afterwards I saw a *Wall Street Week* special on the Montreal Exchange and the Canadian market in general. This gave me an idea I had not considered before. I had always wanted to visit Quebec, so while researching MBA schools I took a look at Montreal. Like most would be MBA's, I wanted to go to Harvard Business School. Failing that, which was a distinct possibility, I looked for alternatives and there it was. McGill University. In the heart of Montreal, well respected school, emphasis on international business, and incredibly low tuition, even for foreign students. Voila! I could learn how to cut deals en francais, ze Tiger way. So, once again TV was a guiding light in my life. As David Letterman said on his late night talk show, "Don't trust so called friends who tell you watching television is a waste of time!"

Not only was I developing a love for the financial markets, I was also growing to love business in general. The Jerry's Sub shop next door to our firm sold beer in addition to sandwiches and soft drinks, so it became our first stop/meeting place any time we headed out on the town after work. We became very friendly with the staff of this Jerry's, especially the manager. This Jerry's location to me was the model of how a small business should be run. I loved to watch it operate like a well oiled machine. The lunch rush was handled with ease, orders would appear in front of customers seconds after they were placed, the location was spotless, and cash seemed to flow in like a waterfall. As we got to know the manager, he would stop by to see us for retail services when he was going on a trip, and he would cut us breaks on sandwiches at lunch and on beers after work. I scratch your back, you scratch mine. A small but beautiful example of capitalism making everyone better off.

So that was that, undaunted by the economic climate after the 1987 market crash, I had discovered what I liked and wanted for a career. I was going to business school and nothing else mattered. I would make any sacrifices necessary to make this happen.

Eyes on the Prize

Have you ever come to a point in your life when you know what you want to do and you are prepared to do anything necessary to make it happen? This was the way I was feeling in my second year working at the foreign exchange firm. I was making plans to do an MBA, and it was time to check out the MBA fair at a hotel in the Washington, DC area. MBA schools from across the country set up information booths with booklets, catalogs, and had representatives there to answer the many questions of would be MBA's. I learned a few things at the fair, but not much more than I already knew. More than anything it was enjoyable to watch each school play out its role, competing for attention against the other schools at the fair.

First there was Harvard. More exactly, there was not Harvard. Harvard did not show up. Harvard did not consider GMAT (business school entrance exams) scores in its evaluation of MBA candidates. Harvard charged more to apply than the other schools. Harvard encouraged students to be "creative" in finding sources of financing to fund the expected $30,000 (this was 1989 remember) annual costs of attending its MBA program. In other words, if you wanted to come to Harvard, be rich first, ok. Harvard did not give a damn and it did not have to. Just about everyone applying to business schools wanted to go there, whether they admitted it or not, and Harvard knew this. Thus, mighty Harvard could not be bothered with some silly little MBA fair.

Then there was Yale. Yale liked to think of itself as a molder of good corporate citizens. The school's program encouraged public service and entrepreneurial employment over careers on Wall Street or with Fortune 500 companies. How noble. We have come full circle back to the Tan Man speech. I would have had to work for about 150 years at the Rainbow Coalition to pay off the loans necessary to attend Yale. I was stubborn though, I told the Yale representative

I still wanted to work on Wall Street, and asked if it would hurt me if I went to Yale. "No, not at all, you know, for all the talk about us being a school for public service we send as many top people to Wall Street as the other MBA schools," he answered. Oh, ok (?)

Then I stopped by UCLA's booth. UCLA had a well respected MBA program, but it also had the attraction of being a California state school. California residents paid the outrageously low in state tuition. All afternoon I heard the poor, frustrated young woman at the UCLA booth trying to stress the educational benefits of the UCLA MBA. All afternoon long all anyone asked her was "How can I go about getting residency in California? Can I do that in my first year, then pay in state tuition in my second year?" I admit it, I was one of the would be California state residents to ask the question. I am sorry.

Saddest of all though was the University of Insurance, or something like that, I do not remember the exact name because I did not stop by its table. Neither did anyone else. All freshly printed booklets and applications sat there in a pile untouched. The guy behind the desk did his best not to doze off. So, even though insurance could be a solid career and a well paying one, in the 1980's people just could not get excited about the actuarial sciences. Gordon Gekko did not have time for insurance.

Many schools had the early decision option, where one can apply early and be accepted or denied admission early. The idea is that if an applicant is interested in one school in particular, he or she could apply to that school first. If accepted, the applicant saves the time, effort, and money spent applying to other schools. My college roommate senior year applied early decision to medical school and he was accepted in late September. The rest of the year therefore became a worry free vacation at Club Hopkins for him. Nothing but TV, beer, and chewing tobacco. And plastic cups full of tobacco spit all over the apartment. It was great though, I did not mind the tobacco spit, I was happy for him. He had blasted through Johns Hopkins' toughest major, biomedical engineering, a combination of pre med and engineering classes, so he deserved a break. Thing was, he was so smart he still got good grades senior year, in between sips of Budweiser and wads of tobacco.

The idea that I failed to grasp fully until it was too late, is that one should apply early admission to a school where one expects to be accepted. I applied to Harvard Business School early admission and received an early rejection before New Year's Day. Alright!!! That was a load off of my mind. And I had been afraid I would have to pay all that tuition. My chances of getting into Harvard had been slim, and I am sure it did not help that the projection of financial need I sent to Harvard came slightly short of $30,000. This is slightly short of the expected costs of a year at Harvard. If you were Harvard, would you give an ex-punk rock drummer $30,000 a year to study at your school. I do not suppose I would either.

At the close of New Year's weekend I sat behind a Hopkins fraternity house in Baltimore. Most of my best friends at Johns Hopkins belonged to this fraternity and they were able to use the house over the holiday for a New Year's/reunion party our second year after graduating. I mentioned to one of my friends who was already in his first year of the MBA at Columbia, that I had already gotten the early bullet from Harvard. He mumbled back, "Harvard is a pipe dream." I should have realized that before applying early admission, oh well.

I really wanted to go to McGill for a number of reasons, but I had also applied to Stanford. I remember worrying what I would do if accepted to both. Ha ha ha, not to worry, Stanford made it easy on me by rejecting me too. At that point I did not bother wasting my money applying to Wharton, which had the latest application deadline among the schools in which I was interested. That was ok, as I said, my true desire was to go to McGill and I was accepted! I could fulfill my dream of living in Montreal, and meeting cool French women like the gorgeous resistance fighter Tiger of the World War II POW camp comedy *Hogan's Heroes*. Put a Tiger in your tank. MTA, Masters of Tiger Administration!

The next problem was money, I needed some. McGill's financial aid office was not a big friend of Americans. If you were a foreign student and a native French speaker from France, Morocco, or Senegal your odds of getting aid were better as I understood it. Since McGill is located in the middle of a French speaking province, the last people McGill University wanted to give aid to were rude, crude, wealthy Americans like me. Except I was not wealthy. Anyway, thanks to some US government loans and a second job I was lucky enough to snag as a waiter at a pizza restaurant in Capitol Hill I would be ok.

It was very difficult and exhausting working the two jobs to save up for business school, but work went well, and I even waited on a table with Senator Joe Biden and some of his aides once. It seemed like August 1989 would never come, but finally it did, and I was able to leave both jobs on good terms and get ready to head north.

Hit the Beach

I knew the McGill MBA would be a challenge after my first week in Montreal. I had just moved into my apartment, and with nothing to do on a Saturday afternoon I decided to take a walk up to the football stadium. It was called *Molson Stadium*, a beautiful name. I was impressed already. McGill's team, the Redmen, had a game that day and I arrived midway through the first half. Too cheap to pay for a ticket, I found a spot along the fence where there was a clear line of sight down to the field and watched the game from there.

The Redmen had the ball on their own 15 yard line and the quarterback dropped back to pass. It was a deep drop back to his own three yard line. As he dropped back, under no pressure at all, no defensive linemen anywhere near him, he tripped, fell backwards, and landed in his own end zone for a safety. Hurrah. Two points for the visitors. "Whoa," I thought, "even Johns Hopkins' football team could not execute plays like that. McGill must be a really good school, they looked like honor roll students in those uniforms."

The football anecdote was meant to be a segue into a discussion of the early days of the MBA program. Actually, it just reminded me of how different football is when you are in Quebec. There was a French Canadian guy with whom I became friends in Montreal, he was a friend of one of my classmates in the MBA program. The guy's nickname was "Capitaine Bonhomme" (Captain Good Man, after an old TV character). The Capitaine was discussing NFL football with me once, and he mentioned that he did not like to sit through the games. But, the highlight shows, they were fantastic! "The music is great!" he said, "and I love that, they show Joe Montana dropping back, and the announcer he says, 'And then, the 49ers made the largest land gain since the Louisiana Purchase!'"

Not quite the same as talking football at a sports bar in DC. In Quebec Joe Montana is called a quart-arriere (quarterback), Vince Lombardi was an entraineur (coach), and the Pats are called Les Patriotes de Nouvelle-Angleterre. Also, there were bizarre rules in Canadian football. Three downs instead of four, twenty yard end zones, and you get a point (called a "rouge") if you kick the ball into the opposing team's end zone and they cannot run it out. During one of my first intramural flag football games at McGill, the other team kicked the ball and downed it in our end zone. Then I watched in amazement as our opponents started jumping up and down, giving each other high fives and clapping. I thought, "What is wrong with them?" Nothing actually, they were winning 1-0.

On the first day of MBA orientation there was a calculus exam, and unless one passed it one had to take an extra class called "Review of Basic Math." Before the exam everyone met for the first time in the lobby of the Bronfman Building, home of McGill's MBA program. The new MBA's eyed each other suspiciously as they waited to enter the testing room, future classmates who might ruin the grade curve for them. One could not help but expect bad things of other MBA's before actually meeting and getting to know them. The first person I met was our future class president, already out shaking hands. Little did I know I would later be a vice president on the student council with him.

Soon enough we were in the room, the test began, and one could see the annoyance on most faces as minds strained to remember the calculus they had studied years before. There was bitterness in the air when after just one hour or so a student got up and handed in his exam. "Probably a math PhD," I remembered thinking. But this was completely wrong. In the coming weeks I would find out that this person tried only a few pages of the test, and seeing that he did not know the rest, packed it in. He had resigned himself to taking that "Review of Basic Math" class.

This person I will call Keanu Reeves, one of the few MBA's directly out of a university undergraduate program. He was a smart guy but his speech and mannerisms were straight out of the movie *Bill and Ted's Excellent Adventure*. He spoke in teenage catch phrases, and used his stinging teenage style wit to have an occasional laugh at someone else's expense. His favorite phrase was "ha… as if," but there was nothing after the "if," that was the end of the phrase. Eventually we became friends as he, like me, had his sights set on investment banking.

I spent much longer than Keanu on the calculus exam, struggling to get partial credit on the tougher questions at the end, but I should have just packed it in too. I spent the summer working two jobs and never had much free time. When I did have a spare minute I could not bring myself to spend it working through a calculus review course. See you in Basic Math! I did not mind really, a lot of the MBA women were in that class ("Review of Basic Tiger Math" yeah!) so it turned out to be fun. The morning after the math exam we had a three hour marathon introduction to accounting lecture, that was fun too. Not.

The first semester was tough in that the workload was heavy, and it was competitive as everyone was trying to make their mark in our class and with the professors. We had core classes like Accounting, Statistics, Management Information Systems, and Organizational Behavior. Our accounting professor knew the subject matter well, and luckily he answered all of our questions. Unfortunately, he always gave us the same answer… "Read the book!" I was interested in Statistics and enjoyed it, but the class was not recommended for those with pacemakers. The exams were like drag races. "Anyone could do my open book tests if they sit there for hours with a calculator and paper, so I just give you one hour," our professor said. True to form, the final exam was a five hour test with a three hour time limit. Afterwards one of my friends said, "My calculator was on fire, eh."

Finally there was Organizational Behavior, a case study class, which was more interesting than accounting (that's a backhanded compliment). It was the same idea as some of those scenes in the movie and the TV series *The Paper Chase* where the professor randomly calls on students to present the facts of the case. This made things competitive. Class participation counted more than exam scores, a frightening thing when you consider that everyone in the MBA program was used to getting A's as an undergraduate.

Have you ever seen Arnold Horshack on the TV show *Welcome Back Kotter*? "Ooh ooh, Mr. Kotter, Mr. Kotter, call on me" Well, multiply that by 60, and you have an idea of what the class was like. The atmosphere became sick when halfway through the semester the professor put up preliminary participation grades with asterisks by the grades of certain students. As I remember more than half the class received asterisks. "Those asterisks mean that you need to participate more," said our professor. More. The following Monday was a nightmare, overachieving MBA's with anxious faces, standing on chairs, waving both arms, setting off flares, anything to get the professor's attention.

Because of the heavy workload, I felt like I had been through a war by the end of the semester. There were some casualties too. About 110 students started the semester and we were down to around a 100 through failures and drop outs by the beginning of the second term. Below a grade of 65 in two classes or below a 70 average overall and it was au revoir Monsieur MBA. After this semester was over I felt like a capitalist marine after boot camp, ready to hit the beach. I became very gung ho and intense about business. I was going to do it all, be serious, do all of those things I never thought of doing at school before. Like run for student council office, for example. All that effort I put into being an apathetic teenager was ruined now. I was a disgrace to my slacker high school. I proceeded to win a vice president slot on the MBA Council.

While a Student Council vice president in the second year of the MBA program, some of the foreign students made a suggestion to me. I should create an organization for international MBA students, since there were a lot of them. So I did. I named it the "McGill MBA International Students Organization" (I had the creativity of a finance major). Technically I was an international student myself at McGill. The group was meant to organize second year foreign MBA's to help new students from other countries tackle the many obstacles involved in studying abroad. We did a few worthwhile things, but like the National Honor Society in high school, and many similar academic organizations, one of the biggest obstacles we tackled at meetings was the problem of coming up with things to discuss at our meetings.

I felt like my greatest accomplishment in furthering international understanding and friendship was when my friend Badri, who was from India, and I went to see the British heavy metal band Iron Maiden in concert at the Montreal Forum. You see although you would never know it by looking at him, Badri was the biggest Iron Maiden fan in India, and perhaps the biggest Iron Maiden fan in the world. The group was everything to him, he knew the words to all their songs, but he never had the chance to see them in concert. As you can imagine, Iron Maiden does not tour the Subcontinent. If the band did, it might face the humiliation of playing support for Ravi Shankar.

When Iron Maiden came to town it was one of the highlights of Badri's two years at McGill. From the windows of the McGill MBA lounge we could see the Iron Maiden tour bus parked in front of the Four Seasons Hotel across the street. As we sat around in the lounge that day Badri kept watch out the window just in case singer Bruce Dickinson and his metal madmen should appear. Badri purchased two tickets for the concert but not surprisingly, none of his MBA friends were interested in the show. None that is until he asked the founder and president of the McGill MBA International Students Organization, who relished the opportunity to make a foreign student's dreams come true, and to do a little headbanging at the same time.

Iron Maiden was not one of my favorite groups, but this concert was a memorable one. I could not help but catch Maiden fever as Badri leaped to his feet with the first few chords of every song. "OH SHEEET MAN!!! DAMN IT!!! I LOVE THIS SONG!!!" he would scream. Badri's fist was in the air and he yelled every word along with Bruce Dickinson as Iron Maiden ravaged Montreal. I am starting to get all wound up remembering the concert, time to cool off. Back to the story. This chapter is supposed to be about the first year of the MBA program anyway.

As I was saying, after finishing the first semester of the MBA I was feeling rough and ready. Looking good and feeling good. So, for our MBA Talent Show I did a joke rap song. The majority of the song's lyrics dealt with individual classes and professors, but in my opinion the following sections summed up the general mood of cockiness I was feeling at the time.

> Right about now I'm going to do this rap about McGill MBA's, Much Bucks Always with the degree that pays, Much to Brag About, with the Monster Bank Account, in charge, living large, Masters of Bond Arbitrage, Making Beaucoup d'Argent (a lot of money) chaque jour (each day), real chill at McGill University in the place to be…
>
> Statistics say that we are smart, degrees of freedom going off the chart, take the mean, take the standard deev, of the calories, the salaries that we achieve, making

dollars and sense, pounds and pence, Deutsche Marks, Yen, Francs that are French

Lots of talk about superior intelligence, being in charge, and most of all making lots of money. Looking back on this, I might buy the intelligence part. Book knowledge anyway, but no one doing an MBA in this era had a PhD in good timing, or else they would not have been doing an MBA. As for being in charge, hmm. In charge of our lockers maybe, our pens, and our school notebooks, that was about it. And the money? Much Bucks Always, degree that pays, Monster Bank Account... ba ha.

Right. As they like to say in the world of finance, we were talking in terms of the sum of expected future cash flows, future being the key word. A few years of weak cash flows later I could do some NPV (Net Present Value) analysis on the investment decision to do an MBA. This is a way finance people determine whether a project or purchase is a worthwhile proposition. Simple, we take the total present value of the future cash flows (money earned as a result of having an MBA valued at the time I began the MBA) and subtract from it the cost of the investment (the MBA tuition itself). It was clear because of the current recession it was going to take a while for the MBA investment to pay for itself.

What did this mean? It meant for me anyway, the money I was to earn in my first few years out of the program did not look like it was going to compensate for the money invested in attaining the MBA. In laymen's terms, the MBA and its promise of a Monster Bank Account seemed to be turning into a Most Bogus Aspiration. In the recession and poor job market of the early 1990's, it did not matter how good a program McGill had. During my first year in the program, however, I felt like I could do anything. I was going to march right down to Wall Street and have whatever job I wanted.

School and classes were nice enough, but let us get on to the real reason most people do an MBA... the search for a fast track career. A large part of the supposed benefit of doing an MBA is the improved access to companies, interviews, and networking through the school. Our first big event was "Career Day," when companies set up booths with corporate literature and MBA's were given the opportunity to talk to representatives about career possibilities. It was the first taste I had that things were not going to be as my rap song promised.

For starters Goldman Sachs, one of the major Wall Street firms, did not show up. Their place was prepared at a table with a name card that read "Goldman Sachs" but no one was sitting there. It was just like the MBA fair I attended in Washington, DC where Harvard did not show up. I suppose this is how it works, the most desirable places just do not show up, that way we can only imagine how wonderful they are and we will not be disappointed. I started to think that perhaps I should employ the same strategy in my job search. I would be the only person not to show up for my on campus interviews. Then I bet the best financial firms and corporations would end up sending recruiters to my apartment to find me!

Soon after Career Day individual company presentations began, and I made sure to go to as many as I could. Not because they were offering fantastic positions, though. In fact, most firms stopped by out of habit. They had come on campus every year before, so why stop now? Many representatives would say, "This year we probably are not going to hire on campus, but if you are really interested you can send us your resume anyway. If someone really stands out, we might consider him or her."

I had no false hopes about the prospects of joining one of these companies, I was there for the food. McGill set up nice spreads of sandwiches, cheese and crackers, fruit, pastries, wine, soda, you name it and I ate it. The words "free food" are magic to anyone who is a student, you do not let those opportunities pass you by no matter what the sacrifice. Even if it meant sitting through a 90 minute presentation by Canadian Pacific Rail about the new marketing breakthroughs they had planned. In fact some of the presentations were even more lavish than the ones sponsored by McGill. Citibank Canada made its presentation at the Four Seasons Hotel in my second year of the MBA and it was the same story, no on campus interviews. Man did they have some food there though!

I made many telephone calls and sent out resumes both in Montreal and New York. Soon after sending a resume to Drexel Burnham in New York, I saw headlines in the newspaper announcing the collapse of the firm made famous by Michael Milken. Next to the news stories were photos of boxes full of documents being hauled away outside Drexel's New York headquarters. I always wondered if my resume accidentally made it to one of those boxes that was hauled off, or if it hit the trash can immediately upon entering Drexel's New York offices.

Wall Street investment bankers Salomon Brothers scheduled a presentation in my first year at McGill for all potential candidates from MBA and undergraduate university programs in Montreal. Salomon actually showed up for the presentation (a definite sign that the firm was in decline!). Like Citibank Canada a year later, Salomon gave its presentation at the Four Seasons Hotel, and I was all over it. The food was good of course but more than that, I hung on every word. Nothing but investment banking talk and money. Speeches given by Salomon representatives turned into a contest of who could claim to have worked the most hours…

"At Salomon you'll find yourself working 12 hour days on average."

"I typically work 14-16 hours a day, and most weekends."

"Well, we are allotted vacation days, but I never take them."

I think all this talk scared the life out of many candidates in the audience who were unfamiliar with investment banking culture. I overheard one member of the crowd talking to another and he seemed very upset, "But... 16 hours a day... but... I mean... when do you eat, when do you sleep?" "What a weenie," I thought at the time, "don't you remember what Gordon Gekko said in the movie *Wall Street* when he woke Bud Fox with a phone call in the wee hours of the morning? Money never sleeps." After the presentations I moved in on a few of the recruiters and talked for a good half hour with them. Finally I found myself alone with one recruiter who was a Canadian born employee of Salomon based in New York City. He said I should stop by and see him when I was in New York over Christmas concerning working during the summer at Salomon. This was it, capitalist marine, D-Day late December, hit the beach!

Before Christmas break I called and set up an appointment with Salomon, then the day came. My recruiter friend looked different. In Montreal he was all smiles, drink in hand, twisting the ring on his finger in a happy go lucky fashion. Now he looked like death warmed over, no smile, bags under his eyes, clearly frustrated about whatever he was working on at the time. Still, he was great in that he took ten minutes to talk to me and helped me set up a preliminary interview. We had established a good relationship and I might have had a chance to work in his area for the summer, which was Investment Research, but the idiot I was, I thought that was not a cool area in which to work! I just *had* to work in trading (because that was considered cool in the investment banking book about Salomon Brothers I had read called *Liar's Poker*). When I told him what I wanted to do he passed me on to someone he knew in Sales and Trading.

I was able to take the obligatory trip to the viewing gallery of Salomon's famous trading floor, I was so impressed at the time. Later I met with a nice young woman from personnel and this went well. Then I was taken out on the bond sales floor to get a preliminary grilling from one of Salomon's bond salesmen. This man asked me some questions about the market, but most of the discussion centered around my character. My favorite question was, "Give me five adverbs to describe yourself." Adverbs? There's a new one. Testing my motivation and my English grammar in one fell swoop. So, I did not try to be fancy, I just picked five good adjectives and added -ly to the end... aggressive-ly, efficient-ly, etc. I suppose adjectives are not cool at Salomon, because adjectives are passive. They can describe someone just sitting there, and no one just sits there at Salomon. The only acceptable descriptive words are words describing action verbs.

The salesman seemed happy enough with my answer, and ended the interview with this... "I want to test how well you listen, early in our discussion I mentioned something about subject X (I do not remember the actual subject), now I want you to tell me what I said about subject X." The fact was I had been listening extreme-ly attentive-ly the entire interview, and he never said a word about subject X, which was the whole point. I was supposed to become nervous and upset and flustered, thinking that I had forgotten something. Hey, I was too sharp for this, he did not realize he was messing with a capitalist marine. I calmly replied, "You never said anything about subject X." "Are you sure?" he asked. "Yes, I am sure I did not hear anything about subject X." As I said this I noticed a slight upturn in the corner of his mouth, a tiny smile I do not think I was supposed to see. I had given the correct answer. He said goodbye and I was led out by the woman from personnel who told me I would be hearing from them soon.

A few weeks later up at McGill I received a letter from Salomon, instructing me to call and set up another appointment. I called and picked a date during my spring break in February. Although I did a bit more job hunting in New York over the break, the main reason I went down was for the second Salomon interview. I prepared myself for a full day's worth of grueling interviews and arrived first thing in the morning. I was taken to a senior human resources woman and I sat down in her office. She asked me a few questions about myself, why I was there, and a few questions about the market. After ten minutes or so she seemed to be wrapping up our conversation. I was ready, "bring on my future coworkers to grill me more, I'm ready for battle," I thought. Wrong. She got up from her desk, gave me her card and said, "Thanks for coming by, you can give me a call in a few days if you like."

What?!?! That was it? Ten minutes, I came all the way to New York for ten minutes with someone from personnel? Two days later I called, but I knew the deal, my goose was cooked. I did not care. I called anyway, every half hour, and every half hour she was busy interviewing another candidate. I kept calling until finally late in the afternoon she took the phone to talk to me. I wanted to hear her say that I came all the way to New York for nothing. With a bit of nervousness in her voice she blurted out, "I don't know Michael, I don't think you are going to fit our needs this year." Thank you Salomon Brothers.

As the year went on, it started to dawn on me that I was in trouble as far as the job situation was concerned for the summer. Less companies paid visits to McGill than in years past I was told, and the ones that came did more speaking than hiring. The placement office at McGill was full of good intentions and tried to remain upbeat, but there was not much it could do.

I scheduled a meeting with the head of McGill's placement office that year. He began our discussion by asking me, "Why this big fascination you have with trading and investment banking? Have you ever considered other things, like working for Ford maybe?" Ford? I was open to suggestions but the whole point of the MBA for me was to try to get a banking job, which was hardly out of the ordinary for an MBA. Later I discovered that our placement officer made the same suggestion to everyone. His last job had been at Ford and that is where he had connections. His advice had nothing to do with each MBA's strengths or career aspirations at all. We nearly became the first class in business school history to all take a job at the same company! Our class reunions could have been barbecues in the Ford parking lot. 100 Ford Taurus automobiles waiting in line to park with drivers rolling down their windows to ask the attendant, "Is this the way to the McGill class reunion?"

The McGill placement office worked hard in putting together a book of MBA resumes every year and mailed this book to various companies. I am surprised our placement office did not catch the wrath of environmental groups for this, because it was a shameful waste of trees. We were urged to put our resumes in, it was very important we were told, so I paid my money and put my resume in. Most people did. I never heard another word about it and neither did anyone else as far as I knew. We did get a handy manual from the placement office, advice on interviews and job hunting which was full of helpful hints like… "Be well groomed, be courteous, don't chew gum (!)" So that was it. If only I had read the manual earlier in the year I would have known not to go to the Salomon interview with a full pack of Bubble Yum in mouth!

This was not McGill's fault. The thing about job searching, especially in a recession, is that it is all about knowing the right people or getting introductions to them. The rest of the placement office's time and effort is of less value. The office can work on providing resume writing workshops and practice interviews, but what kind of MBA has trouble writing his or her own resume?

Oh well. McGill is an excellent school, and the relatively low tuition was a big plus, but there is no such thing as a free lunch. It was going to be harder for me to get a good job in the

United States because McGill's placement office was not geared toward American companies. And, it was hard for me to get a job in Canada during a recession because I was a US citizen. In certain cases the Canadian companies had to prove that there was no Canadian citizen of equal talent and qualifications to the American in order to get the work permit for the American citizen. At the time Canada's unemployment was even worse than America's was, in fact Canada probably had more overeducated and underemployed young people than the US in the early 1990's. If you stopped at a McDonalds in Toronto, you could discuss Voltaire with the person behind the counter while you waited for your Big Mac.

The summer between my two years at McGill I ended up doing paralegal work at an excellent law firm in New York City, but an adrenaline pumped capitalist marine could lose his mind in a place like a law firm – all those legal documents with all those words every day and no numbers or dollar signs anywhere in sight!

Enough about jobs and careers. Whatever happened to Tiger? I was in Quebec after all, and French girls were everywhere. Well, I spent my first year in Montreal dating a nice English speaking Canadian classmate of mine from Ottawa. Unlike native English speaking girls the French Canadian women typically started dating early, and moved in with someone by their late teens. By the time they hit their twenties they were either married or waiting for their roommate boyfriends to marry them. Colonel Hogan did not warn me about this!

I had a subscription to one of Montreal's French language newspapers called *La Presse* which used to have a one page section for teenagers. I read bug eyed as one of the articles discussed "your first time." But it was not about your first time having sex, it was your first time moving in with a boyfriend or girlfriend. In Quebec I suppose it is a rite of passage for a teenager, just like getting braces or taking your driving test.

One of my English speaking Canadian MBA friends in his mid-twenties met a French Canadian girl early enough. A late bloomer, she was around 19 and still was not living with someone. She would spend the night with him in his parents' house and eat breakfast with the whole family in the morning (!) God bless Quebec. What a province! I think this is why the Quebecois do not have a good understanding of football; they are too busy having sex in their formative years to get a solid grounding in basic football rules and strategy.

MBA Year Two

The second year of an MBA program is the time most MBA's look forward to. The core classes are done, and the student is free to concentrate on his or her area of interest. Students usually work on projects in conjunction with actual businesses to gain practical experience. And, or so I have been told, a long time ago in an era called the early 1980's it was a time to be wined and dined by recruiters. A time to make difficult choices between the pros and cons of a multitude of job offers. It must have been tough back then. MBA's of the early 1990's had no difficult decisions to make, our rule of thumb was if you got one job offer, you took it. Just like Pepperidge Farm cookies, the MBA's of the early 1990's will be remembered as products of a simpler, happier time.

I concentrated on finance and investments in my second year, and one class I took was called "Applied Investments." This class actually began in the middle of our first year and continued until the middle of our second year. Groups of students were given actual investment portfolios to manage in consultation with brokers of various investment firms in Montreal. Each group inherited a portfolio from a group in the previous year's class, and the group was free to keep or sell the securities in the portfolio as it saw fit. The portfolio my group inherited was a real winner. A sizable portion of our funds were in Campeau stock, the operation of the famous Canadian developer Robert Campeau. He was a businessman whose operations were rapidly falling to pieces. The stock's price had crashed from the mid-teens to a few dollars per share before we were given the capability to make trades in class.

Our group made some solid decisions as well as some bad ones due to the nature of the class. There was an obvious short term perspective inherent in managing a portfolio for one year only, which is why the idea behind this class was flawed. It sounds glamorous to manage real money, but a business school could put the funds to better use than having green MBA's losing it in risky short term bets on the market. In a class called "Options and Futures" second semester in second year we invested using imaginary funds and it was just as educational for us.

Our Applied Investments group stayed fully invested in stocks throughout a lengthy bear market. Just about everything we did, wise and foolish, went against us. One of our beauties was a ride on a whipsaw called Archer Communications, one of the most volatile stocks in any market anywhere it seemed. The reason for this was Archer's famous "Q Sound." Q Sound was a breakthrough Archer claimed to have made in audio technology, a four way listening experience as opposed to normal stereo sound systems. Archer's true specialty was market rumors.

More amusing than the actual rumors were the silences in between. Q Sound was about to hit the music market like a tornado! Then nothing. Information was harder to come by back then before the internet, so our group began to wonder… were there actually staff at Archer headquarters? Was there an Archer headquarters? I started to suspect Archer Communications was actually just one man who would make calls from payphones in Canada to financial reporters… "Yeah, yeah, Q Sound… that's it… any day now…what's that?...Madonna?... who?... oh yeah that's right Madonna she's great, her album will be in Q Sound… we've been working with her… oh she's great to work with… any day now Q Sound is going to hit the market…

My group in Applied Investments gained some very useful experience in money management. We got a lot of practice trying to explain away our losses. Every few months we had to get up in front of the class again and describe another unfortunate dip in the value of our portfolio. By the final presentation we had it down to a science. One member of my group (he was an Iron Maiden fan from India actually) put up a chart of the Toronto Stock Exchange (TSE) index over the year just ended. It had been a very bad year for the stock market; the index had fallen approximately 25% in that time frame. Overtop of this Badri placed a chart of our group's portfolio value, which had fallen less than approximately 25%, if you do not blame us for the drop in the Campeau stock which was out of our control, we were quick to add. Badri then went on to proudly proclaim, against a backdrop of cheering and laughter from our classmates, that our group had managed to outperform the TSE index. This was without mentioning the small detail that our group had underperformed every other portfolio in the class. The only one who did not appreciate the joke was our professor.

So there we were, shifting the blame, rationalizing poor judgement… we were well on our way to becoming professional money managers.

In the second semester of our second year I had a class called "Options and Futures." Despite the fact that there is plenty to learn in terms of practical knowledge and strategy in this area, our classes devolved into endless, complex derivations of options pricing formulas. The class would sit there glassy eyed as the professor wrote expressions on the board like $\sum 2xyz + \pi xy - \beta xyz! - \Omega xz! + \alpha bcxyz$ and then spent all class deriving other expressions that looked slightly different but just as meaningless to us. One day as this was going on a Belgian exchange student in our class became visibly nervous and agitated. He leaned over to me and whispered, "Do you understand this?!?!" Feeling a bit sorry for him, I whispered back, "Don't worry about it, none of us understands.

The Belgian student pondered this for a minute or two. Apparently unsatisfied with my answer, he leaned over to Keanu Reeves. Once again, but this time loud enough so much of the class of 15 students could hear, he asked Keanu, "Do you understand this?!?!" Keanu's response was much less sympathetic than mine. With a mocking laugh and a look of disgust on his face as he pointed a thumb at the Belgian, Keanu glanced at everyone in the class and said, "… as if." Oh well, I tried to tell him.

There was also an investment portfolio competition in Options and Futures class, thankfully with imaginary money this time and a portfolio of my very own as opposed to working in groups like in Applied Investments. This was Spring 1991, when the Gulf War between the US and Saddam Hussein's Iraq took place. I was able to ride the wave of the mini bull market created by news of the American victory and I came through with the top performing portfolio in the class. Although most of my classmates knew what they were doing, there was nothing for me to be big headed about. A few of the bizarre portfolios in this class gave new meaning to the expression "off the wall."

First there was the student who bought all extremely long term growth stocks, and explained in his presentation how they should start to show gains in the next few years. Hello, hello, the class was only four months long. By the time your stocks show gains this class will be a distant memory. Much better than this however was a priceless presentation given by another student on his portfolio strategy. It turned into a 15 minute discussion of the differences between warfare in Vietnam versus warfare in the desert. The student described how he had correctly predicted a quick American victory in the Gulf War due to his understanding of the dynamics of desert warfare. This led him to execute his one and only trade, to take advantage of this astute prediction. The trade involved Japanese Yen futures, unfortunately the student did not understand the contract size and put in an order for something like USD 10,000,000 worth of Yen when we were each given only USD 500,000 to work with in the class.

During the Pentagon like war briefing the student put up an overhead describing Iraq's "Red Guards." Anyone who lived anywhere near a TV during the time of the conflict heard the term "Iraq's Elite Republican Guards" a few thousand times. As our class' answer to General Schwarzkopf discussed the relative ineffectiveness of the Iraqi "Red" Guards, Keanu's hand went up to pose a question. He was merciless.

"Who are the Red Guards?"

"You know, the elite units, the Red Guards."

"So you're saying the Russian Army was in the battle, the Red Guards?"

"No, no... the Iraqi Red Guards."

"Hmm... do you mean the Republican Guards?"

"Um... yeah... the Iraqi Red Guards, the Republican Guards, yeah."

Stormin Norman's presentation lost any shred of credibility it may have had as he went on attempting to convince us that the Republican Guards were also known as the Red Guards. Lost somewhere in all this was the fact that we were in the MBA, and in Options and Futures class, and presenting the strategies and performances of our portfolios.

One of the big moments of the year for finance majors and finance professors alike was the appearance of finance wizard Fischer Black at McGill. Black was well known as a result of the famous Black-Scholes Options Pricing Formula, a mathematical equation which estimated the value of options. The formula was quite a breakthrough when it was published. Mr. Black was to discuss his work at the time in front of an audience at McGill and our finance professors were clearly excited. One of my professors said in class, "If you think all this academic work we do in finance is not relevant to the real world, the working world, just take a look at Fischer Black. Goldman Sachs has just hired him to do research and they are paying him quite well for his work I might add." I bet a genius like Fischer had been smart enough to not show up for his first interview with Goldman!

The Fischer Black lecture started off with a bang when there was a power blackout at McGill about an hour before the talk was to begin. After relocating to a hall off campus on the other side of Sherbrooke Street all systems were go. The hall full of Jesuits were anxiously awaiting the Pope's arrival. The monks were on the edge of their seats anticipating the words of the Dalai Lama. On to the speech.

No doubt a brilliant man, Fischer Black was no Jack Kennedy when it came to public speaking. Mr. Black spent the better part of an hour mumbling into the microphone and staring down at his papers. Eventually the floor was opened for comments, and my options professor posed a well prepared question on one of Fischer Black's calculations. Fischer's answer was total confusion. He shuffled through his papers for a minute, and then replied sheepishly, "Um…you see…we're still working on this… I… I'm not sure, I don't have an answer for you." My gaze turned from Fischer Black to my finance professors all sitting in a row, puzzled faces, crushed expectations, wondering if some guy had wandered in off the street and was pretending to be their idol Fischer Black. They looked like they were ready to give up finance altogether and join the French Foreign Legion. Or the Iraqi Red Guards, even.

As far as I was concerned, you could have your Fischer Black, Bill Gates, and Michael Milken. My true heroes, the business icons who inspired me the most during my MBA years, were on late night television. The infomercial men. There was Tom Vu, the millionaire real estate mogul, whose classic early 1990's video commercials can still be found on YouTube. And there was Tony Robbins, the visionary motivational speaker to top corporations as well as individuals. These were men of action. Living proof that getting rich is easy, when you know how.

Tom Vu was number one with me and some of my MBA friends. We would watch for hours mesmerized as Tom's most successful students were shown in testimonial clips. Once they learned the Tom Vu system the world was their oyster. These short speeches were just a warmup for Tom Vu's brilliant pep talks which were broadcast periodically in between the testimonials. I never got bored with Tom Vu, Tom Vu was my main man!

Tom's infomercials began with shots of expensive mansions and properties and a narrator's voice declaring, "The majority of millionaires made their fortune in real estate…" The Tom Vu method relied on finding and buying the low priced, distressed properties that others miss. The idea was to buy the real estate and then sell it soon afterward for large cash profits, immediately. This was the great attraction. As Tom Vu said in his brochure, "In my search for a program that would make me wealthy, I attended many seminars and read an endless number of books about making money. I always found one recurring problem, they all teach long term investments. Even though they taught me how to do it with no money down, I did not want to wait five or ten years for my profit! Just like you, I want it NOW!"

I was with Tom Vu. Forget all this nonsense in my investment classes, so called famous money managers like Peter Lynch telling you to research companies. You know, buy the good performers and hold them for extended periods. I fell for this conservative nonsense until Tom Vu opened my eyes. *Wall Street Week* was for wimps. Real men lived dynamic lives like my man Tom Vu, and get their profits NOW!

Tom Vu came to America in 1975 as a refugee from Vietnam and he told the informercial camera that he ended up working as a busboy in a country club. It was then that a nice old man revealed to him some secrets of how to be rich. As Tom Vu said in his brochure, "I sincerely believe that if I had not discovered my powerful money making system – which is now the Tom Vu profit seminar – my family would still be just barely getting by in that same penniless situation, instead of having the millions we now have!"

The thing is, I have watched countless hours of Tom Vu informercials, and I can tell you that somebody helped Tom write those eloquent sentences I just quoted. There is no eloquence about Tom Vu and that was the beauty of the man, the myth, the legend that was Tom Vu. The man who wants his profits NOW! Tom Vu says that everyone told him he could not succeed in America because he was a poor immigrant who did not know the language. To this Tom answered, "You know what I say to them!?! I tell them, you a loser, get out of my way!!" Tom told it straight with a heavy Vietnamese accent, it is all about having sports cars, houses, yachts, and beautiful women… he had them and you did not… but you could have had all this if only you would have signed up for his seminar. "Cometomyseminar!" Tom would shout very quickly.

Tom was so rough that on his informercials he could disrespect you worse than a master freestyle rapper in only seven words of broken English. Cut to one shot of Tom in the infomercial, on a massive yacht, with beautiful, bikini clad women on each arm, a cool ocean breeze blowing. Tom, grinning from ear to ear, would say, "Look at me… and look at you!"

He had a point there. I had no comeback for that, sitting in my tiny Montreal apartment alone. All I had were my MBA textbooks full of useless ramblings of so called "experts" in business. You know Fischer Black did not have cool clothes and a Mercedes for each day of the week like my man Tom. Fischer Black took ten minutes fishing through his papers to come up with answers to the questions of my finance professors. Tom Vu made his profits NOW! In the time I wasted in that Fischer Black lecture Tom Vu had probably bought and sold half of Florida.

In another clip Tom Vu was shown standing on a tennis court, on a beautiful large estate with a mansion, and here he would put us in our place. "You think I at park, right! No! This my court, I own it!" As Tom Vu's biggest fan I liked to imagine what Tom's life was like away from the camera. When my man Tom threw a party at his tennis court (he own it!), I bet Richard Branson and Donald Trump stood by their mailboxes all day praying for an invitation. In fact, I bet Donald Trump received personalized Christmas cards from Tom Vu, with photos of Tom Vu and Donald's ex-wife Ivana in a jacuzzi at the Tom Vu estate. The card would read:

Dear Donald,

Merry Christmas.

Look at me… and look at you!

Sincerely,

The World's *Premier* Real Estate Mogul, Tom Vu

I hate to say this, but I have to. Even my favorite *Wall Street Week* guest Marty Zweig, in spite of his tough voice and sharp threads, still looked like a wimp next to Tom Vu. Marty had a system that called for strategic switching of investments depending on interest rates and market conditions. Kind of cool, but it was still a long term strategy. What I did not understand was, as sharp as Marty was, why couldn't he get his profits NOW!? Marty Zweig and Tom Vu both had operations based in Florida, and I could only imagine what happened when they met while grocery shopping. It must have been embarrassing for Marty. Tom probably said, "Marty Zweig!... move your cart!... you a loser, get out of my way!"

Between my friends and me at McGill, Tom Vu's words of wisdom became our own. We greeted each other in McGill's MBA lounge with "You a loser, get out of my way!" When asked advice on how to complete an assignment we might reply like Tom, "Old American saying for this... get off your butt and do it!" And, if there was any hesitation when it was time to hit the Peel Pub for a few beers, the question was, "What you waiting for? CometoPeelPub!"

I actually did go to Tom's free introductory seminar when it came to a Montreal hotel but Tom was not there. I was crushed. I did not plan on forking over money for Tom's course, I went simply to see my man Tom in person. Unfortunately he sent some of his people to give introductory talks and to make the "come to my seminar!" sales pitch without him. So, I just took a brochure with Tom's picture and story as a souvenir. As I walked home through the snow that night, I tried to cheer myself up by repeating my mantra, "look at me... and look at you... look at me... and look at you."

Another hero of mine on the informercial circuit was Tony Robbins of "Robbins Research International." Tony created mental techniques for success in managing your emotions, your business dealings, and your relationships so that you can have a richer, more satisfying life. The infomercial began with former star NFL quarterback Fran Tarkenton describing how he felt like a failure after leading the Minnesota Vikings to three Super Bowl losses. That is, until he met Tony Robbins and used Tony's techniques to turn his life around. My first reaction to this was, "Turn his life around?! That's Incredible! What is Fran talking about? He was a great quarterback." I remembered when I was an eight year old, crying in front of the TV because Fran had just ripped apart the Redskins' defense and knocked them out of the playoffs. On the infomercial Fran introduces Tony with the words, "Tony Robbins is truly remarkable."

"Wow," I thought, "if Fran thinks this guy Tony is that great he must be something. Hell, I am glad Tony Robbins was not playing quarterback for the Vikings back in '73. It could have been really bad for the Redskins!" Soon Fran would begin a completely staged interview with Tony, asking him to describe the Robbins system. When Tony Robbins talked, I was struck by his exaggerated hand gestures, his incredibly expressive face, and an overall appearance of someone on amphetamines. He was like a man possessed, and he had a very bizarre vocabulary. Tony said things like, "Fran, I want to *energize* people, (makes a clutching motion with his hand), to *empower* them with my techniques, so that they can *turbo-charge* their lives, have *vivacious* relationships, *ballistic* careers, and become *impassioned* about life.

At the time I became impassioned enough to check out one of Tony Robbins' books and finding what the hell he was talking about. It turned out that he was a human development trainer, a motivational speaker used by many companies, sports teams, etc. to maximize personal performance. There were some solid ideas in the book, though most were other people's ideas Tony brought together in one package.

Tony said he began his journey at age 19. At the time he was working as a janitor and feeling sorry for himself because he never had any money. One night he broke down, sitting alone in his tiny apartment, tears streaming down his face as Neil Diamond's record, "I am, I cried," played on the stereo. It made sense to me up to that point. I would cry too if I had to listen to a Neil Diamond record in my apartment.

Tony decided then and there to be a success, and worked nonstop at learning techniques for achieving success. Tony Robbins said the key was to model his behavior after that of successful people he saw. Eventually he achieved all his goals. This sounded reasonable, but what was the deal with all of these words Tony used? The book explained. It was called

"Transformational Vocabulary." One way of mastering one's emotions was to alter your word choice to include only positive and energy filled words. For example, do not say "all right" say "superb." Do not say "tasty" say "sumptuous." Do not say "fast" say "ballistic." Fair enough. I thought maybe this might help me out in my career, or better yet, help me connect with some of those Quebec babes! Maybe I would go down to Montreal's busy Ste. Catherine Street and try to score with the women using Tony's transformational vocabulary.

Anyway, back to the story of my second year in the MBA program. There was a somber mood to the second year of my MBA. On the outside people were generally upbeat, going about their day to day business. But, for some of us, this picnic called school would be over soon and we would be struggling to find jobs or struggling with the frustration of underemployment. Career Day was even more of a non-event than the year before; Goldman Sachs did not even pretend they were going to send someone this time.

To make things more difficult for us the person in charge of our placement office resigned and split in his Ford Taurus. The Dean had to search for his replacement smack dab in the middle of the school year. The changeover included a period when we had no placement office except for the poor administrative assistant who could not be expected to do all of the work herself. Thankfully McGill's MBA program quickly found a super replacement who was very proactive and did a lot for us, even in the recession.

After a presentation made by one of the major Canadian banks, a few classmates and I spoke with two members of the bank as I wolfed down my quota of five or six sandwiches. One of the bankers told us he finished his MBA in the late 1970's. He asked us how the recruiting season was going, and our answer amounted to something like, "Oh, not too well." "It's tough eh, no one's hiring." The banker replied, "That's too bad, you know when I finished my MBA, if you didn't have three or four offers you weren't doing so well." Also, in our year of 1991 the "Business Luncheon," a big annual recruiting event at McGill where MBA's and company representatives were mixed at tables to network, was cancelled due to lack of corporate interest. Each week on campus interviews were cancelled by firms tightening their belts in the recession.

We had plenty of good times though. There were events like "The MBA Games" at Queens University in Kingston, Ontario. This was a weekend full of friendly competitions between the major Canadian MBA schools, and drinking of course. The games took place in January and surprise, surprise, it was snowing. We drove through the snow for several hours to get to Kingston from Montreal. The storm was worse to the west of Kingston but four or five MBA's from McMaster University in Hamilton, Ontario still made it on their own. Their chartered bus was cancelled due to the weather but, like St. Bernards on a snowy Swiss ski slope, these brave party dudes took their own car through the blizzard and followed the strong scent of beer coming from Kingston. In contrast, a group of students from University of Ottawa, closer to Kingston than any other school, decided not to come. We were told it was because they had "too much work to do." And we didn't?

The snow definitely gave the games a different, Canadian flavor, from what they would have been if held by all the new California state residents at UCLA, or at the Tom Vu estate in Florida. No women in bikinis, no water polo at the pool. Instead we had touch football, with hangovers, on Saturday morning in two feet of snow. We had indoor volleyball and a scavenger hunt in town with an edge to anyone in a four wheel drive vehicle. And, a "Trivial Pursuits" board game competition, perfect for nerdy MBA's. Although I was not a participant in the Trivial Pursuits competition I heard about the grudge match between McGill and our arch rivals The University of Western Ontario.

"Western" as they are called, fancied themselves at the time as the premier MBA program in Canada, and even tried writing their own case studies just like Harvard Business School does. Anyway, McGill and Western MBA's are not the best of buddies because as everyone knows, McGill's nickname is "The Harvard of the North" and we were the best MBA's. Given this, it was no surprise to hear that there were sparks a plenty at the gaming tables.

Members of McGill's team claimed that Western asked us a question and when our squad gave the correct answer, Western's squad responded, "No, that's incorrect." Quickly the question card was placed back in the stack before McGill's finest could verify the correct answer. A postgame check through the question cards confirmed our worst fears, the answer was correct, and Western had cheated us at Trivial Pursuits. You see, things like this are bound to happen when you put too many "type A personality" MBA's in a room together at the same time.

Our revenge came in the final event, the "air band competition," where groups of students put on performances to music. Although we came in second to Western in overall points, we gave them a good thrashing in this event with a string of brilliant acts in front of a hundred or so Canadian MBA's. The last of our acts was a rap song that I performed. This rap had a decidedly different tone from the one I did at the McGill MBA Talent Night the year before. The message early on was to avoid worrying about your future by getting drunk…

> Take the 401 down to Kingston
>
> Bring the beer, bring the rum, and then we get done
>
> It's McGill MBA's, swaying in a daze, drinking not thinking all of our days
>
> Champion of the MBA games is the name we claim

> It's McGill's one and only MBA crew, down from Quebec, Montreal, PQ
>
> When we got no beer we get MBA rude, Masters of Bad Attitude
>
> We're not brand loyal, we're willing and able
>
> Drinking Labatt's 50 with the Carling Black Label
>
> We'll drink you down, right under the table

Soon reality creeps in, however…

> From Queens to Western to York to McGill
>
> Concordia, McMaster, it's time to get ill
>
> It's time to get drunk, build self-assurance
>
> Get ready to collect unemployment insurance
>
> We'll be on our knees, planting trees
>
> A summer in north BC just us and the bees

But this is easily solved by changing the subject to women…

> MBA women are smart, there's no chance
>
> They're all crafty and they know finance
>
> They can balance your books, keep you out of the red
>
> We should make our team all women instead
>
> Our McGill women, they're smarter than the men
>
> They make us look stupid again and again
>
> They get A's at McGill, then they go
>
> To work at P&G while we paint at College Pro
>
> And our currency don't appreciate
>
> The way they spend our cash flow when we go on a date

>They're so cool, the women from McGill
>
>They'll earn so much money it'll make us ill

401: Main highway leading from Quebec into Ontario

PQ: Province of Quebec

Brand Loyal: Marketing term for customer preference for a particular brand of product

Labatt's 50: A low end Canadian beer

Carling Black Label: A high end Canadian beer

Unemployment Insurance: Canadian form of welfare payment to people out of work

Planting trees / north BC: A summer employment scheme in Canada where money starved students camp out in remote areas like northern British Columbia and are paid by the number of trees they plant

P&G: Proctor & Gamble, highly desirable place to work for marketing majors

College Pro: Another Canadian summer employment scheme for money starved students where groups of students are organized to paint houses for money

Currency / appreciate: Rise in the value of one currency against another, as in "the dollar appreciated versus the yen today"

When the topic of unemployment came up in one of my first year classes, I told the professor that I thought unemployment was one of the "harsh effects of capitalism." The professor froze, shook his head in disbelief and said, "Wait a minute, did I hear correctly?... The harsh effects of capitalism???" What I was trying to say was that capitalism is the best system man has come up with, but it is a difficult and ruthless system. It improves everyone's lot overall but as it makes some individuals wealthy it can leave others trampled underfoot.

There is a saying "The price of freedom is eternal vigilance." I think one could also say that "The price of capitalism is eternal insecurity." With competing forces and never ending changes in the marketplace of a capitalist country, no one can expect a secure life and a steady career. The price we pay for the benefits of capitalism is that at some point in many of our lives our careers are disrupted, companies close down, and workers are laid off. Priorities change and we are left with education and experience that is no longer relevant. Citizens of capitalist countries must always be mentally prepared for upheavals in their careers. They must be ready to pick themselves up, dust off, and do their best to get back into the workforce, to contribute in new and different ways.

Even with its tremendous hardships capitalism has proven itself to be the best, or least worst, economic system. Societies like the former Soviet Union that tried to regulate trade and legislate job security for everyone only succeeded in extinguishing all incentive for innovation. This results in inferior goods and services… bread lines, shoes that fall apart etc. which in turn results in a lower quality of life for everyone. Given a choice, I would take the capitalism and the insecurity anytime, but it is not an easy system

After the last exam of our MBA careers, a group of about twenty of us went out for happy hour at a bar near school. We sat around, a bit relieved the exam was over but a bit sad that the MBA was over. We began talking about what we planned to do now, and most of us did not have much exciting to say. But, Keanu was in a good mood, or a hopeful one anyway. He managed to get an interview with a Canadian investment banking firm in Toronto, it was for an analyst position, writing reports on the market. We considered such positions as great opportunities in 1991.

Keanu and I were good friends but competitive rivals when it came to the investment banking job search. "Frenemies" as Lindsay Lohan might call it, ha ha ha! I had one good opportunity before graduation in 1991, two interviews with Philadelphia based options firm Susquehanna International Group; the first interview went well and they paid my travel there for a second interview. I flubbed it, missing a math/statistics question they asked me, just one, but that was all it took for me not to be hired. I knew the answer but had become fatigued in the interview and quickly spit out the incorrect response. I wanted to kick myself for it. I was still bitter about it, so when Keanu announced at the table "I've got my second interview this week…" and then gushing with pride, "they're flying me in," I was not immediately happy for him. This meant the investment firm was paying for his trip to Toronto for the second interview, a common practice in years past, but a rare occurrence in 1991.

Just as Keanu said, "They're flying me in," in his best cocky investment banker voice, I laughed out loud. It was a laugh of ridicule, which was not very nice and I felt bad about it later, but I was angry and jealous. I had worked hard and wanted some sort of investment banking job myself, and I was disgusted that this was it, school was over and I had nothing to show for it. The second job in Washington, all that student loan money borrowed, all the hard work and tension of completing an MBA for what? I felt like punching something.

A week later I was at another student's apartment who was having a pre-party before our semi-formal to mark the end of our time in the MBA. Keanu spotted me and came over, trying hard to hide his excitement. He said to me, "Mike… I… got…the…job." Having gotten over my initial jealously, I shook his hand to congratulate him and ballistic, that's right, turbo-charged smiles exploded on our faces. I was really happy for him, at least one of us had gotten what he wanted out of this MBA so far.

I had a job to go to as well, as a paralegal at a great New York City law firm. I was not thrilled about it at the time as I had my heart set on investment banking, but I was better off than many of my fellow MBA's who had no job to go to yet. Living and studying in Montreal was one of the best experiences of my life, but like all good things it came to an end. Now I had to get down to New York City, to pound the pavement more and harder, and pay off those student loans in the meantime. I would become an investment banker in no time. Ha… as if.

But wait. To regain our focus on the important things in life and properly conclude this chapter, we must go back to the Tigerama saga. My last week in Montreal I went to a club on my own to see my favorite Quebec rock band Jean Leloup et la Sale Affaire. I bought a beer and sat down, then a few minutes before the show started a French Canadian woman came up to me and asked me in French if the seat next to me was taken. I choked on my beer and for a moment my tongue lost any French speaking ability it had. Once I came to my senses I assured her that she was welcome to sit next to me n'importe quel jour (any day). We talked throughout the show, then after the show and another drink, we went out dancing at another club. There she asked me to keep an eye on her pocketbook while she went to the ladies room, this person I had only met hours before. The last week of the Tiger safari, Tiger came and found me.

Why am I telling the story? Well, eventually she said she already had a serious boyfriend, but we became friends and French language pen pals for a while when I moved to New York. Still, I want to explain why taxes are so high in Quebec. It is simply for the privilege of living in a place like this, where women spend the night with you in your parents' house and eat breakfast with the family in the morning. Where a woman on her own can introduce herself to you in a club, leave her pocketbook with you hours later, and feel reasonably confident that you're not going to steal it. Imagine this happening in New York City. I will say it one more time… God bless Quebec! What a province!

Lightning Strikes

The alarm went off too early that morning. This was the day. I had to leave Montreal for good, no more Tigerama, and I did not have any investment banking career prospects on the horizon. But, on the bright side, I had a job to go to so that I could pay off my student loans for the next ten years. Things were looking great. When I first got out of bed I glanced out of the window into the alley. There was actually a black cat staring back at me, no writer's embellishment here. I made a face at the animal, then laughed thinking what a load of nonsense superstitions are. I had no idea what this day had in store for me.

Most of my things were packed away in boxes already, except for the TV of course. I watched my favorite channel Musiqueplus (French language music videos) until the last minute before I had to pack the TV and go. I still remember what was on, Musiqueplus was showing a rerun of an interview with an American pop singer named Keedy. She was one in a long line of thousands of female pop singers that every record company hopes will be the new Madonna for them. Unfortunately for these young hopefuls Madonna was still going strong and there were thousands of other female pop singers out there who were not. I liked Keedy though. She seemed like a nice person, and she had a good pop tune called "Save Some Love" that made the charts at the time. I thought, "Keedy, save your money while you are saving some love. Pray for my career and I will pray for yours."

The TV was unplugged, tossed in the cardboard box, and that was that. I was out the door and over to meet the McKenzie Brothers. They were not actually brothers, but two MBA classmates of mine. I am going to call them the McKenzie Brothers after Doug and Bob McKenzie, characters played by Dave Thomas and Rick Moranis on the SCTV comedy television show. The McKenzie characters were stereotypical Canadians in flannel shirts who drank beer, liked their hockey, and said "eh" a lot. My two friends were smart MBA's but also cool, good old down to earth Canadians just like the McKenzie's. The McKenzie MBA's were going to help me move but they had no idea what they were getting themselves into.

For the McKenzie's trouble they would get to visit New York City for the first time and enjoy some sightseeing courtesy of yours truly. Let me give you an idea of what a pathetic trip we were beginning. The worst time for a student's personal finances is the end of the Spring term. The money for the school year has been spent, and no money has yet been earned from a summer job. That went for me at least, I would have more money in a few weeks' time. Neither of the McKenzie Brothers had secured jobs at that point, and like me, neither of them had much money. Luckily Doug had a wife who worked, and Bob lived with his girlfriend who received a stipend for being a science graduate student at McGill. So, the boys borrowed a few twenties each from their women. I was no better off. I had about $100 to my name in the world, it was all in my pocket, and it had to last me until my first paycheck. Or more likely, until I could borrow money from someone. I did have credit cards for an emergency, which is what I used for the rental van, but I was very reluctant to go into more debt.

The trip got off to a rip roaring start as I hopped in the rental van. It was parked in an incredibly tight squeeze between two other trucks, so tight that it had been difficult to even get in the door. As I pulled out there was no space to turn and ssscccrrraaape… oops. We heard the sound of the van scraping against one of the parked vans. It must not have been that bad a scratch, as the rental company man let us keep going out of the lot. After everything was packed in the van back at my apartment, we headed out of the city and south to the USA.

As we approached the border it began to drizzle, but not too badly. We passed through customs, no problem, then continued on toward Plattsburgh, NY. Plattsburgh at the time was one of the small American towns near the Canadian border that had become a big strip mall, catering to Canadians in search of low prices and low taxes on day long shopping trips. As we reached the Plattsburgh area the sky became much darker and the rain started coming down in buckets. The sky exploded. A horrendous thunderstorm began, so bad that it was difficult to see the road and the cars around us.

Traffic was creeping along at about twenty miles per hour as our van approached an intersection. WHAM!!! Suddenly there was a tremendous flash of light around the entire van. A split second later there was a deafening BOOM!!! It was as if a bomb had been detonated right below us. Still, the van sputtered on for another five or ten seconds as the McKenzie Brothers and I glared at each other. Before we had a chance to catch our breath there was a rrrrreeeeerrrrr sound from the engine and that was it, the van ground to a halt. The rain was pounding down on us and we were stuck in the middle of the road. Car horns were blaring as I tried desperately to restart the van.

After several minutes of effort I was able to get the van going long enough for it to limp down the street to a service station. It seemed pretty clear that our van was not going any farther than that under its own power. When we had a second to think about what happened we realized that the van had been hit by lightning. Yeah, you know, a lightning bolt hit the van, it happens all the time. This apparently did some serious damage to the electrical system as we would learn later in the day. The three of us ran through the rain into the service station office to explain our problem. Explaining would not be easy because we were still having trouble believing it ourselves.

In the office of the small town service station three men around the counter were enjoying a lazy, rainy Friday afternoon. They were not too excited about having this lazy, rainy

Friday afternoon interrupted. We stumbled into the room excited and on edge, upset about what happened but excited that we were able to get the van to the repair station. Once we were in the door the men reluctantly stopped their conversation and slowly turned their heads in our direction. It was at this point that I began a run on sentence that would have embarrassed my high school English teacher. "We just came up in that van and we were going down the road out there coming down from Canada and the rain started and it started pouring and then BAM lightning struck and then the whole van lit up and then the electrical system went down and the van wouldn't go anywhere and then we realized we got hit by lightning but then we got the van started and it made it to this station but now it's dead and there's no way it's going anywhere now I don't think."

One of the men gazed up at me slowly and said, "So… what did you say?" We went through the story again and I said I would have to call the rental van company. To this the three men replied at a combined speed of two miles per hour, "Oh… the payphone is out there… if you need the phone." I ran out in the rain to the payphone and called the rental van company's emergency service number. The operator at that number gave me another number which I jotted down with my finger on the foggy glass of the phone booth. The second number worked, and what do you know, someone would come for us with a tow truck in a half hour. The tow truck would take us to the local representative of the rental van company. Alright!

By the time the tow truck arrived the storm had ended. Gosh, it was turning into a beautiful day after all. The young tow truck driver hooked up the van, then four of us crammed into the seats of his truck. As we got out onto the road he asked us, "Where are you fellas headed?" "New York City," I replied. He did not look pleased. "You can have New York," he said, "I lived down there for a while once, in Poughkeepsie. Too crowded and busy for me."

The bustling metropolis called Poughkeepsie is a small town about eighty miles north of Manhattan, a place New York City residents would consider a sleepy little village. Anyway, we made it to the local representative's service station in one piece, and I spoke with the local representative there. I still needed to call the rental van company again because the local representative was only its representative locally, you see. When I spoke with the rental van people who were not just local representatives, they promised a replacement van would be sent down from Montreal and should arrive locally within two hours, at the local representative's place of representation. Got it?

The McKenzie Brothers and I went over to the mall to kill some time. We were back after an hour, we waited an hour, but no van. We waited another hour. No van. I called again, and I was assured that although there had been an initial mix up a van would be sent right away, to arrive locally within one or two more hours. Another two hours passed, still no van. Another call, and a call by our local representative, "on its way, to arrive locally anytime now." Then another hour passed. And another. No van. By this time we had worn out all of the interesting things to do at the service station. We looked at all the different makes of cars parked there. We threw rocks. We kicked rocks. We got soda out of the soda machine. We walked around behind the service station to see what was there. We saw the shopping center several times over. We dined in the Plattsburgh Ponderosa Steak House. Still no van.

Night began to fall, and the service station's employees began to head home for dinner with their families. Some waved goodbye to us, the old friends we had become. By around eight or nine o'clock the owner was preparing to close up the station. He looked at us with pity. "Let me try calling the for you once more before I leave." He made the call, then turned out the lights and wished us luck. So the McKenzie's and I were left alone in the dark, sitting alone outside a deserted service station at 9pm. We tried to come up with deadlines for how long we would wait. "Ok, if there is nothing by midnight, we should go get a hotel room." Credit card debt, just what I needed.

Our contingency planning was interrupted occasionally by the sight of headlights on the road. "There, that could be it!... Those lights look like a van... no...no, it's not a van." After many such false alarms the replacement van rolled up at around 11pm, a lightning quick ten hours after our first call. After smiling, saying hello, and giving a huge sigh of relief, we asked the two men in the van what had taken so long. Apparently they had gotten mixed signals, thinking that either someone else had already come for us, and that we were no longer waiting – they thought the van was by itself. All of my possessions were in the van so we could not have just left it there. Oh well.

We transferred all my boxes and furniture from the old van to the replacement van, and got out on the road a little before midnight. To make the most of the weekend for the McKenzie Brothers, we decided to drive straight through the night and arrive in the city Saturday morning. We each took turns driving as the other two tried unsuccessfully to sleep in the crowded rental van. Hours rolled by on Route 87, cassette tape after cassette tape was played on my portable tape player. Our gaze was broken temporarily by the tremendous glare from all the bright lights of Poughkeepsie's skyscrapers. Soon light appeared on the horizon and we caught a second wind at dawn, stopping at a rest area for mega cups of coffee.

I took over the driving duties for the final short leg into New York, and the excitement had only just begun. My sister always says that the best view of New York is from your rear view mirror, unfortunately I was going the wrong way, away from Montreal and toward New York. Ten or fifteen minutes north of the city, though, the scenery is still rolling green hills and trees. The McKenzie's perked up a bit. "Mike, this is beautiful, I'm really surprised. New York is really nice… I wasn't expecting this at all, eh." I tried to hold my laugh in. New York City, a nature lover's dream. "Just wait, we're not really there yet. Any minute now things are going to look different," I said.

It did not take long. The first indication of our proximity to New York was a man walking along the side of the highway. We were still in an area with nothing but trees and grass and I do not know what the man was doing out there, but he looked drunk. Dressed in ragged clothes, he was zig zagging along the grass area between the highway and the trees. We were getting warm. Like birth pangs, these "indicators of New York proximity" increased in frequency and intensity. The traffic became more congested, cars darted between lanes and passed each other with added quickness. Soon we had broken through the woods and we were able to see the lovely, hazy Bronx skyline in the distance.

As we approached a bridge I noticed cars swerving away from the center lane up ahead. When we were on the bridge I realized why. There was a giant heap of metal in the middle of the road, maybe half a car's worth, bathed in flames. Clouds of smoke were billowing up from the bridge's center. The McKenzie Brothers' eyes popped out, "Whoa, what is that!?!?!" We all stared out the van window at the bonfire as we passed. Now we're in New York. Welcome.

Soon we were cruising along the Major Deegan Expressway, through the South Bronx with Harlem right across the water, and Bob and Doug saw their first serious graffiti. Montreal had a bit of graffiti but it was kind of wimpy, often political, and almost always too intellectual. New York graffiti is the real deal. Massive letters, entire walls and buildings covered in cool three dimensional spray painted works of art, or uncool three dimensional spray painted disgusting filth, depending on your point of view. Then we passed Yankee Stadium. Then it was the Triborough Bridge and another toll. New York's many tolls were already taking their toll on my sub $100 cash fund which was to last me until my first paycheck.

After taking an exit off of the Brooklyn-Queens Expressway we came immediately to a stop. Alright, here we go. Our first squeegee window washer, one of those 30 year old guys who looks about 50. He came up to my window and I was in no mood to play. I waved him away furiously, but naturally he ignored me and went to work. I was getting angry, my blood pressure had doubled already, welcome back to New York.

Every time I made a trip either way between Montreal and New York City during my two years in business school there was about a one day adjustment period. Culture shock. Upon arriving in Montreal, my fist would be cocked, ready for anything, and anyone who smiled and said hello to me would arouse my suspicion. Before yelling, "What do you want?" I would catch myself and realize that Montrealers did not want anything from me, they were just being friendly. Likewise, upon arriving in New York, my pulse would start racing in reaction to the speed of everything after spending time in relaxing Canada.

I was not going to pay this squeegee guy a dime. When he finished washing he looked expectantly through the window at me of course. I just stared back angrily and shook my head. He did not care for this at all and started smashing his squeegee wiper BAM BAM BAM against the side of the van. Just then the light turned green and I hit the gas. Another anecdote for the McKenzie's to tell up in the Great White North. Welcome to the jungle.

Immediately down the street we came to another stop light. I noticed the driver of the car on my left was trying to tell me something so I rolled down my window. "Oh no," I thought, "maybe Mr. Squeegee back there damaged my van." No, the van was fine. The problem was with my morality apparently. A four eyed middle aged twin brother of Mr. Peabody informed me of my deficiencies in a high pitched, nasally New York accent, "Why did you let him wash your window and then not pay him?... He's there all the time... you're supposed to pay him you know."

That was it. I flew into a rage with the mega coffee, the lack of sleep, and the past day's events fueling the attack (all of my many expletives are censored from this quote)..."LOOK, WHO DO YOU THINK YOU ARE? I TOLD HIM TO GO AWAY AND HE WOULDN'T GO AWAY!!! SO WHY DON'T YOU MIND YOUR OWN BUSINESS!!!" Yes. I was back in the New York groove. The McKenzie Brothers stared at me in disbelief. I was a nice, polite guy in Montreal, but that is because everyone in Montreal is so nice and polite. I do not think Doug and Bob had seen me like that before. "Wow, you were pretty ticked off Mike... I think it was the coffee talking there, eh," one of them said. Toto, we're not in Quebec anymore.

Finally we arrived at my new apartment in Woodside, Queens, NY about twenty hours after leaving Montreal, and about 24 hours after we had had any real sleep. Still, we needed to move all of my possessions into the place. Once this pleasurable task was complete Doug and Bob threw down their sleeping bags, I unrolled my futon mattress, and we all passed out. Around noon it was up and at'em. Showers, a quick trip to the grocery store to pick up a hearty breakfast of plastic wrapped dinner rolls, then onto the subway into Manhattan.

The McKenzie Brothers had heard plenty of stories about New York City and they were ready for battle. The "drop the gloves and brawl" hockey player came out in Bob..."Look Mike, if there's going to be trouble on the subway, I'm jumping right in there with you." "Yeah... I brought this knife," Doug said proudly, as he displayed a small pocket blade. Yes sir, the homeboys were going to drop their guns and split when they saw the three of us. Yo, New York, MBA gangstas in the house!

Thankfully we had a nice, uneventful day sightseeing up and down the island of Manhattan. Just looking of course, careful not to spend any money. Later back in Queens we splurged on a beer at the nearby Irish pub. We had a good night's sleep, and we were primed to go see the Yankees play the next day. When we arrived at the ticket window in search of the cheapest bleacher seats, we were informed that the seats would cost us $15 each that day. There was a Beach Boys concert after the game, so we had to pay for the concert too.

Ouch, fifteen whole dollars! We needed to eat, the boys needed gas money for the trip back to Montreal, we agreed that we could not afford it. In a classic case of microeconomics, the Beach Boys had smashed our price elasticity curves. In hindsight I do not know why I did not just get out the credit card and treat the brothers to the game – I could have paid for it with my first paycheck in a few weeks. We were so conscious of not having money I guess that we felt like we could not afford anything. Sorry guys, I wasn't thinking.

Instead, we made the mistake of heading down to Battery Park for a visit to the Statue of Liberty, pretty pricey itself at around six or seven dollars. I had been in New York many times but I never was stupid enough to take this tour. The statue looks beautiful from a distance, but the inside has the ambiance of a submarine interior. That is after you wait two hours to get inside. Then you have another hour or so taking steps up a spiral staircase in a single file line without end. Once you get to the top it's all worthwhile though. Hunch over for a ten second peek out the windows in the crown as the park service guide directs you to "move along, move along."

The McKenzie Brothers drove off back to the Great White North the next day without me, back to beautiful Canada, leaving me there in Queens, NY. I missed Montreal so much I was in denial. I listened to just my French language pop music cassette tapes to the exclusion of anything else the first week. Only after visiting my terrific aunt and uncle at their house in Flushing, Queens the following Sunday did I feel at home again.

King of Queens

One night late in the summer I was savoring the good life in my state of the art Queens, NY penthouse. With a can of Budweiser in my hand, I gazed out my window overlooking a fire escape and a brick wall. The brick wall was part of the large apartment building where I lived. Beyond the brick wall and more apartments was posh Queens Boulevard, stomping ground for the rich and famous. More than a few titans of world business could be found at Billy Dean's topless bar down the street. Also, I was told that everyone from feared corporate raider Sir James Goldsmith to the world's richest man, the Sultan of Brunei, flew into New York to buy used cars from the dealership on my block.

Usually there was advance warning of the arrival of these millionaire VIP's, you see my apartment was directly under the flight path of jumbo jets landing at nearby LaGuardia Airport. When my drinking glasses and silverware started trembling and clinking together I knew right away that Sir James was in town. Yes, my MBA was taking me places I never dreamed of, from Plattsburgh, NY to Queens Boulevard.

Suddenly my pompous thoughts were interrupted by a ring of the telephone, long distance from Toronto. Hey, it was Keanu Reeves (the Canadian MBA one of course). Keanu had received my submission to our class alumni address book which he was putting together and decided to call me. "So, how's work, what are you up to?" I asked. "Oh, you know, just hanging out, buying suits," Keanu answered.

Buying suits? Ha… as if! I tried to imagine Keanu in a limo on a Gordon Gekko style shopping spree at the finest men's stores in Toronto. Gimme three o' those, two o' those, four o' those. Oh well, I did not rain on his investment banking parade, I just said, "that's cool." And it was, it seemed like he was enjoying the job. A few weeks later I received the address book in the mail that listed current jobs as well as contact information for most of my MBA classmates. Keanu had not been able to get complete information on all one hundred or so people in our class, but he put in as many people as he could. From what I could see, Keanu was one of maybe a dozen or so people who were very happy with the job they managed to land, if any, out of business school. Some of the more interesting entries follow…

Financial Analyst, Northern Telecom (Nortel)

Keanu comments, "He can be reached at the office until Christmas Eve. NT decided to give him that night off. He has to work Christmas Day though." This is what I liked to hear, a real macho job. All praise to the most righteous Northern Telecom and Royal Bank of Canada, the only major annual recruiters of McGill MBA's who actually came through for us and hired a few members of our class in that ugly year of 1991.

Unemployed

Keanu comments, "She gave a California mailing address for the summer, to her MBA means Major Beach Action. All right!" Keanu put a positive spin on this. I do not know about her, but I did not put myself through an MBA so I could go to the beach without a good job.

Marketing, Merck

Hey, it's Bob McKenzie. A pretty cool job, but he was one of the top minds of our class. He was accepted into Harvard but he chose the dirt cheap McGill tuition over shelling out $30,000 a year for an Ivy League MBA. He received a $1,000 scholarship from Merck (does not sound like a lot but that was around a year's tuition for a Canadian citizen at McGill) and a summer job with Merck after first year and they were still ambivalent about hiring him permanently. As you might remember he was jobless during our NYC moving adventure and from what I heard Merck finally hired him late in the summer. Excellent, now he could pay back his girlfriend!

Law School Student

Ha! The magic solution for many unemployed Canadians. With graduate school tuition around $1,000 per year for Canadian citizens, why not stay in school forever?

Canadian National Defense / Navy

This was a friend who was in the Canadian Navy, they paid for his MBA and now it was payback time.

Marketing Goddess, Tambrands

Keanu writes, "She is marketing tampons and loves her job, if you come to Toronto she'll give you plenty of free samples."

Financial Analyst, Northern Telecom (Nortel)

Another NT hire, great, but I heard that in less than a year they asked him to relocate. He was married and told them that he could not relocate. WHACK! He got the guillotine...NT had a stack of resumes from people who would have relocated to Mongolia for a job in 1991.

Amusing reading, but these were some of the top job placements from our MBA class. Where was Citibank Canada, Bank of Montreal, First Boston, Merrill Lynch, Goldman Sachs, IBM, Alcan, Salomon Brothers, the big accounting firms, Canadian Imperial Bank of Commerce? What was the deal? This did not sound like the graduating class from a top MBA school to me. The early 1990's were a whole new ball game for careers.

Ok, back to my own career. There I was in New York City, plowing through the paralegal work. Some days I felt lucky to have the job, as I learned a lot by traveling to different companies in different cities, doing document discovery in support of cases handled by my firm. Other days I felt frustrated that I worked at a law firm because I wanted to be a banker. So, my free moments at work were spent calling banking contacts to chit chat. Sundays, if I did not go into work at the law firm, were reserved for coffee, bagels, and the help wanted ads. At first I hated this, it was a repeat of my experience after college which I hoped to avoid this time by doing an MBA. However, soon enough I learned to love it, so much so that a year later when I found a position I caught myself still sneaking a peek at the ads. They are loads of fun if you use your imagination and cheap entertainment at only the cost of a newspaper.

Want ads can be hysterical for reasons I will go into later, but even the serious job ads are fun to read. They give you the opportunity to imagine yourself in various careers and inevitably exaggerate the thrills involved in any position. For example, once I saw an advertisement for a promotions person to work for the Quebec Government's office in New York. This was a job I could have done well I figured, but the piece in the paper called for 5+ years of experience in promotion and public relations. No chance. No dice. I did not have 5+ years of experience doing anything except brushing my teeth. I sent a resume in anyway, just for the hell of it. And just as one buys a lottery ticket to dream about what one would do with all the winnings, it was fun to imagine myself doing the Quebec job. But not exactly that job. More of a fantasy job only vaguely related to the actual opening.

Here is what it is like... since this is the Quebec Government, my staff consists of Quebec rock star Jean Leloup, and a half dozen promotion experts named Tiger DuBois, Tiger Mondoux, Tiger Boulanger, Tiger Dion, Tiger LaFleur, and Tiger Lemieux. The last few Tigers are not related to any hockey stars, I just was running out of French last names. Jean Leloup, like any self-respecting rock star, has a fully stocked liquor cabinet in his office, a loud stereo system, and he just sort of hangs out telling jokes all day to keep us entertained. The Tiger women are super smart, they always have things under control. This is a good thing because although I would like to work with them more, I am too busy. You see I am always heading for the next flight, shuttling between New York, Quebec City, Montreal, and Ottawa. Tonight it is a meeting in Ottawa with the Canadian Prime Minister and the Parti Quebecois to discuss my unique solution to Canada's constitutional crisis. Then it is on to Montreal for a lunch meeting with my favorite Musiqueplus VJ Marie Plourde to discuss the new promotional campaign we are working on.

What is the campaign exactly? Who cares? The food was good, and now it is on to Quebec City. Marie is my escort for a party thrown in my honor by the people of Quebec during the Winter Carnival. There is plenty of beer and live performances by Nirvana, Public Enemy, and the Beastie Boys. Hey, what do you know, Boris Yeltsin is at the party, he likes Public Enemy too, and he needs my help in reorganizing the Russian economy and... you get the idea.

Many help wanted ads encourage this sort of fantasizing. Here are some of the treats in store for the help wanted ads connoisseur, want ads buzzwords. These are some of the exciting phrases meant to catch your eye and promise more than any job could hope to deliver...

ROCK AND ROLL ATMOSPHERE!

I get it, you can drive your company car in a pool like Keith Moon, trash your hotel on a business trip like Guns and Roses, and bring groupies to your cubicle like Prince. Where do I sign up?

NO MORE PUNCHING THE CLOCK!

Fantastic, so what happens is you sleep in, roll out of bed at 11am each day in time to watch *Love Boat*, and the company mails paychecks to your house. Sounds cool.

INTERNATIONAL!

This word is turbo-charged, it should be on Tony Robbins' list of transformational vocabulary. It can make the most bogus of jobs catch your eye and get your heart pounding at double speed. Somehow everyone loves things that are "international." I suppose this is because when you hear the word the first images that come to mind are exciting "international images." Shots of Hong Kong and Paris appear as you might see on a United Airlines commercial with that Gershwin music in the background. The people who write the ads know this, but your pulse rate begins a gradual descent as you read the fine print. Here is an example...

INTERNATIONAL!!!

Work with dynamic people in a fast paced, challenging environment, great benefits, mainly typing and filing, must type 50 WPM, position located at multinational dog food company's Iowa headquarters. (BOOM! SPLASH! United Airlines flight #000 just hit the drink in the South China Sea)

That last part is writer's embellishment. If in fact the ad were for a multinational dog food company the ad would never tell you. In fact, this is something that should set off the warning siren in your head. Many ads do not tell you what the company actually does. Why do they not tell you? Take a second and think about it.

A rule of thumb of help wanted ads is that the quality of the job varies inversely to the amount of energy put into selling you on it. Remember Goldman Sachs? The firm pays mighty well, it is well respected in its industry, it does not show up for Career Day. For the same reason Goldman Sachs does not put ads in the paper, and the receptionist is not nice to you if you just drop in unannounced at the Goldman office looking for a job. Goldman does not have to be nice, it is not begging anyone to work there, you and your resume do the begging, and the getting dissed. On the other hand, take a look at that sample abomination I wrote, all of those big capital letters, all of those uncouth exclamation points, words like challenging, dynamic, great. They all add up to WATCH OUT!!!

At the same time these ads are great fun to read, they can be funnier than Jerry Seinfeld (you never want to Finnish) and they help you enjoy the search for the occasional gold nugget hidden in all that mess. Let us sample some of these tasty, I mean sumptuous, help wanted ads shall we? Even better than the ads from your everyday newspapers are those free job newsletters, booklets, magazines (or worse the ones that cost money!) specializing in the job hunt. Their raison d'etre is to snag you hook, line, and sinker. They are at the forefront of their field, the kings, the rocket scientists of the employment industry. Therefore these job newsletters make the most exciting and gut busting reading. I have one such magazine in my hand now, let's see…

ARE YOU MAKING $150,000 OR MORE A YEAR?

Funny that you ask, yes I am, but I check the want ads anyway, just in case there is something better out there listed in your crappy newsletter!

NOW ACCEPTING APPLICATIONS FOR PEST CONTROL TECHNICIANS, SALES PERSONNEL, AND INSPECTORS, EXPERIENCE IS NOT NECESSARY FOR MOST POSITIONS!

That's too bad, I do not have a CPA, but I have killed many roaches in my time.

LOOKING FOR A STEADY PAYCHECK?

No, I was looking for haphazard compensation, so that I might miss a rent payment or two. It will keep me on my toes.

FREE SEMINAR! TRAIN TO BE A POKER DEALER! ONE HOUR COULD CHANGE YOUR WHOLE ATTITUDE!

What attitude? Are you trying to say I have an attitude?

NEED HELP? STRUGGLING PAYING YOUR BILLS? CREDITORS HARASSING YOU? CALL FOR HELP!!

This is the first intelligent ad I have seen yet, this company knows where to advertise to reach its target market.

HELP! OUR SALES ARE EXPLODING!

They do not mention a company name, but I can venture a guess. It is Robbins Research International, right?

LOOKING FOR THE RIGHT JOB?

No stupid, I want the wrong job. You are thinking of someone else.

WANTED 5 SERIOUS PEOPLE!

Sorry, I cannot keep a straight face, I guess I am out.

SALES AND SERVICE PROFESSIONALS, WE ARE CURRENTLY SEEKING INDIVIDUALS POSSESSING DIRECT SALES SERVICE EXPERIENCE OR A DESIRE TO LEARN AND SUCCEED PLUS A STRONG PERSONALITY, POSITIVE ATTITUDE, EXCELLENT COMMUNICATIONS SKILLS, GOOD DRIVING RECORD…

This could be the one for me, but wait, there is more, uh oh…

AND ABILITY TO PASS DRUG SCREENING

Damn, never mind, it is not for me

GOLDEN OPPORTUNITY, WE ARE A TOP RATED JEWELRY ORGANIZATION

Ha ha ha ha ha ha, do you get it??? The word golden and the word jewelry!!! You see!!! Ha ha ha ha ha ha.

SUCCESS EXPRESS!

I want to ride on that train.

AT LAST! 4 GREAT SECRETARIAL POSITIONS!

Phew... at last indeed. I do not know about you, but I was starting to worry a bit.

WHY NOT? SELL A SERVICE THAT EVERYONE EVENTUALLY HAS TO BUY... WE HELP FAMILIES PREPARE IN ADVANCE FOR THEIR CEMETERY NEEDS. WITH OUR COMPANY WE HAVE NO COMPETITION USING OUR PROVEN MARKETING SYSTEM

Yeah, why not? But what is this proven marketing system? I do not think I want to know (Is Michael Corleone involved in this in any way?).

Here are just a few more words on the subject. Watch out for anything that charges you money for job listings or job hunting advice. This was the gravy train industry of the 1990's. If you want some advice on your resume, on cover letters, and on interview techniques, just give me a call. I will tell you for free because I have heard it all. I am the Tom Vu of help wanted ads. When you have a sex question you call Doctor Ruth, when you have a job search question you call Doctor Mike, I will give you the lowdown. It all starts with "do not chew gum at your interview," it continues with, "learn the company's business before the interview, even if it is dog food," after that it is "lower your expectations," and it ends with "be willing to take any job, as a way to get your foot in the door."

I would have to say that this is my favorite of all job search clichés... "get your foot in the door." How many times have I said that, read that, been told that by the legions of advice givers that come out of the woodwork when word gets around that I am in the hunt for a job? Hell, I think when it is time to put me in the old folks home I am going to agree to eat only one meal a day there, so that I can get my foot in the door. I will just do this instinctively. Like a dog who had been beaten all of its life and ducks down in reaction to any sudden movement in the vicinity, I had been conditioned to approach every employment situation ready to agree to anything. Low pay, no pay, no breaks, no vacation, whatever it takes to get my foot in the door.

The Power of Coffee

A definite highlight of any work day is the coffee break, and at the law firm where I worked this was no different. Normally the trip to get the cup was my break, and upon returning to my desk I would begin work again, sipping as I turned pages. After ten minutes or so suddenly I would look up, gaze out the window, and fall into deep thought. "You know, everything's going just fine," I would think, "I've got a lot of great things to look forward to, things are going to be all right. Life is pretty good."

Slowly my eyes would come back to the work on my desk, and more thoughts would roll through my head, "Gee, that's funny, the way moods can change, I mean. This morning I was not as optimistic about everything as I am now." At that moment my eyes would move from my work and notice the empty cup of coffee on the edge of my desk, laughing at me. "It's the caffeine, you moron," the cup would say. It fooled me just about every day.

The Great New York City Job Search

Now to find a job. First, on to the job placement / headhunter firms. These organizations are the personification of the help wanted ads; they are walking, talking, flesh and blood INTERNATIONALS!!!! and ROCK AND ROLL ATMOSPHERES!!!! I dealt with many such firms after I completed business school, and although they always sounded so encouraging they were not able to set up even one interview for me in the early 1990's. I always did much better on my own. This was a sign of the times really. For someone in that era with only a few years work experience who just completed an MBA, these places were a useless waste of time.

Therefore, I think in order to qualify for a position at a placement firm a person has to be an indomitable Pollyanna, able to see the silver lining on the biggest, darkest of clouds. The placement people with whom I spoke were always so up, they made everything sound so promising. This was their job, but I would have been better served if they would just have cut to the quick and said, "sorry, there's nothing out there we can help you find." It would have saved me countless hours and lots of wasted effort. Of course, that approach does not make the headhunters any money, they do work for the employers not the candidates after all. Placement firms employ the strategy of dangling the potential job carrots out there on a stick in front of the candidate. Unfortunately the candidate never gets any closer to the carrots as you and your headhunter keep discussing how to nab one.

Headhunters had a line for every season and every situation. Mid-summer… "Well this time of year is tough, but in a few weeks to a month a lot of things start to open up." The fall… "It is almost Christmas bonus time, when people do not get the bonus they are expecting they quit and then positions open up." The winter… "Well, we have been in a recession, next quarter is supposed to be much better so just hang on." The spring… "We are working on some executive level placements now, but as soon as that is finished we will be dealing with entry level recruiting from the major firms. Be sure to call back in three to four weeks."

What separates placement firms from help wanted ads is that they have another dimension. They are paid by the number of people they place, so that while they encourage and pump you up with one hand, they quietly knock you down with the other. The idea is to lower your expectations and soften you up so that you are prepared to take anything they put on your plate. New York City placement firms specialize in breaking down job candidates and lowering their expectations.

One day I met with a headhunter in Manhattan and handed him my resume, which was a good resume. While maybe not in the top 5% of the nation, I would say it was an above average resume for someone my age. He looked at it for a minute and started to laugh. Then he said condescendingly, "So what you're telling me here is basically that you're a green kid and you wanna do deals, right?" Funny, I did not remember telling him that. I think what I should have told him was that he was a middle aged, polyester wearing, leaving just a touch of grey with his Grecian Formula kind of guy who was such a hotshot that he worked at a placement firm. Of course I did not say this because like most job candidates out there I was a polite young man who wanted a good career and was willing to work hard for it. Meeting with these types of headhunters simply kept me occupied and feeling like I was doing something while I waited for responses from the real contacts and opportunities I created for myself.

My first big lead in New York City came as a result of cold calling. While still in Montreal I called the New York trading desk of a Canadian bank. I then followed up with another call when I was settled in the Big Apple. A woman on the desk agreed to speak with me in person, and when I arrived she was great. She commended me on my initiative and said that yes, in fact the desk was thinking of hiring someone in the near future. I should call back in a few weeks to set up an interview, she told me.

After a month I had an interview with a man in charge of the desk. It all went well until the very end when I was told, "You are one of the first people to interview for the slot. We have gone ahead and placed an ad for the position in the *Wall Street Journal*..." NOOOOOOO! NOOOOOOOO! AAAAAAAH! A blood curdling scream reverberated in my brain worse than something out of a horror movie. All the while my body listened quietly and attentively. "...so it will take a while to collect all of those resumes, go through them, then arrange interviews. I imagine we will bring you back for a second interview but that will not be for another few months or so."

Oooooh man. MonthSSS. Plural months. Usually it is weeks and that seems like months when you are waiting. More often than not the reward for spotting these job openings while they are still young buds is that you get to wait twice as long for a resolution. And the *Wall Street Journal!* In that job market! The guy had a death wish, he was going to get more crazy mail than a Senator's office. This bank gave the words cautious and conservative new meaning. Many banks are like this, however, and that is better than being thoughtless, impulsive, and jerking around young job hunters like me. I could wait, I was not going anywhere.

Months passed and no need to worry, I had not been hired by anyone else in the meantime. The second interview came and this also went well. But once again, the last few minutes of our discussion put a damper on things. I was told, "We received over a hundred resumes for the position, but many of the candidates were really not suited to the position for one reason or another (dude, I could have told you that months ago). We narrowed it down to five people, you are one of the five, and there is one person ahead of you at the moment. He has good experience doing this same job somewhere else, and if he agrees to take it the job is his."

I did not like the content of what he said, but the frankness was refreshing. Canadian and European firms and banks tended to be better and more professional in this regard than American ones at that time anyway. There are good rejections and bad rejections, I know the subject well, and this was a good one. I liked this bank, and if I ever find myself living in Canada again I think I will start an account there!

Another hot scoop that summer came through the friend of my sister who worked for a fashion magazine in the city. This type of networking was the reason I moved to New York City in the first place, my odds of my getting a Wall Street job were infinitely better if I were living and working nearby. The man she set me up with was a very important and busy man at the commodities exchange in the city, and as New York as bagels and cream cheese. After repeated calls and a discussion with his assistant, the man was good enough to see me for ten minutes one day. I sat in his office as his phone rang every 30 seconds or so, but he did his best to continue the conversation with me. He looked at me skeptically, an MBA? "The trading floor here is a tough place, you know. College boyz don't cut it down there. You gotta be tough."

Yes, I knew this, and it was part of the attraction. I was a young guy with lots of energy and wanted to work in an environment like that. The man did not realize it, but he was talking to a guy who used to enjoy diving off the stage at DOA concerts. I did not mention the DOA shows, but I assured him that I was not going to be intimidated by the floor action. I even threw in a few four letter words to make my point. He came back with, "You know, we had an MBA down there once and one of the boyz looked him right in the eye and said, 'Get outta my way now or I'll kick your ass.'" The MBA reportedly fell to pieces (a trading legend has it) and came to his boss in tears. This anecdote sounded about as truthful as a Donald Trump tweet. In any case, this did not sound like me, or any of the MBA's I knew. Ok, maybe one, my old girlfriend back at McGill. A nice but sensitive MBA she could become upset about things like the laundry or broken lead on her pencil. But she did not want to be a floor trader anyway.

Again, I assured him with even more vigor that I knew the deal, I wanted in, and I was ready to do whatever was necessary to get down there. "Ok," he relented, "give me a call at the end of the summer, a few things should open up by then. But you're gonna start at the bottom, you know, and it doesn't pay much." "I know, that's ok, I'm ready for it," I replied. Whatever it takes to get my foot in the door.

Predictably though, when the end of the summer came he had disappeared off the face of the earth. I eventually found out that later in the summer he had asked my connection, the friend of my sister, to marry him and she refused. If she had said yes to the proposal, I might have had a great career as a floor trader. Amazingly, these are the real things that affect a job search, never mind resumes, interview preparation etc. His marriage hopes were no doubt the only reason he agreed to meet with me in the first place. It reminds me of the story in the book *Liar's Poker* where author Michael Lewis gets a job at Salomon Brothers because he happened to be seated and got to know the wife of a Salomon executive at a dinner he attended. The wife pushed her husband to consider Michael for a job at Salomon, and the rest was history.

I found that many New Yorkers who worked in business, especially New Yorkers who were traders, did not care for MBA's. The contempt of the New York businessman was even more pronounced if the MBA had gone to school outside of the universe as the New Yorker understood it. The only business schools in this universe as the New Yorker understood it were NYU and Columbia, and yeah, that Harvard place too I guess. That was in a different galaxy called New England though. You know, where the Red Sox play. Besides, the Mets beat them in 1986 anyway.

One of my best job contacts was from New England, so let's call him Carl Yastrzemski after the all time great Red Sox player. Carl was a vice president at one of the New York banks and worked in precious metals trading. I received this contact courtesy of Keanu Reeves. Keanu got to know Carl when they shared information on the metals markets, as Keanu wrote reports in that subject area. Carl turned out to be a great guy, he invited me to lunch one day. The food was excellent (I had Maryland crab cakes) and Carl took a stack of my resumes with him.

Carl tried for me, putting a lot of emphasis on my Russian language background which had some relevance in the metals markets. Russia was a large source of precious metals and even retained its own contingent of Russian commodities traders. I never got a job as a result of this, but Carl ended up being one of those rare friends you make along the networking trail. These people really try to help you even though they do not have to. I appreciated the efforts of these people on my behalf, and I always dreamed about being in a position in the future where I could do the same for others. When I had a good job in the late 1990's I did.

I noticed that in general Canadian traders seemed much more receptive to people like me who had multiple academic degrees. So, I kept working on contacting banks and financial institutions in Montreal as well as in New York. I was completely open to living in Montreal again if I could work in investments there. I took one quick trip to Montreal to visit friends and pop in on some job contacts toward the end of the Summer. On Sherbrooke Street I bumped into my old options professor who shuddered when he saw me in a suit and tie. "Whew, you look too corporate for me," he joked. He had worked in the markets himself for a while but packed it in for the academic life which suited him. He knew the markets but he liked to stay up late and sleep in late.

Unfortunately one contact in Montreal recommended that I go visit a job placement firm he knew of (yuck) so I had to do it. This was in spite of the fact that there was no way in hell a Canadian placement firm was going to get a job for an American as a trader in Canada's meager 1991 job market. After filling out my life story on an application form I was called in to meet a headhunter who looked younger than me, I was 26 at the time. The young man was anxious to do a good job and be very thorough in all of his questions, so the pointless interview turned into an interrogation. I was climbing the walls...

"So, what kind of position are you looking for exactly?"

"I'd like to work on the trading desk of a bank or an investment banking firm."

"Could you expand on that?"

"Ok (?) I worked in FX and metals a bit before I did the MBA, but with my MBA studies I would be qualified for an entry level spot in bonds or stocks as well."

"And?"

AND WHAT?!! WHAT WHAT WHAT WHAT WHAT???!!! Every question he asked was like this. Pretty soon he would be asking me about any traumas I had in my childhood. Was this a placement screening or psychotherapy? It was more like a nightmare. When the interview was over I ran for the elevator and headed straight for the Peel Pub. The former president of McGill's class of 1991 and I had a long MBA Council reunion with several pitchers of beer. Like me the ex-president was still waiting for his career ship to come in and had plenty of time on his hands.

This Montreal trip ended up being worthwhile when at Montreal's Dorval Airport I saw the king of the whack rappers, or sucker MC's, or whatever your favorite rap phrase of disrespect is. I am talking about the one and only Vanilla Ice and his entourage. His album was selling well at the time, but hardcore rap fans were not buying. Apparently Vanilla had just done a show in town and was headed back to the United States. The Vanilla man strutted around the airport in his gear, confident that everyone knew he was a star. And, from the comments I heard around the terminal, it was clear that Vanilla Ice had made a name for himself by virtue of his hit "Ice Ice Baby." The music backing up his raps on this song was worthy of note as it was, let us say, heavily influenced by a certain David Bowie tune of years before.

When I was waiting in line for my boarding pass I overheard a conversation between two airline employees. One man in his forties asked another employee, a young woman in her twenties, "Who is that guy?" She replied, "Oh that's the rapper Vanilla Ice… you know, the one who stole his music from another group." Ouch. Vanilla Ice was dissed by Ice-T, dissed by 3rd Bass, dissed by Arsenio Hall, and now dissed by the airline industry!

When I returned to New York I pulled an industrious job search move that would make a school placement advisor swell with pride. I noticed an article on the front page of one of the major papers about an American banker who, immediately after Boris Yeltsin's ascension to power, was arranging deals between Russian concerns and American companies in the newly formed Commonwealth of Independent States. I started making calls and eventually tracked this gentleman down at his bank. After informing him about my Russian language background and my MBA he suggested I send my resume, then call in a few weeks when he would be back from a business trip. Pretty crafty, eh? Lots of spunk, lots of initiative, how could he help but be impressed with someone like me?

Eventually it came time to make that call and I was excited. I punched the numbers of the phone with nervous anticipation. There was one ring... two rings... three rings... four rings... (What's up? This is a bank? How many times do they let the phone ring?) five rings... six rings. No voicemail greeting even? Alright, maybe I dialed the wrong number, try again. Nope. Try a third time. Nope. Try different times of the day. Nope. I had an idea, call a number one different from his extension. Ok... one ring... two rings... three BING "Hello?" A woman answered.

"Yes, may I speak with Mr. Doe?"

She sounded very ill at ease, "Oh... I'm sorry... Mr. Doe is no longer employed by this bank." (What?)

"Well, would you happen to know where he could be reached now?"

"No sir, I'm sorry, I have no idea."

Unbelievable. Where was this business trip, to Argentina with a briefcase full of one hundred dollar bills? So much for this international business superstar and his fifteen minutes of fame. He had just been the subject of a front page story a month before!

Anyway, just when you get discouraged in the job search, many times something else will happen to restore your faith a bit. I was preparing for another visit to Montreal in the fall, for two interviews this time. The week before I left I tried cold calling a few Montreal firms that gave me the brush off in the past just to see what would happen. One of these was a floor trading operation on the Montreal Exchange. I expected nothing and proceeded to go through the motions of the call. Then the contact there began his rejection speech, "No, I'm sorry, we're not looking for anyone right..." but suddenly he stopped in mid-sentence. I heard another voice in the background faintly, "yes... yes..." what was going on I wondered. Then the contact was back on the line. "Ok then, it seems that our man on the floor here is looking for someone like you right away, when will you be in town?" "Next week," I answered, holding my breath. "Ok then, so you call us when you are in town and ask for him, and he'll meet with you, ok?"

JACKPOT!!! I will never forget that call. It was the cold calling equivalent of a jackpot on a Vegas slot machine. How often does something like that happen, once in a thousand calls maybe?

When I arrived in Montreal I had a day chock full of activities, three, count'em, three interviews in one day. The first one ended up being a "get to know you" sort of thing, no job open yet. Oh well, then it was time for the Montreal Exchange. This interview went very well, I was commended for coming to Montreal on my own initiative and at my own expense. As a floor trader used to acting quickly, my interviewer seemed anxious to hire me then and there, but he said he had to clear it with his boss first. Still, he wanted an assistant immediately, so it would be a matter of days. Wow, was there not some sort of law against hiring someone without making them wait a month? I could not believe how quickly this was moving.

Ok, time for interview number three, this one at a small Montreal investment firm. It started inauspiciously, as I walked in a McGill MBA I knew from the year after me walked out. We saw each other and said an awkward hello. Oooh, brutal, competing for the same job. We tried to smile and act glad to see each other, but this person had nothing to worry about from me. I ended up being toast a minute after the interview started. The woman, who was French Canadian asked me the common question, "You're American, why did you come up to McGill for your MBA?"

Among many reasons I added in passing, "… and McGill's one of the best MBA programs in Canada." I said this quickly, and unfortunately to her native French ear it sounded like "McGill is the *best* MBA program in Canada." Her expression changed. She looked angry. She said, "Wait a minute... the best MBA program in Canada?... I'm a Western MBA."

I let out a nervous chuckle. She was kidding around, right? Wait, she still was not smiling... KABOOM!!! There is no truce in the Western vs. McGill gang war, not even after graduation. I had become just another statistic.

Wait, do not call in the cemetery company and its proven marketing system yet. I still had my man at the Montreal Exchange. A few days went by and I pounced on every phone call I got, on the first or second ring. Nope. Nothing. Then a week went by. Nothing. I called. He said he and his boss were still talking it over, but his boss had a problem with my American citizenship. It seems they had taken on a few Americans from their Chicago office to work in their Montreal office for a while who were given work permits for Canada. The Americans left Canada without paying their phone and electric bills, so the phone and electric companies started calling the exchange looking for the money. The boss did not like Americans now.

After another week I called back again. "Sorry, Mike, we can't hire you. There's nothing I can do about it. We're going to take a Canadian," my contact said. There is always a catch, it seems. It was too good to be true. To you Chicago guys who did not pay your bills, wherever you are now... merci beaucoup. I would have gladly paid the bills for you.

Before the chapter comes to a close, I would like to share with you some more fond memories of interviews that were close to my heart. Although I did not end up working at the following firms, each touched my life in a unique way.

I followed up on an advertisement for a Wall Street firm with a slick name. When I arrived at their address, which actually was on Wall Street, I noticed it was a bit peculiar. Where was the front desk, the receptionist, the rows of traders buying and selling? Hmm. There were only two men who turned out to be managers, and one new recruit. That was it. Oh yeah, a few phones, cheap chairs, and one (!) computer.

Yes, this was one of those firms where brokers try to hard sell people on dubious securities, then pack up and hit the road when the complaints start pouring in. Why didn't I just turn around and walk out the door immediately? Later in life I would not have given these guys the time of day. At the time I was too polite and too desperate for a Wall Street job (maybe just maybe this place is ok I hoped… ha, as if). I actually am glad I stayed simply for the entertainment value, it turned out to be my all-time favorite interview. It was less like an interview and more like a trip to a used car dealership. They were selling the job and I simply sat and listened to the sales pitch.

One of the two men was to interview me and he talked a mile a minute. He was amazing, he could say fifty words at a clip without pausing for a breath. I, on the other hand, probably did not manage to slip in more than ten words total the entire time I was there. All I could do was sit, listen, and try hard not to laugh. It went something like this… "Alrighttherelookatthis, seethis, thisistheplan, understand? No? Ok, littleinvestmentbankinglessonforyouthen. RTCright? ResolutionTrustCompany, allthepropertiesmortgagesbonds wayundervalued…webuy'em…youcanbuy'em…rightthereseeinthepaper, allforsale, webuy'em thensell'emformore…" and on and on it went. What he was trying to say was that the Resolution Trust Company, the government's organization handling the assets once controlled by all the newly defunct savings and loan companies, was trying to sell the assets. The prices were very low. Ok. I did not bother to ask him why he thought that people would buy these "propertiesmortgagesbonds" from him at a high price when they could buy them from the RTC at a lower price directly. Unless of course he planned to force them on little old ladies who did not know what they were buying.

The verbal onslaught continued but it was starting to make me dizzy. So, out of the corner of my eye, I began watching the second man with the new recruit on the other side of the room. The new recruit had managed to get someone on the phone, and suddenly the atmosphere was transformed. You would have thought we were in the upper deck of Yankee Stadium in the ninth inning of World Series Game #7. It was electric. The man interviewing me broke off his speech, and joined in with the second man. Two thick New York accents, yelling at the top of their lungs, "ALRIGHT BABY C'MON C'MON!!! LET'S SEE YOU SELL LET'S SEE YOU SELL, LET'S DO IT LET'S DO IT, ALRIGHT ALRIGHT ALRIGHT!!!

The new recruit tried to concentrate on the call, but his eyes kept darting over to the two Yankee fans. He looked as if someone were holding a gun to his head. I suppose this was what help wanted ads meant by a fast-paced, dynamic work environment. After this circus was over I thanked the two men, shook hands, and said goodbye. This interview was worthy of note in that it was the first interview where I actually told the interviewer that *I would call him* after I had thought about it. Pretty cool.

I interviewed at another "investment" firm which ran an advertisement in a business paper. The ad said "investments" so I sent in my resume, I received a call, and then I set up an appointment. When I arrived I was treated to a company video in a high tech multimedia conference room. It became clear to me from the video that this was a firm of semi-independent insurance salesmen. The firm was apparently doing well and its business was selling insurance policies to individuals. Cold calling, pay based on commissions. Fine, but why were they calling it an "investment" firm? I will tell you why, because that was a cool thing to call yourself in the 1980's and 1990's.

I told my interviewer that because of their ad, I thought they were involved in the stock market and mutual funds like Fidelity or Charles Schwab. I was looking to do stock analysis or work on a desk, something of that sort. I had not realized it was an insurance firm. Her reply was, "We're an investment firm." I said, "But your whole business is based on selling insurance to individuals, according to that video I watched." "But we do some investments also," she said. The woman just would not say the word "insurance." Not once. Insurance was not cool. I tried to imagine this firm's employee manual...

FIRM CONFIDENTIAL

Rule number one, never use the word *insurance*. When you have understood rule one, please shred this page. No one is to retain any document within the firm which contains the word *insurance*. In office conversations members of the firm must employ the word "investment" rather than the word *insurance*. If it becomes absolutely necessary to convey the concept embodied in the word *insurance*, and this becomes impossible to do simply with the use of the term "investment," at that time employees may use the following expression: "the I-word." Under no circumstances are members of this firm permitted, in written or oral form, to use the combination of syllables that make up the word *insurance*.

This wild goose chase of a job search was starting to take its toll on me mentally. Finally one day I had an interview for a back office position with one of the well known investment firms doing paperwork relating to its commodities business. It turned out the interview was to take place in the firm's personnel office. Ick, a long, drawn out, multiple screening interview affair. After filling out one of those personnel applications for a half hour I was in a rotten mood. Although I had given my name to the receptionist, there was no sign that I was to be called in for the interview any time soon. Forty-five minutes elapsed since my arrival. Then an hour. Then an hour and fifteen minutes and no one seemed to know I was there. There was no one else around waiting to be interviewed as far as I could see. Still, proper interview etiquette says that you sit there with a dumb smile on your face and wait.

It was getting ridiculous though, I could not stand it any longer. I went up to the receptionist and asked as tactfully as I could, "I'm sorry, I wanted to check that you do have my name for the interview. It's just that I work and I'm on my lunch hour." The receptionist glared at me, "Yes... I have your name here." No smile. No understanding. Just that rudeness that many young New York receptionists have made into an art form. After another half hour, an hour and forty-five minutes after first arriving, I was shown in for the interview. The first nasty words out of my interviewer's mouth were, "I'll make this quick, that way you can get back to your job soon."

This rudeness was a function of the job market at that time. I noticed a distinct change in the late 1990's, when candidates were scarce and good jobs were plenty; companies were much more polite because they needed candidates at least as much as the candidates needed the jobs.

The Big Cheese

During one of my forays through the help wanted ads I came across a listing titled, "Assistant to Director, Moscow Office" with Russian language ability required, for a New York import/export firm. The Soviet Union had fallen of course and new business opportunities were opening up in Russia at the time. I applied and soon had my first interview at the spartan offices of this company, and everything went well. My normal routine in the era before the internet was to hit the Manhattan business library to research companies before I went on interviews, but I could not find a word about this company. I knew what the people at the interview told me about the job and that was all. Still, it seemed like it might be a good opportunity; import/export firms were generally a little more rough around the edges than the pristine Manhattan law firm where I worked, so I tried not to pre-judge. I would go forward with the second interview.

This second interview went on for a long while. There were meetings with several individuals, then the CEO and vice presidents. Later there was a period where the executives discussed my candidacy in private, then I was brought back into the room and offered the job right then and there. This blindsided me, it was a shock in many ways. I had not expected them to make a decision that day, and to get any kind of an offer after the year of job searching I had just had blew me away.

I should have asked for a day or two to calm down and think it over, but there was a desperation in me at the time. I quickly accepted and for not as much money as I should have asked for. The truth was I wanted an international business job like this so badly I did not care about the money much. It was all about prestige and ego for me; I was sick of trying to explain why I was a paralegal even though I had an MBA from a top school. Proof of this fact was that one thing I was sure to do once I accepted the offer was to brag about it indirectly. I made dozens of copies of the company's sheet listing the contact information of its international offices and mailed these to friends and colleagues, especially business school ones. The new job placement officer at McGill got one, as did Keanu Reeves and other MBA friends. Stupidly, I had something to prove to everyone at the time. A job in Moscow sounded stunning and exciting, and that was the clincher for me accepting the offer.

Unbelievably, the *same week*, I received a call from London, UK. A contact I had pursued since my time in business school, for two and a half years, called out of the blue to see if I were still interested in working for him on the commodities exchange in London. I originally spoke with this person during my first year at McGill, and then kept in touch but nothing came of it until this week of all times. I had to tell him no, I was taking another position (!) Unreal.

My friends at the law firm knew that I did not plan on a career as a paralegal but a job in Moscow was something else. My boss had always given me a hard time with lines like, "This guy, he came for the summer, then he never left!" So, when I told him I finally found another job he was surprised. When I told him where it was he thought I had lost my mind.

"Michael, with your background, JohnsHopkinsMcGill, you will do well for us." That is how he would say it, in one word… JohnsHopkinsMcGill. This was the CEO of my new firm speaking, I will call him The Big Cheese. He was welcoming me to "Imports R Us," where I was to be Assistant to the Director/CFO of the company's Moscow office. If you were to ask, he was quick to assure you that Imports R Us was an American company, but I was quickly learning that the company was American in name only. Its main office was in New York, with other locations in Moscow and the Far East, but most of the employees and all of the movers and shakers were Asian, Chinese mainly.

I realized it would be an adjustment for an American like me to fit in at what in truth was a foreign company. Imports R Us had a culture and a work environment very different from what I was used to, but I had no problem with that. I had lived and worked in many different places, and considered myself fairly easy going and adaptable. I was very gung ho about this opportunity and anxious to do whatever it would take to make things work out. In any case, soon I would be working in Moscow, with an American supervisor and a staff of about a dozen Russians. I actually expected to feel more comfortable in that situation than at the New York office. The Russian way of doing things was different from the American way of course, but it was much closer to the environment in which I was used to working.

I was stunned to be offered the position in the first place. I felt well qualified, but I was well qualified for plenty of jobs during the past year and that never prevented me from being turned down by other organizations. Because of this I was suspicious of everything. What is wrong with this place? Why did it work out? In other words, like the old expression goes, "I would never join a club that would admit me as a member." That is how I was feeling at the time. Still, I wanted the opportunity to work out so badly that I was hoping against hope that everything would be ok.

I was constantly weighing the positives and negatives of this company and the position in my head. The second interview had been grueling, and after I received the offer an American woman who was the office manager was very nice to me. She gave me some yogurt and a banana to eat because the interview had gone on for hours, and that was very thoughtful. This was a relatively small company so I had not expected any lavish treatment.

Later in the week I was taken out to dinner at the restaurant on top of the World Trade Center by The Big Cheese and a vice president who seemed to act as his right hand man. Thus I will call him The Little Cheese. The two of them may have thought I smiled an awful lot that night but I was actually straining to understand the lengthy discourses of The Big Cheese in his heavy Chinese accent. Often I did not understand, but I learned to just smile and nod when he spoke. The climax of the evening was when The Big Cheese took me to a large window and we looked down on the city from 107 stories high. This was kind of weird to me and struck me as funny at the same time, like Lucifer showing me all that could be mine if I joined him.

I had a lot to think about once I accepted the offer. I used every minute of every day to prepare myself for the new job during my two week notice period at the law firm. I was cramming with Russian language instructional cassettes and my old college textbooks because my Russian skills were rusty. Also, I was trying to arrange all of my personal matters. There was not much time. I was expected to leave for the newly formed Commonwealth of Independent States (CIS) – what they were calling the no longer communist former Soviet Union at the time – within a month and a half. I had many questions about what to expect, what to bring, and how to arrange my finances to receive pay while in Russia.

Unfortunately I was quickly learning that no one in the New York office had a clue about the logistics of the Moscow operation. The few guidelines I received turned out to be off the mark, but this was all right. I was assured that Lenny, the director of the Moscow office, would be calling me on the telephone within a few days or so to fill me in. Soon enough I was given a little background information on the American director in Moscow, and although I was not told his age I realized that he must be younger than I was. Oooh. I considered myself on the young side at age 27 for an assignment as CFO of an overseas office. Uh oh. I was very anxious to talk to this director over the phone, to get to know him a bit, and more importantly to get some answers. Well a week passed and he did not call. Then another week went by, and still no call. What was going on?

Before my official start date I called the office manager for the first time with a few minor questions and to find out why our man in Moscow had not called yet. No more yogurt and bananas, mood change! She sounded very annoyed at my questions and when I asked about the call from Moscow she became more annoyed. Lenny was a busy guy, I was told. I heard this over and over, from the company and later from Lenny himself. Too busy to make a phone call? For weeks? This should have been the company slogan… "Imports R Us, we're busy."

Lenny eventually did call and I got some answers, but it was like pulling teeth. It had taken me weeks just to learn what type of set up I would have to receive pay for my work. I asked for Imports R Us' help in setting something up but they were baffled and made it pretty clear that this, like just about everything, was my personal problem that I had to figure out myself.

Direct deposit was an alien concept to Imports R Us, they said they just could not do that for me, I could only receive paper checks for my pay (!) The problem was I would be in Moscow, and there really were not Western style banks in Moscow in 1992. I would have to have an account in the US, but I would not be in the US to put Imports R Us paychecks in the bank. I struggled to come up with a solution to this problem, talked with the representatives of several American banks in New York City, but it seemed there was no way to have an account of my own that would work for this without direct deposit. The only answer was to have checks sent to a family member in the US and have that person deposit the pay for me. When I finally was able to speak with Lenny he told me that this was what he did with his checks.

A slight hassle, but not that big a problem really. What amazed me was that even though Lenny was paid from the New York office, not one person at the entire New York office was able to tell me what his simple arrangement was.

The first seeds of worry were planted in my head. I expected a move to Moscow to be full of problems and headaches, but these could be overcome. What worried me was the trust factor. To take a remote overseas position without confidence in my company's willingness to support me was a frightening prospect. A name kept popping into my head, "Joe Clark (A)." As I began dealing with my new company, I could not free my mind from the nagging presence of a certain MBA case study (the "A" in parenthesis was a case study's way of designating the first section of the case study, which might continue with Joe Clark (B), Joe Clark (C), and so on). Joe Clark (A) is a Harvard Business School case study we discussed in my Organizational Behavior class at McGill about a man in his late twenties. The young man is finishing his MBA at Harvard and after trudging through many interviews and weighing numerous job offers (this was an old case study!), he takes a position with an Asian-American clothes manufacturer.

The case is a lovely tale of American employees dropping like flies through dismissals and resignations. One is denied a bonus he was promised, fired soon after relocating to another part of the United States, and has to fight for the reimbursement of moving expenses he was promised. This all hit a little too close to home for me. Still, what could I do but keep a watchful eye on events and hope that this type of thing would not happen to me. I suppose the purpose of the case was to allow MBA's to benefit from the knowledge of Joe Clark's bad experiences. Unfortunately I did not have the choices Joe had when he was offered his position, I was an early 1990's MBA. The phone call from my London contact was not an offer, just an inquiry about my interest and a possible interview. I had never even met the London contact in person. In any event the call came too late to save me, I had already accepted the offer from Imports R Us. Was I going to turn down the opportunity to work in a job perfectly suited to me in an exciting new international market, simply because I feared that there might be problems?

Not me, Mr. Gusto MBA. Are you kidding? Whatever problems there were, I would work them out, roll with them, accept them, this might be a once in a lifetime opportunity. I had to find out for sure whether this position would work out for me; I imagined the possible alternative to accepting the offer. Turning down the job could have resulted in my spending another year as a paralegal, wondering what could have been if I had only had the guts to take the position in Moscow.

My first week at the New York office was spent getting my feet wet and learning the Imports R Us accounting and inventory procedures. Once in Moscow I was to work toward implementing similar procedures in that office and to improve the flow of financial data between New York and Russia. Most of the staff in New York were quite gracious and made every effort to relate their work procedures to me.

While the business side of things proceeded normally in the first week or so at the office, I had other major worries. I could never get the straight word on what medical care would be available for me while in Russia. Moscow was a different world from the United States as far as health care was concerned, my understanding was that some if not most people in Russia did not have access to a level of care considered satisfactory in the West. I expected inconveniences and I realized that Moscow would not have well stocked pharmacies on every corner. Still, I wondered if there were any arrangements at all for medical care at the Moscow office, support from the New York office, and preparation for serious medical emergencies. Would something like simple appendicitis turn into a life threatening ailment for a member of the Moscow office?

Lenny the director had not been very specific on the phone, and when the subject came up in New York it was quickly brushed aside. "No problem, we fly you out." That was the extent of the answer. Yeah, I bet. Looking at the company's employee handbook, benefits were minimal. In fact one day in New York a man who was doing mechanical labor in the warehouse area cut himself badly while working. He came into the office area holding his wound and surprise, surprise, the company did not even have a first aid kit available. The office manager yelled to no one in particular, "Could we please see that we have some kind of first aid kit for accidents like this!" Sounds like something for which an office manager herself should have been responsible. This made me wonder what a mess the Moscow office might be.

Part of my training in New York consisted of an afternoon long briefing by The Little Cheese on the structure of Imports R Us, its family of companies, and the current projects of these companies. He went up to the writing board on the wall, took a felt marker, and said to me jokingly, "It's a sham." Your company is a sham. Boy, that's funny (?) By the end of the briefing I was not laughing. He drew an organigram chart on the board, which looked like an umbrella with a lot of appendages. This company was part of this company, this other company belongs to this company etc. etc. This was not unheard of in business but the location for most of these Imports R Us companies was the building in which we were sitting, which consisted of a small one floor office area and a connecting warehouse and storage area. Only a few dozen employees worked there. There were almost as many companies as there were employees it seemed.

The Little Cheese then proceeded to brief me on the current business partners and clients of the New York and Moscow offices that were relevant to what I would have been doing. Whenever I asked what exactly it was that Imports R Us had done with these partners and clients, the answer was always, "We are trying to work out a deal with them, nothing concrete has happened yet," or "We are going to set up a store with them, we don't have a location yet."

Yes, just like Joe Clark (A) promised, I was finding Imports R Us to have quite an exotic work atmosphere. The corporate culture was certainly different from anything I had previously experienced; this really did not affect me much in the first few weeks, but I guessed it would when I became a full fledged employee. There was constant talk of entertaining people, "entertaining clients is an art, you see," The Big Cheese liked to say. He always spoke of office politics, conflicts, and avoidance of interoffice romantic affairs that might interfere with business. "As an American businessman, Russian women are going to want you," he repeated to me many times. There seemed to be a lot of funny talk about women. My favorite statement in this regard was made by The Little Cheese who said, "It's ok to have girlfriends, as long as you love your wife."

One day I was riding in The Little Cheese's car and noticed that he had an old, ragged box of tissues on the dashboard. This was just a decoy he proudly explained. He showed me and another passenger in the car that inside the tissue box was a radar detector. This gave him a warning in case there were any police in the area who might be handing out speeding tickets. Thinking about the corporate structure, the talk of women, the radar detector and other relatively minor examples led me to believe there was a culture of cheating at Imports R Us. This led me not to trust them much compared to other companies where I have worked.

At the Imports R Us office I came to realize that my responsibilities were not going to be made clear, and at any time something could end up being my fault. For example, to go to Russia I was going to need a work visa. I was led to believe that the firm was going to take care of this as it did for all employees who made the trip to the Moscow office. A short time before I was to depart for Moscow all hell broke loose because no one had taken care of it. I felt the heat from The Big Cheese, "Michael, I don't understand how you let this happen! You must have the visa ready, how could you let it not be ready yet."

I had been led to believe otherwise, but if the visa were my responsibility then fine. In an effort to resolve the situation I stopped by on my own after work to have a visa photo taken. This would save someone at the office the trouble of driving me to a photo shop the next day, and allow me to spend the entire day at the office as well. When I brought the photos in the following day with a receipt, the office manager's response was, "Why did you get them taken at a place like that, where they charge you $15!!! Pictures should not cost that much!!!" Oh man, I am supposed to be CFO of your Moscow office and you are berating me like this over $15? Never mind, I'll pay for it with my own money, geez.

The Big Cheese's administrative assistant was under stress from this atmosphere I could see. He kept insisting that I have her type up a calendar of meetings and events for the following few weeks. When I would bring the dates I had taken down in my discussions with The Big Cheese to his administrative assistant, she would become flustered. "He's given me four different calendars to type, the dates are all different, I don't know what he wants." The dates I had were included in the calendar she had already begun work on, so we agreed to let that calendar be the standard. Soon I was reprimanded by The Big Cheese anyway, "Michael, you still have not prepared the calendar for me!" Most of these issues were more amusing than worrisome, but I was concerned about the future. Important issues and problems were sure to arise and I would be halfway around the world, dependent on a company like this for support.

I was briefed by many different people in the New York office but none of the discussions were helpful. I received all sorts of different information and opinions about the

Moscow office. When one vice president in New York discussed the implementation of an inventory system in Moscow with me, he concluded the discussion with this comment, "Bring a lot of change of underwear, ha ha ha." He found this a lot funnier than I did at the time, but in hindsight after having experienced the Moscow operation firsthand I am better able to see the humor there. The main message I received from these briefings could be summed up in the following phrase, "Moscow does not know what it is doing."

If I had not gotten the message in my individual briefings, not to fear. One day there was a big meeting between the CEO, the vice presidents, a few other employees, and me concerning the operations of the Moscow office. Lenny the Moscow Office Director was not present to defend himself, so it was open season. They ripped the poor guy to shreds.

> "Lenny does not understand business, you see."
>
> "How does he sell a shoe for $5, then say that we make money… the shoe costs $3.75, shipping costs $1.50, you have to pay salaries to the workers, how does he say we are making money?"
>
> "You go to Lenny's apartment and he stops you at the door. He says, 'that's ok you do not have to come in,' and he closes the door very quickly like he's hiding something in there. What is he hiding?"

Imports R Us had a consultant at the meeting, an older American man who apparently was retired from a career in the garment business. If you have ever watched the show *Seinfeld* think Jerry's dad on the show, Morty Seinfeld, and you can imagine what this guy was like. Mister retired old school NY garment business person. This man visited the Moscow office on one occasion and his version of its operations made the Asian employees descriptions sound kind by comparison. In a nightmarish tale, he spoke of a "kid" (Lenny) who was, "bright, don't get me wrong, but he's never had to do anything for himself in his life. He's way over his head, too many responsibilities, he just can't handle it. One day we got in the car to head for the airport, and the smell was incredible. Lenny had not bathed for days, he wouldn't get dressed, he just wore the same sweat suit all the time." He continued on, tearing Lenny to bits.

The consultant's account made Lenny seem erratic. The account was incredibly dramatic. Too dramatic. It became clear to me over time that this consultant was known by many people at Imports R Us for his skill in exaggerating events and stretching the truth. The day I left for Moscow the consultant pulled me aside secretly and told me to watch myself in my dealings with "the kid." Terrific. I had trouble believing most of the consultant's description of the Moscow office, but the meeting as a whole did not do much to assuage my fears about this company. Any way you sliced it, whatever combination of stories I chose to believe, there were a lot of strange things going on at Imports R Us.

In our discussions The Big Cheese made it clear that my job was going to be to fix all of the problems and inefficiencies in the Moscow office, but I was not to challenge Lenny's authority, and I could not ruffle the feathers of any of the Russian staff. Ok all you MBA's out there, by this point you have come to love Imports R Us, you have heard the highlights of the meeting, and you have gotten your instructions from The Big Cheese. There's a business case study for you... now come up with an action plan!

In any event, I would get to judge Lenny the Director for myself, meeting him for the first time in New York later that week. When I did meet him he seemed like a good enough guy, a fairly normal 26 year old. This confused me to an even greater extent, I guess I was expecting too much. No one could live up to the hype of that meeting we had earlier in the week. Lenny certainly was *busy* though. He had to rush back to Moscow almost immediately to continue working on a big oil deal. You know Imports R Us had been working on the big oil deal for a long time, nothing concrete has happened yet, they needed to keep working on the big deal (!) To this day I wonder if they ever closed that "big oil deal?" Somehow I doubt it.

Since Lenny was in town, the first order of business was to have a meeting. The Big Cheese had Lenny, me, and some vice presidents meet in the conference room in various combinations. In the most memorable of these meetings we discussed how the finances should be structured in the Moscow office. The Big Cheese stressed how the finances of the office must be organized into proper accounts with an accurate accounting system. If not, there could be serious problems. "This must be done! Some day the KGBCIA (just like JohnsHopkinsMcGill, in Big Cheese's English very disparate organizations became one) come to the Moscow office you see. KGBCIA is not looking for me… they are looking for Lenny, they are looking for Michael… you are in charge of the Moscow office, not me!"

"Holy shit, would you listen to this?" I thought to myself.

Anyway, one of the many Imports R Us ventures was a new bank in Moscow which was to be set up by a Russian businessman named Pechorin with help from Imports R Us' Moscow office. This young Russian appeared to be about my age, and he had come to New York to talk with some Imports R Us people. The businessman was visiting New York to learn about American business first hand courtesy of Imports R Us. Lenny, The Little Cheese, and I were to take the Russian businessman to several banks in the New York area for demonstrations.

First we showed up at one of the major commercial banks in Manhattan's financial district. We were to meet a woman there who was to expose the Russian to some of the inner workings and procedures of a major bank, and then we were to set up a relationship with that bank. By virtue of this relationship, the Russian bank would gain the capability to transfer funds and data internationally. However, when we arrived the woman was not expecting us for more than a very brief visit. Oops! The Little Cheese had not specified the purpose of our visit with her on the phone. He made an unsuccessful attempt to explain away this oversight, and I remember the woman looking at me with a confused expression. Her face seemed to be asking, "What is the story with you people?" Sheepishly, I just kept my lips zipped. The Little Cheese was running the show here, not me.

Later that week there was a big meeting between Pechorin and The Big Cheese. It was a high level tete-a-tete at Imports R Us and the atmosphere in the office was akin to that of a Reagan-Gorbachev summit. Pechorin and The Big Cheese, separated by different cultures and languages, were planning the startup of the Moscow bank. Lenny was back in Moscow working on the "big oil deal," so my presence was required at this meeting to help Pechorin understand and convey ideas in English. Pechorin was too proud for this, however. He understood some English, but he pretended to understand everything The Big Cheese said at the meeting. Anytime I offered a helpful "ponyatno?" (understand?) or "ladno" (Ok?) Pechorin would roll his eyes and say in English, "I know, I know." I am sorry, but there was no way he understood everything. I had trouble understanding The Big Cheese's English!

So there we were, the conference room was filled with smoke, the tension was high, and the meeting was priceless. Here are a few highlights…

>Big Cheese: "To have bank, should have computer."
>
>Pechorin: "Yes… yes"
>
>Big Cheese: "Also, want to print out pamphlet, that tells about bank."
>
>Pechorin: "Yes, of course… yes"

Look out Citibank, there was a new force to be reckoned with in the global banking community!

If one were to ask what Imports R Us did in Moscow, I would suggest that a better question was, "What didn't Imports R Us do in Moscow?" Just like a big box superstore, it was a one stop location for all you CIS business needs. The Moscow office offered everything from shipping, freight forwarding, sales of food, shoes, clothing, Asian souvenirs, real estate, a visa service, legal aid, business consulting in the CIS, computer sales, oil purchases, and on top of this there was the jointly run bank with Pechorin. This was an office of about a dozen people with one person running things; this person was in his mid-twenties and had no particular business or legal expertise.

As far as I could fathom up to this point the office seemed completely out of control, trying to do everything and accomplishing nothing. Actually there was one thing it was definitely doing. It was definitely spending money. How much was anyone's guess until the cutting edge accounting system from Imports R Us New York was implemented in the Moscow office. This was to be my job.

I had another assignment one day in New York, I was to call some people from other companies who were requesting information about Imports R Us. Incredibly, Imports R Us had placed an advertisement in a widely read business paper which boasted of the many services offered by its Moscow office. It could do just about anything for anyone in the CIS. Predictably though, months passed, many letters of inquiry piled up in the New York office, and none of these letters had ever been answered. Imports R Us was a *busy* company, remember. I made a few calls, and found myself at a loss trying to explain what the Moscow office did, and make it sound believable.

Russia is... Casino

This chapter concerns the young Russian businessman Pechorin. It was my job to show him around New York City for a week and keep him entertained, and he turned out to be a great guy. Pechorin was not his real name of course, it is the name of the main character in the classic Russian novel *A Hero of Our Time* by Mikhail Lermontov. This Russian businessman, like Pechorin in the novel, had a sharp mind and a bold personality. But also like Pechorin of the novel, he had a very fatalistic view of life. One night over drinks he said to me, with a melancholy smile on his face, "Work... it is my life. I work always... then one day, I will die." What do you say to that? "So... Pechorin... how 'bout those Orioles?"

The Little Cheese and I picked up Pechorin at JFK Airport on a Saturday afternoon. He was dressed in a suit and although this was his first time in New York City, he did not seem too excited. This was probably the result of a long, tiring flight. He sat in the front seat of the car with a look of quiet exhaustion as we rounded the Belt Parkway in Brooklyn. Pechorin snapped out of his trance when we passed the Verrazano Bridge, staring out of the window in awe at the huge suspension bridge connecting Brooklyn and Staten Island. The Russian shook his head slowly at the sight of the imposing structure and whispered to himself, "amazing." I had to agree, it was amazing they would build a bridge to Staten Island.

Pechorin was right, though. There are many incredible sights in New York that are taken for granted by those who live in the city. Sometimes one needs to see these sights through a visitor's eyes to truly appreciate them. Soon New York's skyline came into view and Pechorin was fascinated, whereas upon seeing the same view New Yorkers would likely complain about the congestion of Manhattan and wish for a week at the beach. Eventually we made our way into the city and checked Pechorin into his hotel, then we went out for some steak.

First on the agenda the following day was a search for some business suits for Pechorin. Another vice president from Imports R Us named Joe took Pechorin and me to some men's clothing shops in northern New Jersey. Joe was a member of the company for whom I had a great deal of respect; he was a Vietnamese man who was raised in the United States and went to an American university. Joe was very intelligent, easy going, and full of common sense, so sometimes I wondered how he made it to vice president at Imports R Us!

Pechorin was very particular about the clothes we saw, very definite about what was "gooood" and what was "nogooood." His reaction to most of the suits that day was a disgusted "no, no, no." He was able to spot the stores that were not top of the line instantly, and when we did find some of the best cut suits his eyes lit up, "yes... is gooood." Pechorin had surprisingly good taste in suits, he was definitely a member of a new breed of Russians. A Russian yuppie. This Russian yuppie certainly came prepared for the United States, bringing US $5,000 cash (!) for his week in New York. Russian biznes had been very good to him.

Money and symbols of wealth seemed to be an obsession with Pechorin, but not in a greedy or spoiled way. It seemed to me that they were symbols of achievement and status to him. As we rode around in Joe's car the conversation centered around the other autos on the road. "Yes... Mercedes... gooood car," "Volvo, da, Swedish car, gooood in Russia, with snow." Sorry Honda, Toyota, Ford, and the rest, American and Japanese cars got the thumbs down from the Russian. Judging from what Pechorin said, and from what I saw when I arrived in Moscow, American and Japanese vehicles were considered second rate in the CIS. If you lived in Moscow and you had the dollars to afford it, you got a Mercedes, preferably with a car phone. Failing that, maybe a Volvo, a Saab, or a Bemweh would be your choice. A Bemweh was how Pechorin said BMW until Joe and I clued him in to the correct English pronunciation.

Joe drove us to some of the more upscale residential areas of metropolitan New York so that Pechorin could have a look at the lifestyles of the rich and famous. Pechorin would always ask "Skolko?" (How much?), so I got some practice with my Russian numbers, "Pyatsot tisyach dollarov, moshet bit," ($500,000 maybe) – that was a very expensive house in 1992. Naturally the subject turned to where Pechorin lived in Russia, and Joe and I learned that he made his home in a country house of a former Communist Party official. This house in the Moscow area included a tennis court (!) out back. Immediately my mind raced to the idol of my business school days, "You see, I not at park to play tennis, this court is mine, I own it." A tennis court of his own! Tom Vu would have been proud of Pechorin.

Around the middle of the day we became hungry, so we took a break from the shopping to chow down. The three of us bought sandwiches and salads in a bistro of an upscale mall's food court. Pechorin was perplexed by some of the food, and I could relate to this. I remembered the times I had eaten in Soviet cafeterias and I was clueless as to what I was getting and how to go about ordering the food. Pechorin was given two small plastic cups by the man behind the counter of the bistro, one was full of French salad dressing and the other was full of ketchup for the fries. After we sat down I noticed Pechorin out of the corner of my eye as he proceeded to pour ketchup all over his salad, but I was too late to stop him. He had already begun dipping his fries in the French dressing, and he seemed to like it, so I just left him alone and did not say anything.

We ended the day by seeing Liberty State Park with its view of the Statue of Liberty, then we took a quick tour of the sights of Manhattan, but what Pechorin seemed most interested in was the heliport. His main wish during his week in Manhattan was to take a helicopter ride over the city. Pechorin never got a chance to do this thanks to all the things The Big Cheese and The

Little Cheese decided he had to see during the week, things like a Broadway play, and of course lunch at the top of the World Trade Center with that view. "Entertaining client is an art, you see."

The first in depth discussion I had with Pechorin was at the bar in his hotel. We talked about everything from business to differences between Russian and American lifestyles. There is an anecdote in Russian literature, it is in one of Dostoevsky's novels I think (Alright, you're thinking, *another* reference to Russian literature, what is this crap? Look, I do not care, that Hopkins education cost good money, and we did a lot of literature in my advanced Russian classes, so I am trying to get my money's worth, ok?). The anecdote speaks of the difference between German and Russian students at the time, the 1800's. It says that if you give a German student a map of the universe he will return the next day with the map memorized. If you give the same map of the universe to a Russian student he will return the next day with the map and his corrections to it.

Pechorin could be like that at times, very sure of himself, and very opinionated. One topic we discussed at the bar was the tobacco industry. Pechorin argued that it was the great industry of the future, that more and more people were smoking every day. I responded that this may be true in Russia but in fact the opposite is true in the US. He just refused to believe this, everyone smoked in America he assured me.

Another night we went to see the Broadway play *CATS*, and at intermission we went out for some fresh air. Many audience members were smoking cigarettes near us and Pechorin nailed me, "You see, you see, everyone is smoking, I told you." Pechorin had a sentimental side which came out occasionally as well. At times I could tell he was homesick for Russia, and during one of Andrew Lloyd Webber's tunes from *CATS* I noticed Pechorin wiping away a few tears. When I arrived at the hotel to pick him up for the play that night he was watching cartoons on TV and having a blast. The Russian wore the biggest grin I had ever seen on him. He turned his head toward me sitting in the chair and pointed at the TV screen. "Look!" he said, laughing out loud.

During the week I took Pechorin along on the subway with me a few times to show him what a New York commute was like and the Russian was unfazed by the subway and New York in general. Pechorin was not completely impressed by the America he saw either, he kept telling me how much nicer Russia is, a country where friends gather for long meals and good conversation. I assured Pechorin that he was only seeing one small part of America by remaining in New York City. For his next visit I would have to invite the McKenzie Brothers down and take him out to the Ponderosa Steak House in Plattsburgh, NY.

During the commute one day Pechorin asked me, "Are you angry with life?" "Nah, not really. I am happy with life," I responded. "I am angry," he replied, "you must be angry with life to be successful, working always." I suppose Pechorin meant something more along the lines of driven, ambitious in life, but at the same time "angry" was not such a bad choice of words. He did seem to be on some sort of a mission, and he said once that the pressure took its toll. Pechorin told me he saw a doctor for a sickness, he had problems with his nerves. As he said this I could not help noticing that he was chugging black coffee and chain smoking cigarettes like there was no tomorrow. I wondered if this was his "nerve problem." The big Russian was still young and not terribly out of shape, but he did not look like a regular at the gym either.

Like many foreign businessmen Pechorin was keen on hitting the strip clubs, as there was nothing comparable in Russia he said (I'm sure this changed over the course of the 1990's). So, we made that obligatory trip to "Flashdancers," the famous Manhattan strip club after seeing *CATS*. At one point Pechorin asked me about the prostitute situation in New York City, and I do not know if he was just curious or truly interested, but I told him it was an area where I just could not help him. I did not get involved in it and therefore I knew nothing about it. His response to this answer was very funny. I suppose he thought I was playing dumb, that I would not give him the scoop for one reason or another, and he demanded, "Why?! Why is it that you do not know?!" What did I look like, Hugh Hefner?

Pechorin had a ball at Flashdancers, and although I do not often visit these places I had to admit it was a breath of fresh air after three hours of "wholesome, feel good" Andrew Lloyd Webber entertainment. But, I think the happiest people of all that night were the women who came in our direction. Unfortunately Pechorin did not understand being entertained as a client or at least did not like the fact that I was paying for everything with company money. By the time we arrived at Flashdancers he absolutely refused to let me pay for his drinks and entertainment any longer. The dancers and hostesses at strip clubs like Flashdancers are crafty, the only thing they like better than a foreigner with a drink is a foreigner with a drink and too much money on his hands. They can smell it a mile away.

One woman at Flashdancers was paying particularly close attention to Pechorin, and he really liked her. He asked her, "What is your name." She replied, "Oh, my name is 'Baby.'" Of course, all the girls take on fake names to protect themselves from the whacko contingent of New York's population. Unfortunately the word "baby" was part of Pechorin's limited English vocabulary, and this only served to confuse him thoroughly. "Ba-by?" he asked her. "Mm-hmm," she answered in her steamy voice, no help at all.

Eventually Pechorin's facial expression changed from bewilderment to one that said, "Oh, who gives a damn anyway, give me another drink." I felt a little responsible for him there and said to him in Russian, so that Ms. Baby would not understand, "Ostorozhno, potomu shto ona znayet shto u tebya mnogo deneg." This loosely translates to "Watch yourself, Baby's working on taking you for a lot of child support." Pechorin snapped back in English, "I know, I know!" That was cool, no problem, I did my duty. He was having a great time so why not? By the night's end he witnessed countless dances, he had his picture taken with Ms. Baby for a souvenir to show his Moscow drinking buddies, and he had probably paid for Baby's new Camaro.

The last day I spent with Pechorin I took him to a few New York electronics stores and he made some store owners very happy. I think the Russian single handedly revitalized the New York City economy with his purchases during the week he spent in America. Pechorin picked up a sound system and a new Sega Genesis video game set with some cartridges, and while on our shopping spree we saw the headline dancer of the night before at Flashdancers. She was signing an autograph for a policeman. Great, at least now Pechorin could say he saw a celebrity while he was in Manhattan.

That night we had dinner in an Italian restaurant and Pechorin was more talkative than ever. He went on at length to describe the state of business in Russia. He asserted that, "Russian biznes… is better than American biznes… it is fast, there is deal, lots of money, quickly… American business is slow, meetings, plans, more meetings." Later Pechorin described a theory of his that Russia in the future would be the world's greatest economic power. "America… Europe… Japan… is like 1929, depression… Russia is just beginning. We have resources, we have smart people." Pechorin expected that IBM, Citibank, all the big corporations would establish a considerable presence in Russia in the future, but not yet. According to the Russian, this time of free markets before the entry of the large western companies was the best time to make a killing. Pechorin said glowingly, "Now is *wonderful* time to be in Russia. Russia is… casino."

I don't know. My money was on real estate mogul Tom Vu. When he starts investing in Russia, so will I.

Back in the CIS

"Back in the CIS" does not quite have the same ring to it as the old Beatles tune "Back in the USSR." But, having been in both the Union of Soviet Socialist Republics in 1986 and the newly formed Commonwealth of Independent States in 1992 I can tell you that the CIS was a much friendlier place to be if you were American. Upon my arrival in Moscow in 1992 the passport agent smiled at me and asked, "American, yes?" Wait a minute, did we get off in the right country? The last time I had been at the Moscow airport in 1986 passport control gave me one of those "guilty until proven innocent" Soviet stares. Once through that touching encounter our student group was herded down dimly lit corridors like a cattle drive, airport security people forcing us to carry our baggage at a gallop shouting, "poshli, poshli!!! (move along, move along). Poshli poshli poshli… keep them doggies rollin'… poshli poshli poshli… get'em up, move'em out, poshli, rawhide.

Things were different in 1992. The wild east had been tamed and the old cattle drives were history. After passport control I was greeted with brightly lit signs, advertisements for business, telecommunications, and travel services just as one might see at a western airport.

Pechorin was with me on the flight, which included a thrilling three hour layover in the small Helsinki, Finland airport at an off hour. We paced back and forth, sat, got up and paced again, then I decided to buy some orange juice. The Finnish woman behind the counter politely informed me that she would gladly take American currency, but she did not have any American currency to make change. I had nothing but $20 bills in my wallet. No thanks I don't care for no $20 cup of orange juice! Never mind.

I was loaded down with things from New York. At the Moscow baggage pickup area I grabbed the two large cardboard boxes jammed full of all my luggage and supplies from New

York. Then there were little bags, papers, and various other items people in the New York office gave to me at the last minute. ("Oh Michael, please take this to the Moscow office for me.") On top of this was over $10,000 cash for the Moscow office, for which I had to fill out a US customs declaration along the way. Since there were no western style banks in Moscow at the time it was not an uncommon practice to carry large sums of cash in and out of the CIS. However, considering how little I trusted Imports R Us this only made me feel more ill at ease.

As Pechorin and I picked up the last of our belongings some men appeared, a few to pick up Pechorin and one named Ilya who was the Russian driver from Imports R Us' Moscow office. Ilya and I threw the boxes and bags into the back of the car and we were off into the city, passing more advertisements, these on billboards lining the airport road. On the highway heading toward downtown Moscow it was just as Pechorin had described to Joe and me. Interspersed with the Russian cars were… a Mercedes… and a Volvo… and another Mercedes, this one with a car phone. Would you look at that. Yo Tito, I mean Toto, we're not in the USSR anymore.

Ilya and I got to talking soon enough, and he was a funny guy, really friendly. He did not seem to know much English but my Russian, while not fantastic at that point, was good enough for us to carry on a conversation. After some small talk about the price of gasoline in Moscow the conversation turned to more serious matters… Russian women. Ilya went on at length, just as Pechorin had, about how incredible Russian women were. They were the best. He'd been all around the great big world and he'd seen all kinds of girls, but Ilya couldn't wait to get back to Irkutsk, back to the cutest girls in the world.

I decided to take Ilya's word for it. I had not come across any Vogue models on my last stay in Moscow, just bad teeth and no Right Guard. But sure enough as we made our way into the center of the city Ilya pointed out the window and said "smotri" (look). My eyes followed the direction of his finger and there she was, an incredibly good looking young woman pushing a baby carriage, dressed in a mini skirt with heels. Welcome to the CIS! I turned to Ilya, smiled and said, "… i ona mat!" (…and she's a mom!)

Unfortunately it was downhill from there. Ilya took me straight to the apartment which was about a fifteen minute walk from the Russian "White House" where Boris Yeltsin held out against the conservative coup a year before. After a bit of a struggle with the door we managed to get in, and I was left on my own to get some rest while Ilya went back to the office. The apartment looked fine, it even had a TV. Excellent. I took a quick walk around the place and then decided to open up the large cardboard boxes full of my luggage and supplies for the office.

I removed the Swiss army knife from one of my bags and began to cut at the tape on the box. Whoops, the entire blade penetrated the cardboard. No problem I figured, odds are the blade did not touch anything inside. Wrong. When I finally opened up the box what was on top but my garment bag containing my trench coat and two suits. Quickly I zipped open the bag and… lovely a huge slice through the back of my trench coat, and the back of the jacket of the better of my two suits. Hmm, I would just run those down to the tailor on the corner of the block and he would fix them right up for me. Wait, I was in Moscow in 1992, tough luck. Never mind. Welcome to the CIS!

I had a few hours rest and then Lenny the director showed up at my apartment to take me to dinner at a Russian restaurant. This sounded great. I hoped and expected that since Lenny and I were away from the New York office he and I could begin to establish a good working relationship. In New York, Lenny was held accountable for a lot and certainly took his share of criticism, but there in Moscow I assumed he would be more relaxed. I had plenty of questions to ask him about work and life in Russia since, as I already mentioned, no one in the New York office had a good understanding of what the Moscow office was about.

Lenny and I arrived at the restaurant and settled down at a table. The director ordered some drinks and appetizers and we began to talk. I asked Lenny a question concerning the office and he snapped at me, "I make it a rule here, when we're not at work we don't talk about work!" Oooookay boss, I guess I will ask tomorrow then. So I cooled it with the questions and just enjoyed looking around the restaurant, which was an interesting place. There was a groovy Russian band playing whose members looked and sounded like they belonged on one of those old K-Tel disco music compilation albums. For a lot of Russians it seemed the 1970's never ended when it came to music and style.

As the night went on it became clear to me that Lenny's conversations typically consisted of giving orders, this came from Lenny being in Russia on his own with no one to answer to for his actions. Well, there was the fax machine and the telephone with daily messages from the New York office, but he ignored those when he wished. What were they going to do, fire him? No one else in the entire New York office could speak a word of Russian, so without Lenny their connection to the Moscow office was in trouble. I think part of The Big Cheese plan was to get me over to Moscow as another American to put a bit of a leash on Lenny. I remembered something The Big Cheese mentioned to me in New York, "Lenny says we do not understand Russians, but we think maybe he himself is becoming Russian. You must not become Russian, Michael, you must maintain American corporate structure!"

Simple… stay American and maintain Chinese corporate structure with all Russian employees, or was that American corporate structure with Chinese employees? But do everything your American boss, who is Russian, says, and do not challenge the Russian employees. But make sure the entire office changes its way of working, it is all your responsibility, Michael!

Ha... as if.

Dinner ended, and Lenny and I headed home in his car. We seemed to be getting along moderately well at this point so I decided to pop the medical question. It had been bugging me all along but now I would get the facts. "Lenny... I'm curious... what happens if someone gets really sick or hurt here? What do you do?" The director replied, "That's a good question, I suppose one of the Russians in the office could recommend something, but even then most of the doctors here are bad, they don't always have access to all the medicine they need. I thought about setting something up with one of the western style medical clinics in Moscow, but I didn't because they have a long waiting list to join. Really though, it's never come up, and I don't worry about it because *I don't get sick.*"

What?

It was safe to say I was a bit concerned about what Lenny said when I arrived back at the apartment. I put the key in the apartment door and guess what, it stuck. It would not turn. I pulled at it, tried to ease it out, nothing worked. "Ok, just take it easy," I thought, "sit down for a minute and calm down." I struggled with the lock some more, a good ten minutes until finally the lock opened. From then on I only locked the bottom of the two locks, which seemed to work ok. The next week Lenny was over and he had his own set of keys to this apartment. His keys worked just fine, no doubt he had the original set and gave me a copy set made by "skilled" Russian locksmiths.

Work at Imports R Us was, well, a piece of work. As one walked in the door there was a receptionist with a computer, a telephone, and a fax machine. On the right there was a room jam packed with Russian employees, less than ten or so, with several computers which they all wanted to use very badly. In fact to make a photocopy in the office one had to use the fax machine as there was not a copier available. I knew working in Russia would mean many inconveniences, so be it.

But then, on the left was the director's office. Very nice and comfortable relative to where the Russians worked, with a bookshelf, spacious desk, and a computer. On my first day of work, when I was able to speak to Lenny for a minute (he was a *busy* guy, remember) I asked him where I could sit. "Hmm, let me think, where could you sit?" he answered. It was good to see that a lot of thought had gone into preparing for the arrival of his American Chief Financial Officer. Lenny continued, "I guess you could pull a chair up to that table where Vladimir and Gleb are working."

When the men politely cleared a space for me, the number two man, CFO of Imports R Us Moscow had about a two foot by one foot area on the table to use in his task of revamping the finances of the Moscow office. At least the Russians were very nice and polite to me after Lenny went back into his office. One Russian worker informed me that there was an employee who was not in that day, and actually had not shown up very often lately for unknown reasons (that was reassuring), so I was welcome to use his table for the time being.

Lenny the director was a busy bee that week, running in and out of the office, out more often than in. On one occasion I was graced by his presence for 30 seconds or so and I used it to the fullest, blurting out a question quickly before I was interrupted by a more pressing matter. "Lenny, one second, how do I receive mail at my apartment in Moscow?" This was not a question I would normally waste time on at work but I had no choice, anytime I could get a word with Lenny was precious. "Oh, there is a mailbox there, I have the keys to it. I guess I could give them to you," Lenny quickly said to me, and then he was off again. That was great, he was going to give me the keys to my own mailbox at my own apartment at some point.

I began working with a Russian woman who was in charge of the accounting in the office. I was delighted and fascinated to see that although her Russian manual of bookkeeping methods seemed very different at first glance, it actually contained many of the same concepts embodied in western style accounting. She was quite smart and cooperative and we went about developing a true accounting system for the office. It was going to be a bit tough at first, as I worked on absorbing all the Russian vocabulary for accounting terms, but not impossible in the least.

Lenny had the two of us come into his office for a short meeting once. At this meeting he informed me and my Russian coworker that he required daily updates on our progress on the accounting system, in person. But, in case you had been in Siberia for the past ten years and did not know, Lenny was a very *busy* guy. Thus, the director said, it was *our* responsibility to track him down every day and give him the update when he had the time.

The three of us did have an interesting trip one day. We took a ride to the "exhibition center" which featured many of the fine goods offered by Imports R Us in Moscow. To my eyes it was like a scene from *Mad Max Beyond Thunderdome*, a post-apocalyptic vision, because the center was located in what used to be called VDNX in the Soviet Union. VDNX was short for "Vistavka Dostizheni Narodnovo Xozyaistvo (The People's Exhibition of Technological Achievements). This was a park with various buildings containing displays of Soviet achievements in rocket and aerospace technology. There were also monuments to the cosmonauts, centering on one of the greatest Soviet heroes Yuri Gagarin, the first man in space.

I remembered being led around the exhibits by the Soviet guide Natasha six years earlier and how proud she was of everything on display.

In 1992 the park was a disgrace, run down and ignored. Some of the old exhibition buildings were being rented out to entrepreneurs with goods to sell, and part of one building was reserved for Imports R Us. Some Soviet logic had survived at the park, however. To enter the park one had to pay a fee, even if one was from a company selling goods at the park. Essentially, we had to pay to get into our own store.

Inside the building, the Imports R Us area was basically a mess. Boxes of shoes were all over the floor, and clothes were hanging or lying about for Russian wholesale buyers to take back to their shops. As far as I could see the opinion of the New York office was correct, there did not seem to be any way of knowing for sure how many of each of these items Imports R Us had at any given time. I would have been surprised if some of the Russians hanging around the building were not robbing the place at their leisure.

The apartment building where I lived was the stage for some of those bizarre Russian situations that make westerners shake their heads in disbelief, but that is what makes Russia an interesting, and sometimes funny place to be. For instance, every day there were men doing construction work on the rear of the building. One day as I walked by I saw a man standing on the scaffolding about four stories high, he was removing large old chunks of cement and stone from the side of the building. As he removed these heavy cement pieces he proceeded to toss them off the scaffolding down to the ground four floors below. There was another man working on the ground, squatting with his back to the building and completely absorbed by what he was doing. Both men seemed oblivious to the fact that the cement chunks were landing dangerously close to the man on the ground. One unlucky cement toss and that Russian construction worker would be a Russian pancake!

Lenny was strangely secretive about this company apartment. This was where I had to live, albeit rent free, but I had no privacy there because it belonged to Imports R Us. Lenny had his own place and still, as I mentioned earlier, Lenny had his own (better) key to "my" place. I did not care for this arrangement at all. I was told by employees in the New York office that Imports R Us had secured the apartment through a Russian employee's connection with the government. There was an extensive library of books in the place which was located in a nice area of the city, and I wondered if the apartment had previously belonged to a Communist Party official or some other privileged Soviet. In one exchange I had with Lenny the apartment was mentioned. I made an off the cuff remark like, "Oh we got this apartment through so and so at the office, his father has government connections or something, right?"

Lenny snapped back, *"No, that's not it… that's not it at all!"* But he gave no further explanation. My mind went back to the meeting at Imports R Us in New York… "Lenny says you don't have to come in, and closes the door quickly, like he is hiding something in there, what is he hiding?" Remember that? What was the deal with these apartments and why was he secretive about them?

The whole situation was so strange with this company. There were obviously hardships involved as an American living and working in Moscow, but I was prepared for those. I felt the opportunity was well worth the sacrifices involved. But all this nonsense with Imports R Us was a different matter entirely, there was no one in charge in New York or Moscow that I trusted. There were so many crazy things happening in and around the company. It seemed the idea that

I would be able to muddle through this mess, do some worthwhile work, and get some good experience was unlikely.

These thoughts ran through my brain one day as I stared out the back window into the big courtyard behind the apartment buildings. Russians from the neighboring buildings were playing a pick up soccer game. How great it would have been to just go out there and meet them, jump in the game, and become part of the city. Unfortunately I was in no mood for that, given everything with the company and all the weirdness that went along with it.

Between the soccer game in progress and the window there were two dogs wandering about, incredibly, unnaturally large dogs. Each had short, curly hair of a poodle except that the hair was all matted together, thin, stringy, and dirty. Both dogs looked sickly as they stumbled around the rocky, unkept courtyard. I was queasy as I watched them and pondered my situation. My mind shifted to that polar bear I had seen six years earlier in the Moscow Zoo, flustered, pacing back and forth as a flock of birds ate his food. I felt like that bear.

I had seen enough of Imports R Us, both in New York and Moscow, so I caught Lenny as soon as I could and said, "We need to talk." I told him that things were just not working out, that I was thinking of heading back to New York. In his world everything was fine, and he reasoned that I simply must be overwhelmed by the new environment. Not true, I just could not trust Imports R Us and trust was crucial in this situation, in another country half way around the world from the United States. I tried my best to diplomatically explain why I was leaving, and there were plenty of reasons from which to choose. I worried that criticizing him personally might anger Lenny and he might make it more difficult for me to arrange the trip home through Imports R Us.

"If you are not overwhelmed, then what is the problem?" Lenny asked.

"Everything, this place, everyone trying to do all these things and not making any money," I said.

"How can you say we're not making any money, did you see that warehouse? What did you think it would be like, why did you come here in the first place?"

"I thought it would be more professional. I don't mind Russia, I wanted to come here, but I wanted to be with a professional firm, like it might be working for a big American company here."

"I tell you what, take a couple of days and go visit those companies here and talk to them, see what they're like. They don't know anything, they don't know what they're doing. You know… the one thing I've learned here… is *that nothing bad can happen.*"

That was the clincher for me. Nothing bad can happen. I was headed back to the States as soon as possible. I was going to call New York myself from the apartment but I suppose Lenny beat me to the punch. That evening I received a phone call from The Big Cheese who was baffled by the news. I told him my reasons and I asked that the New York office arrange a flight for me as soon as possible. The Big Cheese argued, trying to convince me that I had to adjust to the new environment and he advised me to just stay put. Once again I asked that work begin on setting up a flight and I stated clearly that my mind was made up. The Big Cheese finally agreed.

The Big Cheese and I spoke again a few days later and I asked if there was any progress made on the plane ticket. He advised me to stay, relax, and try to enjoy Moscow life. I liked that one, "enjoy Moscow life." Arrangements were made for the senior vice president to fly in to Moscow from New York to see me. The Big Cheese told me that when this senior vice president arrived I could discuss the matter with him, so I asked that this man have a ticket for me in his hand when he arrived in Moscow. The Big Cheese agreed.

The senior vice president showed up at the apartment in another day or so. He was not that old, but he had the demeanor of a wise old man. He spoke very calmly, in a soft voice that was anything but threatening. This was no doubt why he was sent, the nice wise man of the company was going to patch things up. No surprise, when I asked about the plane ticket he said he did not have one for me. "They were working on it, but no flights were available for another week," I was assured. Another week? So he could fly in on a day's notice, but to fly out it takes a week?

The senior vice president and I sat in the living room of the apartment and had a lengthy discussion about the situation. I voiced my reasons for leaving in detail, and they went in one ear and out the other. The senior vice president attempted to convince me to stay on, and his justification went something like this, "I am a careful, organized person. You are the same. Lenny is an entrepreneur, you cannot attempt to control such people. I could not do what he does, neither could you."

Hmm, I do not know about that. I think I could have run around Moscow and spent money like Lenny, his situation did not seem so tough to me. Running an office is a lot easier when turning a profit is not necessary, did Lenny have any kind of budget at all? Imports R Us worked on the premise that all this nonsense going on in Moscow was giving them some sort of foothold in the new Russian market, therefore Lenny did not have to make any money. The senior vice president assured me that, "Some day Lenny is going to be a big shot, he is his own man. You must be your own man. The company is not going to take care of you." The company is not going to take care of you… that was for sure.

Leaving Moscow

From what I could see, the leadership of Imports R Us was hoping to just wait me out. I would change my mind if I stayed a while longer and just "enjoyed Moscow life." After the discussion I had with the senior vice president, Lenny stopped by and the three of us went out to dinner. It was grand, as you could imagine I was a pariah at the table.

As I mentioned in the previous chapter, during my meeting with the senior vice president I raised the issue of the plane ticket back to the United States. I mentioned the possibility of my going to the American Express office in Moscow and purchasing a ticket there rather than waiting for New York to arrange a flight. The senior vice president's words were, "They are working on a flight for you but nothing is available for another week, you can check on your own if you like, but all flights are booked up."

I could not understand this statement, at the time it seemed to me that he simply was not telling the truth in an attempt to deter me from leaving. From what I knew of The Big Cheese and the crew back in New York it would not have surprised me if they were not working on getting a flight at all. They probably figured that they could change my mind within a week and I would stay. I had no way of knowing for sure. Still, I could not imagine the senior vice president would be so naïve as to think I would believe all flights were booked for a week.

The senior vice president was staying at my apartment which had a second bedroom, while Lenny had his own apartment in another location. Early the next morning Lenny arrived to take the senior vice president over to the Imports R Us office, and I went out for a walk without disclosing my destination. I headed straight for the American Express office which was about a half hour walk from the apartment. There were no other customers there at the time, so I went through the door and right up to the counter. When I asked the Russian woman behind the counter about the availability of flights to New York her answer was simple, "Sure, when would you like to leave? There is a flight this afternoon, and one tomorrow also." Imagine that.

Who could say what was going on in the minds of the men who ran Imports R Us? Maybe they wanted me to buy the ticket myself and planned on refusing me reimbursement? I could not tell, but it was time for some action. I pulled out the American Express card and reserved a flight that afternoon on British Airways to London with a connecting flight to New York a few days later. Maybe it was not too late to nail that London job after all.

When I arrived back at the apartment it was empty, apparently the senior vice president was still over at the office with Lenny. What to do? Should I call to say that I had a ticket and ask for a ride to the airport? If I did that, they might then try even harder to convince me to stay, and maybe make me late for the flight. I started tossing the remainder of my belongings into bags, luckily I had been smart enough to pack most of my things the day before the senior vice president's arrival in Moscow. I had four bags and they were pretty unwieldy, so unwieldy that for a second I considered leaving one behind to make my trip easier. Never mind that, I decided to take them all as I figured I only had to make it out to the main street to catch a cab.

Unfortunately the only entrance to the apartment faced the courtyard, so it was quite a haul to go all the way around the lengthy building with four bags. I managed to do it by pulling the one rolling suitcase along the ground and throwing the largest bag on my back with the strap around my shoulders. The two smaller bags I carried with one hand; it was not fun nor pretty to make it like this all the way out to the street. To say I must have looked strange is an understatement, dressed in American clothes, Nike basketball shoes, my black trench coat, dragging four bags along at a snail's pace with a concerned and slightly desperate look on my face.

There happened to be a middle aged Russian woman out in the courtyard and she caught sight of the spectacle. The woman stared straight at me for thirty seconds or so, no doubt puzzled by the scene but not reacting at all. She just kept staring. I really did not give a damn what she thought of me at that point, I had places to go, so I kept plodding on. But just like a good New Yorker, or a good Muscovite, or a wise resident of any large city, she was not going to get involved. I could only imagine what she must have been thinking.

After what seemed like an eternity I made it around the building and to the sidewalk of the main thoroughfare. I dropped the bags with a thud and took a minute to catch my breath. Five or six Russians at the bus stop about twenty yards away watched curiously as I attempted to hail a cab. Good luck. Official cabs were not that easy to come by in Moscow, even on the busy avenue where I lived. My flight was to leave Sheremetyevo Airport in the afternoon and I needed to get going, so I decided to take an unofficial cab ride. Many Russians who were fortunate enough to own cars at the time used them to ferry people around, it was basically Uber without the smart phones.

It was not long before I noticed a Mercedes car door open down the street, and a Russian man got out and walked toward me. Soon he was in front of me and he asked, "V aeroport, da?" (To the airport, yes?) No, actually to the Bolshoi Theater, *War and Peace* is playing so I'm bringing a few months' change of clothes. I just said, "Da." We settled on a price in US Dollars and he seemed happy. The guy helped me throw my bags in the trunk and I was out of there. The Russian was friendly and talkative from the get go, though he spoke no English. The Russian immediately asked me what I was doing in Moscow and I replied simply, "biznes." "Ax, kontrakt napishen, da? (Oh, the contract is signed / the deal is closed, yes?) he asked. "Da," I smiled.

We arrived at the airport in plenty of time and I paid him the amount of dollars we had agreed upon, plus some of the unspent rubles in my pocket for good measure. Now to the next hurdle, getting on that plane. I had worries about getting through the passport check and customs clearance, mainly because I did not know what to expect. All I knew was what I had faced leaving the Soviet Union six years previously and that was a hassle. I hoped the Commonwealth of Independent States would be nicer about things. The Soviets were quite strict, travelers were made to carry forms detailing how much hard currency was on hand when entering the country, how much they still had when leaving, and receipts to show where the cash was spent or exchanged for rubles during the stay. Soviets were also fairly particular about the dates on visas, visitors were supposed to enter and leave the USSR on the days specified.

My visa had a US return date for a random amount of time like six months or so in the future as I remember; whether this mattered in the CIS I did not know. I suspected this would be ok but I could not be sure. If I were unable to make it onto the plane I would have had an awkward return back to the Moscow apartment, having to explain to the Imports R Us crew that I tried to skip town.

I grabbed a customs declaration and filled it out with the amount US Dollars and Russian Rubles I had in my possession, then stepped into the passport line dragging my four bags behind me. The line was long and I waited about a half hour, or at least it seemed like a half hour. As I moved within earshot of the Russian immigration agents I listened carefully to the dialogue as each person was checked. This only added to my worries. My mind went wild imagining tricky questions they might ask me about the purpose of my visit and why I was leaving on this day in particular.

Finally it was time. I braced myself, went up to the agent and handed over my passport, visa, and customs form. The agent took a long look at my papers, much too long for my taste. Then she called another agent over to ask a question. Uh oh. After a minute their discussion ended and the agent turned to me. "You cannot bring rubles out of the country, you must change for dollars downstairs and bring the receipt back," she said. I realized then that I should have just given all the rubles to the cabbie as I only had five or ten dollars of rubles left. Unfortunately the rubles had been the last thing on my mind that day.

This was a hassle, to go downstairs with my four bags, change five dollars of rubles, then come back up and get in line again. But if this were my only issue with the passport agents, I was in good shape. When I came back up everything seemed all right as far as I could tell. Then it was the moment of truth, another long look at my papers, my ruble transaction receipt, and… that's it? I can go? Yes. But wait, there's another checkpoint, it looked like airline personnel there… oh ok, a baggage check. So I gave him my bags, and… yes! He did not even open them to have a look inside. He smiled. I can go, over the second hurdle. Alright, what is next?

I turned right and headed for the British Airways gate. There it was. What a sight! No, not the British Airways gate, but an Irish pub. *An Irish Pub?* Was it a dream? Was I going to wake up at KGB headquarters, or even worse, at Imports R Us headquarters? No, it was real. Those great Irish folks who make a science of running duty free shops back in Ireland had moved into Moscow. Not only did they have this pub strategically located at the British Airways terminal of Sheremetyevo Airport, they also had a complex in Moscow near the Imports R Us office called "Irish House." Irish House was a beautiful western style grocery store where I bought food while in Moscow.

That day the pub at the airport was full of rugged British soccer fans clad in Manchester United gear, throwing back the pints. I learned later that they were in Moscow to see their home side face one of Moscow's professional soccer teams. The pub, the soccer fans, the Irish barmaids, the whole scene was indescribably beautiful to me at that moment. No more Imports R Us! I dropped my bags at a table, walked up to the bar with a smile, and ordered a pint. I was met with a sweet Irish brogue, "A pint of Guinness coming up sir!" It was the best Guinness I have ever tasted, and probably will ever taste.

Big Bob

The flight to London was a good one. Still winding down from my adventures in Moscow, I ordered a dark beer from the British Airways flight attendant. She was very nice and after a quick look through her service cart she apologized, there was no dark beer left. "Oh, that's ok, whatever you've got is fine," I answered. The attendant smiled, leaving me with a plastic cup and a can of regular beer. Five minutes later while I was still enjoying my drink, the flight attendant came back down the aisle and stopped next to my chair. I looked up and she was smiling at me again. "I found a dark beer for you, have one for the road!" she said as she placed the can on my tray. No charge. Ahh, the sun was shining on me this day. It was like a leprechaun was sitting on my shoulder, magically controlling events around me. Irish pubs were appearing in the most unlikely places, and dark beer was free.

After checking into a London hotel near Heathrow Airport I called my job contact Bob to tell him that I was in London. We spoke once while I was in Moscow so he knew I might be leaving Russia, but he was a bit surprised to hear I was already in town. "Ok, the first thing we need to do is to get you out of that hotel. Stop by my flat tomorrow, you can leave your things with my wife, then come on down to the exchange. Tomorrow night we can set you up over at Wilford's flat, he's got a lot of room over there."

Bob was an American, someone with whom I had spoken by phone on several occasions but never met in person. His wife worked with my sister in New York City for a time and that is how I was able to connect with him, in fact the first time Bob and I spoke I was still in the MBA program at McGill. Wilford was also an American; he worked for Bob on the exchange and was living temporarily in a two bedroom flat, so he had a place for me to crash. Bob and Wilford were options brokers, buying and selling combinations of options and the underlying commodity futures for various clients.

Futures are agreements to buy or sell a commodity like gold, silver, oil, or foreign currency for a set price at a particular date in the future. Futures can help investors or companies using commodities in their work, such as a multinational company receiving payments in different currencies, to hedge against the risk of price changes over time by locking in prices in advance. Options are contracts that give the buyer the right but not the obligation to buy or sell the futures at a given price at any time before a certain date. Combinations of options and futures give firms and investors many different ways of either hedging against risk or speculating on the rise or fall in the price of a commodity. The large exchanges where commodities were traded in the United States were located in New York and Chicago.

Bob and Wilford were a few years older than me. They were both midwestern guys who got their start in Chicago, and this was evident to me as soon as I arrived on the London exchange floor the next day. There was a photo taped to their booth of Chicago Bulls star Michael Jordan puffing on a cigar, and their conversation that day centered around Kansas City Royals legend George Brett. It was interesting to meet Bob in person after only knowing him as a voice over the phone for so long. He seemed like a sharp, no nonsense type of guy, more of an urban Midwesterner than Wilford.

Wilford was a Missouri guy. He also seemed smart, and although his name was not really Wilford of course, he was friendly and exuded solid midwestern values like Wilford Brimley in a Grape Nuts cereal commercial, so I'll call him Wilford. Brimley's famous line in the commercials was, "It's the right thing to do." That's the way Wilford the options broker spoke, simply and honestly. This slice of middle America in London made me feel at home as

Bob and Wilford talked with me and explained the workings of the exchange for a while between trades.

I met two other people who were working for Bob as well, a third midwestern guy named Craig and a young woman from New York named Colleen. Craig was about the same age as Bob and Wilford and he was new to London. He had experience trading in Chicago, and he was now preparing to trade in the futures pit in support of Bob and Wilford's trades in the options pit. Colleen on the other hand had been in London for a time, she was Bob's sister in law. Fresh out of college Colleen was offered the opportunity to work in London by Bob. In describing his operation Bob seemed very excited about the success of his team and its prospects for the future. He said of Colleen, "She's as good as anyone out here," meaning any of the traders in the options pit. Bob and Wilford were also pleased to learn of my ability to speak French, which could possibly come in handy. There was a company from France with whom Bob always hoped to do business but had not been able to attract any interest from so far.

This visit was just an interview, not a job offer yet, so I returned to the United States and stayed with my family in the DC area awaiting the decision of Bob and Wilford. While I waited I exchanged letters with Imports R Us to secure payment for my flight back to the US. After several rounds of letters my "friends" there did in fact reimburse me, and returned a few boxes of belongings I had sent on a shipping container to Moscow. Within weeks Wilford called and broke the bad news to me, he and Bob were not busy enough at the moment to make use of me in London. But days later, before I had the chance to work myself into a good funk about it, I received a message that Bob had called. I returned the call the next day and was offered a job.

I took off for London even though I did not have a work visa for the United Kingdom. Bob's plan was that I begin work on the exchange and then wait for the papers to come through while I was in England. Not a great plan, but he was the husband of my sister's friend, so I trusted him on this. One is not allowed to work until the papers are in order, but the only people who typically asked about a work permit back then were immigration officers at the airport. The "illegal" worker had only to say, "I'm just visiting the UK" when he arrived at the airport and he was home free. Of course I would have preferred to have all my documents in order beforehand, but I was not going to argue with Bob. There is no doubt he would have taken care of the problem. Simple. Hire someone else who would not argue about it.

I spent the first week in London hunting for a place to live and stopping by the exchange to observe when I was free. I found a flat I liked, the price was right, so I signed a lease by the end of that week. The flat was on Abbey Road in St. Johns Wood, blocks north of that famous crosswalk shown in the photo on the cover of the Beatles' *Abbey Road* album. My first day in the Abbey Road flat I met a friendly, gregarious older man named George on my floor. George was a retired civil servant who lived on his own and knew the scoop on everything.

He clued me in on all I needed to know about the area, from the fact that canned peas were cheaper at Sainsbury's grocery store than at the nearby Europa Foods, to the fact that there was an unmarried British Airways flight attendant about my age who lived on the floor below us. George was the man. He also told me that local council representatives stopped by his place periodically to check on him, his flat, and to drop off a bit of monetary assistance to help him make ends meet. The older gentleman offered to talk to the council people for me if I were interested in some welfare assistance from the council as well. As an illegal worker in the UK still in my twenties, I guessed that I would not be eligible for council assistance, but I thanked George for the tip on the flight attendant anyway.

I also became friendly with Wilford while staying in the spare bedroom in his flat the first week. Just as George briefed me on the ins and outs of St. Johns Wood, Wilford was nice enough to give me a rundown on what to expect at work during the week I was at his flat. Wilford would quiz me on what had taken place on the exchange each day to make sure I was clear on everything. When the conversation turned away from work, the man from Missouri showed me his tape collection which was quite different from mine. My tapes went from the Beastie Boys to Daisy Chainsaw to Public Enemy while his went from Garth Brooks to Randy Travis to Suzy Bogguss.

In my second week at work I was given an exam on options and trading procedures by the exchange. I had studied a book provided by the exchange, and I had also had a class in options while at McGill, so I did not have any difficulty with the test. Still, learning to trade in the options pit was a different story, it was tough and more a matter of practical experience, learning by doing, and by screwing up occasionally. Still, the exam was one less thing to worry about, and I was primed to get my feet wet down on the floor. Everything seemed to be going well and according to plan, but then it occurred to me. Where was Craig? Where was Colleen? They were not working on the exchange with us, and I had not heard a word about them since my arrival in London. What was up with that? I did not ask but I found out soon enough.

During a slow period one day on the floor Bob and I were both seated by our firm's booth waiting for trading to heat up again. Bob said to me in a matter of fact way that, "It was tough calling my father in law and telling him that I needed to fire Colleen, but he was ok about it. He told me to do whatever I needed to do. She couldn't cut it down here, that's all."

Uh oh. I had jumped out of the Moscow frying pan into a midwestern barbecue pit. Remember when I met Bob for the first time on my way back from Moscow he told me that

Colleen was "as good as anyone out here." Now, a short time later, "she couldn't cut it." Things sure could change quickly. I suppose that is why Bob first told me there was not enough business for them to hire me, then a few days later he offered me the job. I guess I was Colleen's replacement. Bob was an impulsive guy as I was to learn later.

Bob continued on, "You know, I've said it before and I'll say it again, women can't make it in this business." That was true, as long as most male decision makers down on exchange floors carried ideas like this in their heads, women never would make it in the business. Another day the second half of the riddle was revealed. Wilford and I were alone by our booth on the exchange floor when a British broker from another firm asked Wilford, "What ever happened to that other broker you had, Craig was it?" "Oh, things didn't work out. I don't think he liked Bob much, ha ha ha," Wilford replied. Uh oh, fire up the grill.

So, judging by the fate of those who worked for Bob in the past, my future as a floor broker looked dim, but I was there and needed to give it my best shot. Wilford seemed to get along with Bob, so maybe there was hope. As a new and inexperienced floor trader I knew it was going to be rough for a while, open outcry floor trading could be competitive and stressful. There is typically no love lost between brokers from opposing firms trading in a pit as the business is a zero sum game to a certain extent. A trade executed by one brokerage firm is often a trade missed by another so tensions can run high. Bob warned me time and again that the British brokers "aren't your friends," that they were out to screw us, and that in disputes it was their practice to gang up on the Americans.

In fact, one of my first days on the floor I was treated to an amusing scene when Wilford was involved in a dispute with a British broker. As promised by Bob, when exchange personnel set about resolving the dispute brokers from various British firms sided with the British broker.

All pit action was recorded on videotape so Bob went to check the instant replay with officials from the exchange. A few minutes later the door to the viewing room flew open and out came Bob with two fists in the air, running a victory lap around the pit. The replay had shown that Wilford was in the right and our team won. Bob, who was a happy guy for the remainder of the afternoon, taped a piece of paper to our booth with the inscription:

Yanks   Brits

1   202

A short while after the incident two British brokers asked me what the sign was all about and I explained, "Bob says it's the first time we Americans have won a dispute here." "What? You always win," said one of the Brits, with a confused look on his face.

I had not been around long enough to argue one way or the other, but now, looking back on the time I spent on the exchange, the British did get the nod in most decisions. It was their home field. Still, I think it seemed to many of the British brokers that they were getting the short end of the stick because the Americans were doing a large part of the business in the options area of the Brits' home field. The British could be bastards like everyone else in the pit when a trade was up for grabs, but other times they were surprisingly friendly to me.

Bob, however, was all over me early on, yelling at me like a football coach yells at a rookie player. I suppose he considered this the best way to turn an inexperienced floor broker into a tough and wise floor broker in the shortest period of time. At times I brought a cascade of criticism upon myself with some rookie mistakes, other times the abuse came when I had done nothing wrong but Bob decided I had. I must have screwed up something he assumed, simply by being there in the pit. At times it was difficult to keep from laughing as I was berated for things like handing Bob a trade ticket which had one of its corner's bent slightly. In fact it was a big day for me after my first month or so when Bob actually began calling me by my name "Mike" rather than yelling "hey!" or "look man!"

Some days were difficult but the grief was worth it to me. I am sure I did not seem happy on the outside but inside I was feeling *impassioned* and *turbo-charged* (pick any Tony Robbins word). I liked the job, and I liked living in London so much that I was fine with the yelling each day, happy simply to keep my spot on the exchange. And, although I resented some of the criticism as it occurred, deep down I harbored no ill feelings toward Bob. I figured this was just what he felt he needed to do to get me up to speed on the trading floor. When the yelling became especially intense Wilford would take me aside for a little pep talk. "Bob's like a coach, he'll run you, he'll make you sweat. Don't take it personally, if there's a problem we'll correct it and that's all. Don't dwell on anything."

All the while I concentrated on keeping my mouth shut and kept plugging away at learning the job. I was so happy to finally be doing something I really enjoyed and to have a potential career to look forward to that I cared about little else. Most Saturday mornings, sleeping in after a taxing week with Bob, my eyes would open and it would dawn on me where I was. This was my flat, I lived in London, I worked on the floor of the exchange! I would bounce out of bed and strut around my empty flat with my arms raised in triumph.

Nonetheless, when this nonstop yelling was coupled with what I had learned of Craig and Colleen leaving, I could not help but fear for my job. A week out of each year members of the business converged on London for meetings and parties, one of which as thrown by our firm and I attended with Bob and Wilford. Later that night Wilford had to head home and Bob and I ended up going out to a restaurant for a late dinner. We discussed how things were going at work and with me in particular, and Bob reassured me, "All we're looking for is 15%

improvement a week. We've gotten that from you and in the past week or so we even got about 25%, so don't worry about it. Keep on doing what you're doing. Less than a year is too short a time to judge anyone in this business."

Yup, in no time I would be "as good as anyone out here." Part of me felt reassured, but the wiser part of me did not really believe it. Oh well, there was nothing else I could do anyway but just work as hard as I could and let the fates decide. Jumping to another firm, which traders did quite frequently, was out of the question for me. First of all I was not experienced enough yet, and second of all I still had no working papers for the UK.

On top of this, if in the future Bob's actions were to prove that he actually was giving me a fair chance, then I would feel a certain loyalty to him. He was the one who gave me a chance to work on the floor, and that was worth something. So, I really wanted to stick it out with him if at all possible, for as long as possible. But if he did not mean what he was saying, well break out the barbecue sauce, Mike the rookie trader would be on the menu!

It was very interesting to be on the floor, even in my first few weeks when I understood the least about what was happening. One thing I learned was that Wilford was correct, the abuse I took from Bob was nothing personal. At times Bob raged on everyone in the options area, from brokers at other firms to pit referees and price reporters. In any case there were plenty of cool things going on at the exchange to take my mind off the yelling. Besides my interest in the markets and the pleasure of being at the center of the action during trading hours, our exchange like any exchange had its share of characters who made each day entertaining. These personalities were not restricted by the rules of decorum one might find in an office environment.

In the middle of the trading floor mayhem was a young woman who stuck out like a sore thumb. She was the best pit referee working in our area, but she was also the epitome of English propriety, like a princess in the pit. The closest thing to a representative of the royal family at the exchange. Unlike most people in the pit, she did not raise her voice to make her point. Instead she corrected improper conduct with the demeanor of an English grammar school teacher scolding naughty ten year old children. This princess let me have it a few times in the pit and I cannot say I was pleased with her at the time, but she always did her best to be fair. The best was when she stepped in to stop a British broker who was arguing with and yelling at a French broker. The princess cut in, "Jonathan, don't blame others for your own inadequacies." Ouch. That was more lethal than any stream of four letter words!

To learn early on, I listened in as Wilford shot quick bursts of market information into the phone with clients, and relayed buy and sell orders to Bob in the pit. He had the voice of a midwestern airline pilot, and the dialogue would sound like this...

"Got a 2 bid, 2 bid on the puts now, Pierce & Pierce looking to buy also..."

"Who's on the offer?"

"Dean Witless... 200 at 3, Frogs got a 100 more at 3..."

"What's futures?"

"At a quarter... lots of action in the futures pit now... there it goes, look out below!" (futures market starting to drop)

"Pay 3! Pay 3!"

"Buy'em Bob!!! Buy'em!!!"

Let those truckers roll, 10-4 good buddy. Whenever I listened to Wilford on the phones it made me think of that timeless trucker tune of the 1970's, the pop song called "Convoy" that made the CB radio famous.

In case you have not guessed it yet, Wilford meant the French brokers when he said "Frogs." At the exchange in London, Frogs had to have thick, thick skin. The abuse these poor guys took at times made my experience look like a picnic. When there was a dispute in our pit the British brokers had each other, the Americans had power in the amount of business they brought in, and the French had nothing. Well, they did have a little broker I will call LeBeau. I am naming him this in part because he reminded me of Corporal Louis LeBeau, French prisoner of war in my favorite show *Hogan's Heroes*.

He was a cool little guy with a good sense of humor, the kind of person who is difficult to dislike. LeBeau could laugh at the frog jokes all day long and smile. The French brokers even had a British newspaper with an anti-French article taped to their booth with the headline "Hop Off, French Frogs!" Sometimes when the phone rang in the French booth LeBeau would jump to his feet and run around in a panic yelling, "Frog alert! Frog alert!"

One of LeBeau's favorite things to do was exaggerate his French accent while speaking English. His English was good, but he enjoyed talking in a goofy French accent just to be a clown. He also liked the British slang word for sex which was "shag," so when he and his Parisian girlfriend planned to be together for Saturday and Sunday he announced out loud, "Eeet weeel beee, a shageee weekend!" (It will be a shaggy weekend!) LeBeau's accent met its match one day when an American broker from the futures area came over to check an option price in our pit. This American had a very thick New York accent, and here's what happened (I do not remember the exact numbers so I have chosen some of the best sounding ones).

"Watts Mawrch toity-tree cawwls?" (What's March 33 calls?)

"Zeee zirteee zreee cools oof Maaarch iz zirteee too beeed at zirteee zevennn"

(The 33 calls of March is 32 bid at 37)

"Wayta minnit heah… watt da fuck's dis guy tawkin'?... fucking tawk English!"

(Wait a minute here… what the fuck is this guy talking?... fucking talk English!)

The entire options pit erupted in laughter. I do not think the British brokers heard one word in the entire give and take between LeBeau and the New Yorker that they could identify as belonging to their native language.

It's the Pits

As with any new job, the first days in the pit and on the phones were the toughest for me. Mistakes happened less often over time, and my confidence grew each week. I will never forget my first day in the pit though. For whatever reason, Bob decided to lean on me harder than at anytime before or afterwards and he flew into a rage. Yelling louder than ever, he demanded every tidbit of market information present in that pit from me. He screamed for everything from the price of a miniscule ten lot offer that had no chance of being bought to the lot size of every quotation in the pit regardless of whether it was even close to trading. Many of the brokers, the pit referee, and the price reporter in our pit just stared at the spectacle.

I had already learned to let Bob's screaming bounce right off me and to just do the best I could at any given time. I actually thought it was pretty funny after the fact. A few days later I was talking to one of our clients on the phone who said to me, "Bob was giving you hell in the pit the other day!"

"How do you know?" I asked.

"Because I could hear him," the client said.

This client spoke with us by phone from an office that was not on the exchange floor at all. He meant that he could hear Bob's yelling on the exchange floor through his telephone above all the other background noise at the exchange. That was loud yelling.

When trading was slow, Bob and Wilford used to read the *USA Today* as it was the best source of American sports news in London. From the NFL to college basketball to major league baseball, sports dominated the conversations at our booth. Sometimes in between pages Bob liked to go on about some of his favorite things, like the jet fighter scenes in the movie *Top Gun*. Bob said once, "When that song starts and the fighter planes take off… vroom! Man I get a chubby." Our booth was like a piece of America transplanted into English soil. I never became homesick on the exchange because although I lived in London, I felt like I worked in Chicago.

One time Bob was fooling around on the floor, playing air guitar and singing the circa 1980 new wave hit song "Turning Japanese." As he did this he asked various brokers, "You ever heard that song? It's by the B-52's or something, you know, 'I'm turning Japanese I think I'm turning Japanese,' have you ever heard that?" One or two brokers shook their heads, then Bob turned to me and asked, "You ever heard that?" but quickly corrected himself, "No, you wouldn't know that song, you were too young."

I just shrugged my shoulders. As I shrugged my shoulders I remembered watching the music video to the song on television when I was in high school (I was only a few years younger than Bob) and I was old enough to remember that a group called "The Vapors" did the song, not the B-52's. Still, I kept my mouth shut because nobody likes a know it all rookie floor broker, or one that knows anything for that matter. It was all part of the deal and that was all right with me. It did strike me how Bob and Wilford treated me like I was some kid on an internship, when this was a serious job to me. I had several years of work experience and an MBA, and I had uprooted myself to move to London in my late twenties for this position.

I was never an official employee of the company because of the work visa issue, and Wilford actually paid me my salary with a check under the table written on his personal account. I wondered when this would be straightened out, and when the visa would come through. One day a British executive from our firm paid a visit to the exchange floor and started asking Bob questions. Traders in the pit at that time carried paper pads to jot down a record of the trades they did; the cards from these order pads were ripped off and submitted to the exchange as a record of all transactions in the pits. Each card had a space at the bottom for a trader's signature, but we never signed the cards. Our normal practice was simply to draw a line through this space with our pens after filling out the card rather than waste time signing each one. The executive from our office was curious about these signatures.

"He hasn't been trading, has he?" the executive asked Bob (doh! he was talking about me) "This line in the signature box of the cards, is that your signature? Do you do all the trading in the pit?" "Yeah, I do all the trading," Bob answered. That was not quite true. Bob did the majority of trading in the pit for us, but I had been doing a little bit of trading most days for a while so I could learn. And although Wilford specialized in working the phones, he did plenty of trades in the pit as well.

"Well, it has to stay that way for now," the man said, "He's not allowed to do anything but observe until he's registered with the SFA. If he trades, we could be fined by the exchange." What our British boss was telling Bob was that since I had not been registered as a floor broker with the British Securities and Futures Authority (SFA), our firm could be fined if I traded. This was a tough one, because in order to register with the SFA I had to have a British Social Insurance Number (I did not, I was American) or a work permit (I did not of course). Hmm. There was no telling how long it would take for my working papers to come through, it could be months.

I went on the trading floor on a Friday soon after that and Bob had spoken with our British boss again – I still could not do anything at the exchange but watch. Bob suggested that the best thing to do was just to have me take the day off, so I would be out of sight of exchange personnel. That way there was no chance of our firm being fined. I was told to go over to our company's office in another section of London, meet with the British executive, and fill out all of the SFA license application that I could. That took me the first part of the morning, unfortunately there was still that sticky problem of the Social Insurance Number. The form asked for it, and the British executive was at a loss. He asked me, "Do you have any idea when your work papers will come through?" "Not really," I answered.

So, Bob and our British boss had a problem on their hands and they were going to try to figure out what to do. I was to check with Bob after the weekend to see if I could work again Monday, but I was given the rest of Friday off. Needless to say I was not too excited about getting a day off, not for this reason anyway.

When I came back to my flat late Sunday night there was a message on my machine, it was Wilford saying that I did not need to come to work Monday and that he would call me in the morning. When I answered the phone at 9am Monday, Wilford's voice had that same tone as when he gave me the pep talks after Bob finished yelling at me. I was in trouble.

> "Well Mike, you know how things haven't been going well here lately?"
> "Uh, ... no?"
> "It's just not working out. This has nothing to do with the SFA thing. Now Mike, this is better than if we kept you here a full year and then let you go."

That was certainly true. If I had stayed a full year the firm was supposed to pay me a bonus. Now they would not have to pay anything. But, I also had to pick up and move back to the US without a job, and what was my resume going to say – I worked for part of a year at a job where I was not an official employee? Right, it was better this way. I do not think Bob and Wilford gave this much thought, as I said they treated me like I was some sort of teenager on an internship so what did it matter to them?

So this was it, I had tasted the guillotine. Not one to easily give up however, I made some feeble attempts to secure a job with other firms while I was still in London working on ending the lease on my flat. I had a lot going for me... *no* working papers, *months* of experience in the London commodities markets, and worst of all, an MBA. MBA's do not make good traders, remember the legend of the crying MBA in New York?

I bumped into my friendly neighbor George the retired civil servant one day in the stairwell. He was surprised to see me at our building on a weekday when the sun was still out.

"You on vacation, Mike?" he asked.

"No George, unfortunately I don't have a job anymore."

"You're telling me they made you redundant Mike?" George asked with an angry voice.

I am sure he had experienced more of life's disappointments than a youngster like me could appreciate. Again he offered to call his friends at the local council to see about getting me some monetary assistance. I said thanks, but I did not expect to be in London much longer.

One bright spot of my stay in London was the music. London has always been home to some of the newest and best in rock music. I was present for an important period in alternative rock music in 1993, when a group of American and British women who called themselves "Riot Grrrls" played great punk rock in either all female bands or at least bands led by women. I went to two different London shows of the "Bikini Kill" and "Huggy Bear" tour; the American band "Bikini Kill" and British band "Huggy Bear" played some harsh music and caused a ruckus in the British music scene.

At one of the shows I remember singer Kathleen Hanna saying during a break between songs, "Right now I'm on stage with a microphone, I'm a lead singer, and the leader of a band...

but that's tonight… tomorrow I have to be a waitress again, or a secretary, or a homemaker.." she continued with a pained expression on her face, "you always have to go back." Yeah, everybody has problems, and mine were not as bad as those of many other people. I thought of this as I left London, trying not to feel sorry for myself. Things would work out for me eventually.

  I decided to visit and stay with my sister in California for the summer, wait some tables and try to figure out what I was going to do next. I knew I was taking a risk by going to work in Moscow and later London, and if one of those opportunities had worked out it could have been life changing for me. But those opportunities did not work out, and I had to start over. Free market capitalism presents great opportunities and great risks to workers, and I was still young in my late twenties, so there could be better days ahead. I remember my father telling me at the time, "You don't realize how young you are," and he was right. At the time it seemed like my world was coming to an end, but that was hardly the case.

Rags to Riches

After spending Summer 1993 in California I came back east to live at my father's house in Northern Virginia. I was determined to be smarter about my career from now on. I learned a lot attending an informal reunion of high school friends in 1993, many of whom seemed to be doing better than me career wise even though I had gotten better grades than they did in high school. I was also fortunate enough to have gone to a big name school. What was I doing wrong? My high school friends found jobs with solid companies and stuck with them.

Instead of going with the flow of the job market and working for a good general business organization, I had been obsessed with investment banking. I read the book *Liar's Poker* during my first year of business school. Reading that book, as well as seeing the movie *Wall Street,* was the worst thing that ever happened to my career. Lost on me and other MBA's was the fact that the book and the movie were critical of the Wall Street lifestyle; we actually idolized Gordon Gekko and Bud Fox (!) Before 1993 I had been determined to get exactly the job I wanted and it had to be something high paying and stunning, just like in the book and the movie. Anything else was not "cool" to me. I was only in my mid-twenties and was expecting too much too soon, listening to a few college and business school friends who supposedly were already making big bucks in the investment world. Technology would soon make it so that an individual could invest on the web from home anyway. Later in life I made investments a hobby because I liked it - I did not need the Gordon Gekko Italian suits.

From my father's house I would have easy access to public transport for jobs in the Washington, DC area, and I did find some temp assignments here and there, even though the economy was in the doldrums. After a few short assignments I was able to secure a better, long term assignment in the legal department of a big corporation in DC. The work was similar to what I did at the law firm where I worked in New York City two years earlier. The assignment lasted six months or so until the case settled, and the army of temps got the boot. It was worthwhile in that I learned a few things, got references that helped me get another position, and I even met a new girlfriend who had been a coworker. The temp assignment was also memorable for a gaffe that I remember to this day; one of the managers at the company told us that we would have the next Monday off work for Martin Luther King's Assassination Day (Oops, I think he meant to say Martin Luther King's Birthday!) None of us corrected him at the time, we just had a good laugh later, wondering as temps often do – "why are we the temps and someone like that is a permanently employed manager?"

Soon I got lucky (not with my new girlfriend, silly rabbit!), I secured a contract assignment doing finance work for a large Canadian company in Northern Virginia. My MBA was from McGill University in Canada! This was a good start. And more money. And I moved out of my father's house to an apartment in Arlington, VA with my girlfriend. Movin' on up to the east side, to a deluxe apartment in the sky!

Yes! Things were getting so much better, I felt just like George Jefferson. I worked really hard at the company, nights and weekends, I did not mind! Eventually it paid off. My big break came as I was doing a lot of photocopying for an American manager. As the copy machine churned out page after page, I drank coffee from my McGill University mug. A Canadian manager named Mr. King happened to walk into the copy room, and he saw me. He did a double take, and then asked me, "is that *McGill* University written on your mug?"

"Yes, that's where I did my MBA," I replied.

"That's where I got my accounting degree," he said. "You have an MBA, and they've got you in here doing all this copying?"

"Yes" I answered.

"We need to rethink the way we do things around here," Mr. King said.

The next day an American manager came to me and said, "Mr. King wants to know if you'd like to help him with some of his work." Ha! It was off to the races!

This Canadian manager Mr. King became my mentor and taught me many important things they don't teach you in your MBA. Like luck and a stupid coffee mug can mean more than years of hard work. I mean, you still have to work hard, but working hard just gives you a chance to be lucky. After this I made sure to drink from a McGill University coffee mug every day at work, it is my good luck charm.

I put in hundreds of hours crunching numbers and building Excel budget spreadsheet models for Mr. King, it was a great opportunity to improve my skills and learn. Partly as a result of office politics, Mr. King was never able to secure me a permanent spot at that Canadian company but after two years or so I would get even luckier. With a great reference from him, I scored a permanent position in the treasury department of a large entertainment company. I had always wanted to work in the treasury field, which concerns managing company cash flow, as opposed to the straight accounting and finance of the Canadian company. There was also an international finance element to this new job, which I loved, and I was able to use the French skills I picked up from Johns Hopkins classes and from living in Montreal while at McGill.

No longer a contractor, soon I was doing things I remembered middle class adults like my parents did in the 1960's and 1970's – holding down a so-called "real job," using my new health insurance to go to the doctor and dentist, going on business trips. I bought a new car for the commute to work – no more subway to bus connections in the rain and snow! I paid off the credit card balance I had run up buying a home computer and other things I needed for work but could not afford when I was a contractor. In the years to come I would pay off the student loans from graduate school. My girlfriend and I were so used to living for years with no benefits and low pay (even though we both had graduate degrees) that I suddenly felt like a millionaire.

1997 in particular was a banner year. When my boss left the company, I was working extra hours every day to pick up the slack, without a formal promotion. It just so happened I was there by myself early in the a.m. when the new Chief Financial Officer arrived for his first day. He caught me there working hard all alone in our department, and soon I was promoted to supervisor with employees reporting to me. I received a raise and a bonus, and I had fun.

It was just the sort of work I was passionate about, executing money transfers and trying to predict future company cash flows. I would borrow and invest for the company based on my projections and I did very well at this. Plus, the internet had recently exploded on to the business scene, and we found creative ways to use it for our work. I found free real time spot foreign exchange rates available on the web to use in keeping our forex dealer banks honest when they quoted us prices. No need for an expensive financial reporting service like Reuters. Also, one of my employees used internet mapping sites to send our touring groups easy directions to the bank branches our company used in each city.

Outside of work I played basketball with coworkers every week, spent nights out with friends on the Arlington, VA Wilson Boulevard strip, and went to see my favorite bands at the Black Cat and the 9:30 Club in downtown DC. Music is one of my top interests in life and it was gratifying to start buying CD's on a regular basis where previously I bought cassettes because they were cheaper. It was like a dream come true.

Through 1998 and 1999 the weeks and months flew by. I feel like my department improved, doing more work in less time. Still, years later when I read the entries in my journal from that time period, something strange is apparent. In what on paper was the best year of my career, the highest paying, the year my department was running like clockwork, my stress level was rising. I was doing too much, not getting enough sleep, burning the candle at both ends, and more than half the days in the journal I kept I sounded bitter and unhappy. There is even an entry one day that speaks of a "sense of impending doom" about my job and the company.

This may have been me suspicious of my own success, after short assignments at multiple companies where annual downsizing was common. But this was 1999, height of the internet economic boom, and I even had my own brokerage account with Fidelity that had grown in value the previous two years. And although my company had had a few minor failures in its operations, by all accounts it was doing fine. Years later a friend who stayed with the company told me that things had not changed much there. What was going on with me and my "sense of impending doom?" Time would soon tell.

Things Get Ugly

Convinced that the company was in trouble and my job might be in jeopardy, I came up with a plan. Brilliant. Always a plan with me. I make plans of plans, and to do lists of to do lists. Organizational Behavior was my best class while doing my MBA, a class where you analyze office situations and the politics of different corporate departments. I was a self-proclaimed expert at this, but I think you can over analyze things sometimes; in many cases the best course of action is to just show up at your job and try to do the work on your desk. 90% of success is just showing up, one saying goes, but sometimes I forget that.

The first step in my plan was to pass my CCM (Certified Cash Manager) exam – similar to a CPA but for cash flow management professionals. Normally a company pays for a person to take a review class and pays for the exam fees as well, so that the company's employee can upgrade his or her skills. I was too smart for this! I would pay for it myself, and take vacation days during the review course so my company would not know what I was up to. My company was going to collapse soon after all! You see, I planned to put the CCM on my resume and use it to get an even better job without my company knowing.

I passed the CCM in mid-1999, and started firing off resumes. It was quite a change from the early 1990's, I had a better resume now and man, everybody and their brother was expanding and hiring in the internet boom year 1999. I had initial screening interviews over the phone with several of the top companies across the country. It was all going to happen for me now, I just knew it! The two jobs I worked to pay for my MBA, the years of study, the years of contract work, it was payoff time for me!

One of the highlights of my career was being flown out west for a second interview (the first interview was by phone) with a top brewing company. The job was to fly around the globe and audit the company's cash management in its many international brewing locations. In this job I would be Master of the Universe as far as I was concerned – never mind bond trading on Wall Street! The pay was double what I was making. The cost of living out there was half! And I would never be spending that money because the company was going to pay for me to travel the globe.

Well, it came down to three candidates and I did not get the job. I was crushed. I sometimes wonder if I would have avoided my future illness if I had gotten that job. Instead, I continued burning the candle at both ends in the DC area, killing myself working and not getting enough sleep while sending out resumes and interviewing as much as possible. Work was getting weird for me. Top managers were having meetings, wasn't that suspicious? Then a memo came out that, holy shit, our Chief Operating Officer who just started with us a few years before was taking a job somewhere else. I knew it! I knew it! We were Titanic, Inc. I needed to interview more and quickly. Everyone was acting weird at work weren't they? What's this, another email, my good friend Andrea in accounting was "no longer with the company." What's that all about? No explanation.

One of my best friends in the company named Fergus was a manager in accounting. He gave me the scoop later. Andrea was charging on her personal credit card and cutting company checks to pay her personal credit card bills. Andrea was in big trouble. Wait, I was good friends with Andrea. And you can bet they were suspicious of Fergus too, Andrea was his star employee, and he was one of my best friends. Upper management knew this. And guess what. Guess who moved the most money in the company by himself, by wire transfer not check! Guess who was a signer on all the bank accounts, domestic and international. Guess who could move a million US Dollars, a million British Pounds, 100 million Japanese Yen with a few clicks of his mouse. ME!!! Upper management knew this. You can bet they were watching me now.

People were acting weird at work, laughing at me behind my back. That was it. I needed to leave this company. Each time I took an afternoon or a day off for an interview I'm sure they thought I was up to something. I couldn't tell them of course. Any day now I would be in trouble. For what? Well I'm sure one of those clicks on the mouse sent some British Pounds somewhere, upper management would figure it out. I hadn't done anything wrong ever, had I? Everyone knew I was going to be arrested, it would be just like when Bud Fox gets handcuffed in his office in the movie *Wall Street*. It would be humiliating. I hoped I wouldn't cry like Charlie Sheen did when it all went down.

Pretty soon the pressure at work had gotten too great with all this stuff to worry about, and no new job yet from those interviews, so I did what any sensible person like me would do. I kept my cool and quit. No two week notice, just quit. I was actually pretty cool and calm about it. Better to quit than to accidentally send some British Pounds somewhere, and then they'd figure it all out.

I even had to do jury duty around that time. Each of the three days I went to the Arlington Court House I kissed my girlfriend goodbye, thinking that might be the last time I ever would kiss her. This was probably when they were going to make the arrest so I just faced up to that. Luckily they never did. I felt like I was playing a cat and mouse game with the staff of the court house, though. They were hoping that I would just crack and confess, but I did not know what to confess! I was starting to hope they would just arrest me so I could know what the hell was going on, you know, what I would be charged with. But nothing happened.

I kept having nightmares one weekend and there were people talking to me, even when I was awake – I thought they must be in the next apartment or outside our window. My girlfriend did not hear the things I was hearing, so I finally told her that I knew everything, I mean I knew that she knew what was going on with me. She just kind of shook her head, got up and went to the kitchen. By that Monday I was so exhausted from the nightmares and not having slept all weekend that I called out sick from the contract assignment where I was working. Then I spoke to my father by phone, and I told him that I knew everything. I mean that I knew that he knew what was going on with me. My father asked me who told me this. I told him it was the "network administrator." He told me to sit tight, he was going to drive up from North Carolina to see me, and I said ok. I figured it would be good to see him to straighten things out.

My father arrived eventually and took me to Arlington Hospital. He sat down with me as I told a therapist what I had been experiencing, and it slowly dawned on me that things would be all right and that I actually had just had a mental health burnout. A lot of what had been going on with me was just nonsense in my brain.

In the last few pages I tried to recreate the way I was thinking when I became ill but had not started on medication. Those were actual thoughts I had, and they seemed logical to me at the time. I had drifted gradually from feeling normal to thinking in that nonsensical way, and did not realize anything had changed within me, everything around me seemed to be changing. (Remember that Joe Walsh song lyric: "It's tough to handle this fortune and fame, everybody's so different, I haven't changed.") Now that I am healthier that time period seems like a dream, you know the feeling of having a strange dream where everything makes sense until you wake up, then it becomes clear that none of it made sense.

When I first arrived at Arlington Hospital and saw the psychiatric area I freaked out, thinking my father might be leaving me there, like something out of *One Flew Over the Cuckoo's Nest*. That was not the case, however. My situation was totally treatable, I was just to take the medication they gave me and make an appointment with a professional for outpatient care. I could even start a great permanent position I accepted at an international nonprofit in Washington, DC!

Muddling Through

My new job was as a budget analyst with a nonprofit organization in DC which worked on civil society projects in the former Soviet Union and Eastern Europe. Just like the treasury position I had before, this was a dream job for me, with an opportunity to use my Russian skills and even travel to some of the former Soviet republics. The job was fantastic, I was offered the position based on my past experience and qualifications. Unfortunately I was not the same person or the same worker as before.

Thank God the work was relatively easy and the people were so nice at the nonprofit. I do not think they had any idea what was going on with me. If they had known Mike Pollard the worker from the 1990's they would not have recognized me now. I was not as sharp, I was kind of slow actually, but I still got the job done early on in my time at the "International Nonprofit."

Why was I slow now? The medication mainly. I was not all hyped up and frantic like my last days at the entertainment company. Now I was listless at times, some days I would sit for 30 minutes at a stretch spaced out, staring at my computer screen. But, I had my own office, so I got away with this. And, I got the work done. All I really had to do was check and approve disbursements and then submit financial reports on our projects to the government and other donors (and only once every three months!).

Working trips to the former Soviet Republics were part of this job and these were super interesting in spite of my health woes. Moscow was quite different in the early 2000's from what I remembered from previous visits, there was a fancy underground shopping mall near the Kremlin. It had a food court which inclued Sbarro pizza and a Cuban cigar shop, plus there was a Benetton store in GUM (a mall much changed from the Soviet days) as well as a fancy McDonalds near the International Nonprofit office.

Not all was change for the better, however. There was the fact that many Russians could never afford to shop in such stores, and lots of people had lost their social safety net from Soviet times. While staying at a hotel in Kiev we were treated to a disturbing but somewhat amusing scene. There was an office next to the hotel bar, and the sign above the door said, "Service Office." Oh, must be an administrative office of the hotel I thought. But then we noticed that we could hear the office phone ring through the open door.

After the man at the desk finished each conversation and hung up his phone, he would walk out to the bar and whisper in the ear of one of the many women who seemed to be hanging out a very long time at the bar. Immediately the woman would get up from her seat and head straight for the elevators. Ukrainskiye prostitutki (Ukrainian prostitutes). That was a "service office" alright.

It was sad to see these women doing this, and even worse when they would talk to us. I tried to be polite and respectful to them but they would give us the hard sell. I felt terribly guilty as I puffed on my Cuban cigar, and one of the women at the table next to us told me she would "love to be with a cigar man such as you." Another said, "c'mon guys... how much money?" wanting to negotiate a price with us.

One goal of our nonprofit was to improve life for the average person in the former Soviet Union through civil society work and student exchanges with the US. Maybe that would help put an end to women being forced into these situations; we had high hopes, but as Putin consolidated power over the years in Russia it was clear that American nonprofits and Peace Corps volunteers were not so welcome by politicians in the former Soviet Union anymore.

Back in the DC office the first medications I took made me very drowsy, like sleeping pills I suppose. A few cups of coffee helped me through the workdays, but I could not overload on coffee either or else I would get too jittery and that was no good. Some days I came to work late, other days I could not make it at all. Weekends were ok because I would just sleep a lot. No problem.

Work was a problem, though. I was getting paid and I owed it to my employer, my bosses, and my coworkers to be on my game. The International Nonprofit had an email general message board which everyone used instead of calling in sick or announcing they would be late. I would shoot an email in from my computer at home with no explanation why I was late or out. It was ok, everyone did it sometimes, and I was still getting my work done.

However, concerned coworkers sometimes asked if I was ok when I came back in and this was tough. I tried to be as vague as possible. Once a coworker kept pressing me, asking "What kind of cold was it? Were you coughing, did you have a head cold?" After her third question I almost bit her head off with my response. I think then she knew what was wrong – I was a jerk! I later apologized to her and we remained friends.

My doctor encouraged me to have a normal social life, but this is where I got into some trouble. To me a normal social life meant happy hours, and my doctor warned me to just nurse a beer or so when I went out, but I wanted to party like it was 1999, literally. In later years I realized it was imperative for me to rest a lot when not working and to stay away from any alcohol. This was the only way I could work successfully, albeit for short stretches of time.

My social situation at the time was a toxic mix for my health. In 2000 I moved out from the apartment I was sharing with my girlfriend, since I did not know what my future would be like health wise. We were not married, our relationship had run its course anyway, and I did not want her to feel responsible for taking care of me in any way if I got worse. This was the right thing to do, but afterwards I should have hunkered down and rested most of the time, conserving my energy for work. Instead I had what I like to think of as a pseudo midlife crisis, but in my late thirties! I did not do anything out of the ordinary, but socializing as I had in the early 1990's was bad for me in the 2000's.

Nights out were exciting. I was not in a committed relationship anymore and my office was full of cool, intelligent, attractive twenty-something women, as well as fun, twenty-something drinking buddy guys. Problem was I was in my late thirties. It was time to cool it, especially with my health issues, but you could not tell me that at the time. I thought it was all good for me to get back to the "normal" life I had in the 1990's, but health wise and age wise I should not have become involved in this in the 2000's. I was not the same person anymore but it took a few years for me to realize that.

Even worse for me than the happy hour socializing with my coworkers, I discovered one bar in particular called "The Royal Lee" in Arlington, VA that would host bi-weekly punk rock shows. It was almost like reliving the early to mid-1980's again with many powerful bands. I noticed something interesting about this scene, however. The crowd was mostly teenagers, but the bands seemed to be mostly old fogies in their twenties and thirties. Some were veterans of the 1980's punk rock wars! One of these was Kent Stax, who had played drums for one of my favorite 1980's bands called Scream. (Kent eventually quit Scream back then and was replaced by Dave Grohl who later went on to Nirvana and the Foo Fighters in the 1990's) Kent had a family and a regular job in the 2000's but was still playing punk rock with a band called Spitfires United. This made it seem normal to me that I could play drums in a band in my thirties too.

Unfortunately my thirty-something self was sucked into this scene as it became more and more fun. I looked forward to those Friday nights as I struggled with my health at work each week, but I should have been resting instead. I was really making my health worse, I just did not realize it at the time. Then one foggy Friday eve, a guitar player came to say, "Mike with your drumming so tight, won't you drum for my band tonight?" Ok, he did not say that exactly, but his band had broken up and he knew I was a drummer. He asked me if I wanted in. Why didn't I say no!?! Instead I was having so much fun in the scene I said yes. I did not feel self-conscious about my age because this guitar player was a year older than me. With two twenty-somethings on vocals and bass, Cheerleaders of the Apocalypse was born. Though fun at times, the band ended up wasting my time, money, and denied me the extra rest I needed to try to keep working at International Nonprofit.

My doctor actually told me he thought the band would be good for me, an active social life can help some people's mental state, but I could not always hack it. I missed a few shows and band practices when I did not feel well, and I missed days at International Nonprofit when I had stayed out too late with the band. At the time it seemed like a good thing to do, but I really regret it now. I have learned since then; I always make resting up for work my number one priority.

Cheerleaders of the Apocalypse cut a CD, we played shows from DC to Baltimore to Philly to Boston, and even flew at our own expense (so stupid!) to Houston, TX to play a show and record some tracks with a local record company there. I sure did not get rich doing this. But my ego was gratified when the *Washington Post* did a story on us and "The Royal Lee" in its Weekend Section with photos too. A female coworker came by my office at International Nonprofit that day unannounced and said "So you're famous now!" She had read the article in the *Post*. Like I said, at times being in the band was fun, but it was not a good thing for me to be doing. After a year or two of this I could not cope with being in the band while working at the nonprofit so I had to quit the band.

Unfortunately work got harder for me after two years with more and more on my plate. My boss was good and in her eyes I was succeeding, she gave me raises and good reviews, and she thought I could handle more work. I had moved on to better medications which did not make me drowsy. The new medicine helped some, but it made me sick to my stomach all of the time. This made work more difficult. As my stress grew at work, my performance dropped, and my calling in sick too often caught my boss's attention eventually. In 2003 I used all of my sick days and kept calling out anyway.

Finally I got a call from human resources at International Nonprofit one day, and was asked to come over there for a meeting. I had become such friends with everyone at the organization that instead of being too worried about this, I suspected they were going to express concern for my health because of all the sick days I took. Maybe they would ask if I were an alcoholic, or had cancer maybe? I would just tell them no, of course not.

When I got to the HR manager's office, she was sitting there with my boss. The two of them let me know that International Nonprofit was going to lay me off. Soon I realized that they were cutting a different position in the finance department (my position was safe), but that that person was going to take my position. I had to train her to do my job in exchange for some severance pay. I suspect if I had performed better and not taken so many sick days in 2003 I might have been able to keep my job. I had tried my best, but my poor health and side effects of the medication ruined this great job for me.

Downward Spiral

After a short period of feeling sorry for myself at losing the International Nonprofit position I started the resumes going out. Soon I had a temp assignment (yes, back to that) doing "cash management" in a treasury department I was told by the temp agency. They weren't lying, it was true, they had yours truly the 100 Million Yen Man photocopying small checks and writing up deposit slips at a big government contractor in Northern Virginia. I did my best with the Excel report they gave me to do as well, but this was really more like working for a collection agency than a treasury department.

Still struggling with the side effects of the medication I found the transition to the new job more difficult than it would have been normally. What was really difficult was dealing with an older woman who was just a coworker; this woman would come to my office every afternoon and start to yell at me. She would tell me I was not doing the report right every day, but she would not tell me why. I was just "not getting it."

My boss did not have a problem with my work, but my boss was also too timid to stop this woman from yelling all the time. This sort of thing had become the hardest part of work for me, I started to crack when in constant conflict with others in the workplace. It was so lucky for me that I worked at International Nonprofit in the few years previous to this – the people were really nice and so professional that conflict was not usually a problem. That is why I was able to last close to four years there in spite of my health problems. It was back to the real world for me now.

Fortunately I got out of the government contractor assignment soon and found a position as a finance manager with six direct reports. It would be similar to my first job out of college, when I managed foreign currency tellers. The job sounded good but deep down I knew it would be a struggle for me. They had the seven of us crammed into the basement office, about as big as a walk-in closet, of an international organization's building in Washington, DC. I did my best but the pressures, the phone calls, the emails, the constant interruptions at this hectic job were too much for me. There were plenty of wealthy, overprivileged international customers complaining about everything, including some who ordered sketchy wire transfers to international banks without sufficient details about themselves and the beneficiaries. This went on from time to time and I really did not want any part of that anyway.

    My manager was a nice guy who went from branch to branch so I did not work with him on a daily basis. When I resigned this time the difference was I trusted him enough to tell him it was due to health problems. In retrospect I do not think telling him this was a good idea, but I did not want him to think he was responsible in any way for my leaving. My boss did not really get it, thinking maybe I should just try to be more positive about things, and he even told me I should try reading Tony Robbins' motivational books (!) If I had not been feeling so bad and distraught I would have bust a gut laughing.

    I was definitely in trouble at this point. I was well qualified for that job but it was so demanding that my poor health and medication made it impossible for me to do it. What could I do, I wondered? Weeks went by as I sent out more resumes out of habit, but things were looking gloomy. I was not getting many responses anymore, my resume was starting to look questionable again – too many jobs in too short a time.

    With the encouragement and financial support of my family I ended up working over half a year at a bookstore for seven dollars an hour. This helped me get myself together, but even the bookstore was challenging and stressful to me at times, especially around the holidays. One low point was spending Christmas Eve at the store putting sale stickers on books until later in the evening after the store closed. I went right from the bookstore to midnight mass! I always have a lot of respect for retail workers when I go into stores. The conditions in which they work and the situations with which they have to deal are tough when you consider what they actually earn for their efforts.

Hyper Capitalism

A few thoughts on economics and capitalism (talk about mood swings, right!). Technology can be great, I can not even imagine writing a book without a computer. Still, I think that technology poses some challenges for us in terms of stress. I do not know how much it has to do with my poor health and medication, but as the 2000's continued I seemed to be struggling with technology more and more. Productivity expectations at work became higher and higher, and that it is very difficult for everyone I think.

One of my brothers is an architect, he told me later in the 2000's that people would say to him, "you have a computer, why can't you get the drawings to me now?" The bookstore where I worked was understaffed to save the company money, and I do not know how many times I heard from customers, "I found it on Amazon, why don't you have it in the store? Just look on your computer screen." At one of my jobs in the 2000's, a boss of mine was under pressure from his boss, and so my boss sent me an email. As I opened his email, he sent me an instant message (IM). I looked away from his email to read his IM, and then noticed he was standing right in front of my cubicle asking the same question in person. This all happened within the space of a minute!

What I think it comes down to is when you are a consumer, things are getting better and better. New technology makes everything so convenient. When you are a worker, things are getting tougher and tougher. We are killing ourselves in the name of productivity gains. Something has to be done to reduce the stress at work as technology advances, but I do not have the answer.

Once an MBA always an MBA, but I have to say as the years have gone by I have become less and less fond of this capitalism thing. We need the proper balance. It is great when you are playing the consumer, and especially if you have a lot of money, but for most of us it is a tough business.

Out West

I was getting through each day at the bookstore, in part because the hours were good for me. I worked four or five days a week, and many times my shift started in the afternoon, so I could get a lot of rest. No 50 to 60 hour work weeks like back in the 1990's. The job was not easy, we had our share of difficult customers of course. I was sending out resumes for professional jobs again but I was not getting any responses on these. Except one I remember. A woman called from a nonprofit in regard to a finance position. Going over my resume job by job, she asked me, "what are you doing now?" "I work at a bookstore now," I replied. "Oh, ok, thank you," she said, and then hung up the phone. That was the last I heard from her!

As winter turned to spring in 2005 I became more and more concerned. I was not earning a living because DC and Northern Virginia are expensive. My rent was more than my monthly income at the bookstore, and I could not keep doing this forever. My brother out west had an idea – why not move to Salt Lake City where he lived. Salt Lake is a very peaceful, beautiful place in the mountains. A small city where rent is cheap and the living is easy. Maybe this would be better for me. My brother said, "Salt Lake City is the place you want to be," so I loaded up the truck and I moved to SLC. Of course he did not say it like that. That was the *Beverly Hillbillies* show.

Anyway, I decided to give it a shot. I really had nothing to lose. I was scared to drive myself across country, though, what if I started feeling worse on the way? What if I lost my medicine? What if I could not find a good doctor out there? What if what if what if? Sometimes in life you just have to go and do something and see what happens. I did not know what else to do. It turns out the drive was ok, it was not much different from staying in my apartment all day. I just got a good night's sleep, sat in the car and drove for eight hours a day with my favorite music playing. Six days later I was in Salt Lake, amazed that I had pulled it off.

It was great to see my brother and his family, and I immediately started sending out resumes. One job in the paper sounded like some sort of data entry job where you needed to know French (French? In Salt Lake City?) I was curious, so I faxed in a resume. Within days a call came. A call? I went months without a call back in DC. Maybe moving to Salt Lake was the right move after all. The next day I had an interview, that afternoon I had an offer, and two days later I was working there. They must have been desperate to get a warm body, I had never gotten a job that quickly before.

It turned out to be a great, successful mining company with very nice people and a good work atmosphere. "Mining Co." had operations around the world including Quebec, and that is where the French came in to play. I worked with two other people procuring parts for the Canadian group. The kicker was that they seemed to have a ton of work to do, and three people were probably not enough to do everything for which the Canadian group was technically responsible.

Bad news on the home front was that I was having trouble getting a doctor in my new city. My sister in law was a surgical assistant and she gave me the names of three whom I called and called and called. I should have pursued this further and maybe gone to a hospital for a referral if necessary (I did not have insurance), but I got busy with work and hatched another plan. What if I blew off getting a doctor, kept the medication I had left ready just in case I started feeling bad, and tried life without the meds? After all, I was feeling better in the past year or so, and my main problem seemed to be the side effects from the medication. These were the main cause of my difficulties at the bookstore job. Weighing on me was the pressure to earn my own living. I needed to succeed at this new job, Mining Co. seemed a good fit for me. And, I had to know. It had been five years on the meds, would I ever be able to live without them?

The result... phenomenal! Within days no stomach problems. No excess nervousness, no worries, no jitters. No problem getting up for the early morning start (we worked Eastern Canada hours). It was like being Rip Van Winkle, asleep for six years and suddenly waking up. I told my brother I had not felt this good since early 1999. The world was utterly beautiful again. Weeks, then months went by without the relapse I expected might come.

The position turned out to be quite taxing, very busy at times, especially a month into the job when one of us three people in the Canadian group went on vacation (his honeymoon) for two weeks. Not finished learning how to do my own job well yet, I had to cover his area and mine, and by the second week of his vacation I was reeling. Unfortunately he had set his email software to pour every one of his emails into my inbox, and all of his phone calls were forwarded to me, for two entire weeks. Emails were coming in faster than I could prioritize them, let alone read them. The fax machine was spewing out nonstop orders, it was difficult to keep the paper stocked, forget about reading those either! When I tried answering the phone I noticed a second call would come in and that caller would leave a message. As I tried to listen to the message, another phone call would come in and leave another message.

Health wise I was ok but I was overwhelmed with this. I could not believe the guy now on his honeymoon handled so much work. Later I realized that he did not, a nice and smart but Pollyanna-type Mormon guy, he just smiled all day while drowning in work, leaving most orders undone. Management was happy with him there, but the managers did not seem to understand the details of our French speaking group of three people, the Canadian team. Most days the managers focused on the local mine in Salt Lake and left us three to our own devices.

The first week of my coworker's vacation I told my direct manager that I was falling behind fast. Instead of calmly asking what he could do to help, he just said in a loud voice "ask her!" meaning the other member of our Canadian group. This boss was typically a good guy but I think he was a little insecure about managing the three of us because he was not familiar at all with the details of what we did. Unfortunately the other member of the Canadian group was not able to help me either. A Belgian woman, her specialty was the Quebec operation. I and the guy on his honeymoon handled Labrador City because we were native English speakers and her French was better than ours.

Drowning in work, I panicked during the second week of my coworker's honeymoon and resigned (I did not think this was such a big deal, I was still a contract employee waiting for my months long background check to finish). I did not want to worsen my illness over this and I figured I would be fired anyway when they discovered all the unresolved orders and issues. It is a shame, if my coworker had only taken one week off I might have survived this crisis and I might be working in Salt Lake City to this day. It was too early in my time at the company and I did not understand the big picture yet, otherwise I would have hung in there and kept my mouth shut.

The worst problem was the ensuing drama over my resignation. Up until this point I had had a great relationship with my boss and my boss's boss. When I lost my cool one morning my boss was not at the office, so I went in to see his boss and resigned to her. She was visibly upset. Later when my boss came in to work he had a conference with her in her office that I could not hear. He was really pissed off after that. I suspect she blamed him for my quitting, and given that he had snapped at me the week before, he probably thought I told her about him getting angry with me. I did not, I just resigned for my personal reasons, the stress of the work volume was eating me up.

Things got worse from there. Mining Co. quickly found a replacement for me in the Canadian group, and when it came time for my last day, my boss was once again out of the office. So, his manager invited me in to her office that day, I suspected she wanted to wish me well. But no. She said she was going to create a new position for me (as a contractor, not permanent yet) and that the Canadian group was going to be four people strong now. This was fantastic, and I accepted her offer. There would now be more of us to finish the mountains of work and I went home ecstatic that Friday.

Then Monday morning came. I sat working at my desk when my boss came in and he looked at me like he had seen a ghost. "What are you doing here!?!" he said in a loud tone. "Wasn't Friday your last day?!?"

"No," I said, "she (his boss) created a new position for me, I'm staying." Uh oh. It quickly became apparent that his boss had done this without telling him, and he flipped out. From that point on my boss hated my guts and there was nothing I could do about it. This would have been a case study for my MBA Organizational Behavior class! What do you do when something like this happens through no fault of your own, and your boss hates your guts forever?

I just came in every day, kept my mouth shut, and worked as hard as I could. It did not matter. He hated me so much from that point on that I could do nothing right. It was miserable and I struggled to make it in to the office each morning, but I am proud to say I did for half a year. This probably was the worst work situation I have ever been through in my life. I never experienced a boss's hatred like this in my career. I hoped if I did a good job and kept quiet over time things would get better.

After some months on the job the true test was coming. Two of the Canadian group were going on a business trip for a week to Labrador City (a trip I would have gone on if not for the fiasco with my boss, doh!) and I was to cover both of their jobs. To me this was it... I had had enough time to learn the job, I was off medication, could I work like the Mike Pollard of the 1990's? I actually looked forward to the week like a pro football player anticipating his first Super Bowl.

The week came and I nailed it. 5am to 4pm every day for five straight days. Lunch at my desk every day, phone calls, instant messages, and emails pouring in. I am sure I made mistakes along the way, but in my mind I redeemed myself for initially quitting the job, and more importantly – the old Mike Pollard was back! Five months med free baby and not a worry in sight! My mind was awash in the significance of this. A new life. A good career? Dating again? I could live wherever I wanted. I could earn a living! Ha! ... My boss still hated me, though.

Another Crash

There were a few worries in sight, however. The six month lease on my apartment was coming due, and my status at work was still as a contractor (without health insurance). Would they make the position permanent? Was it worth the risk to sign a new lease if Mining Co. would not make the position permanent? Did I still want to live in Salt Lake City now that all things were possible for me health wise?

I had some time to think about these things, but I was leaning toward heading back East. The holiday season was upon us and I would enjoy Christmas and New Year's, my sister was visiting from California, then I would decide in January 2006. Anyway, Christmas was great, we went to midnight mass and I enjoyed the time off work. My sister, her husband, and my nephew arrived in town a day before New Year's and we all met at my brother's house. I was feeling good, excited about the weekend, and even brought two bottles of wine to the gathering. I will have a glass of wine myself if I don't mind (I'm med free now) I thought!

Later that night we headed for our cars and my sister was acting weird. I wanted to know when we were going to get together tomorrow and she would not tell me what time! Why not? Were they going to get together without my knowing? Anyway, we spent the next day with my little nephew and this exhausted me. Hours and hours with him. Lots of fun but mentally exhausting. I was getting really tired. Then we had some wine with dinner. This was not a relaxing weekend I thought! I am so tired. My brother dropped me at my apartment this time, I did not feel much like talking, yeah yeah, Happy New Year I said and I went in. I was so tired but I could not fall asleep, so I watched the Dick Clark New Year's Rockin' Eve. I could not get to sleep for a long time.

The next day my brother and sister took the kids skiing without me. Later that night I spoke to my sister on the phone and I was distraught. What the hell was going on? Everyone was acting weird. My sister said she was sorry to say it, but I sounded like I did six years before when I really got sick. She said I should see a doctor. I did not want to go through all that shit again, I said. She said I still should. Later my brother agreed. My brother said he would help me get a doctor in the coming week.

The next day I felt even worse, I could not think straight. It was scary, I could not remember things. I started writing down how I felt and what I should do in case I forgot and could not think straight anymore. I needed to call my brother. He answered the cell and said he would be right over.

When we got to LDS Hospital I was so out of it. I felt terrible, like I would pass out. I could not remember my address when they asked me. I sat down, my head was down but I could see out of the corner of my eye people kept wandering in and out of the room, looking at me with very worried expressions on their faces. One woman who was some sort of social worker, I could tell she was not a doctor, started talking to my brother. So obnoxious. She said, "I do not think it is medical at all, I think he has a social problem, look at the way he is sitting."

What?!? I did not say anything but just glanced at her with a dirty look. I was in such a state I was not able to muster more than that. I was missing the medication, and the exhausting weekend with the wine and everything else wiped me out. My brain was a mess. Finally a real doctor arrived and he was good. I was able to tell him about what medication I took, and that I still had a few week's supply of it at my apartment for an emergency. He encouraged me to start taking it again that afternoon, and he gave me contact information for a specialist in town that I could see right away that week.

My brother took me back to my apartment, hung with me a while after I took my meds, and I started to feel a bit better. I needed *rest*, desperately. I crashed after my brother left and spent days doing next to nothing except eating, resting, and taking the medication. Finally I recovered.

Anyway, I felt pretty stupid. I was embarrassed that I had to make a trip to the emergency room but I learned my lesson. I needed the medication – it took months for the full effect of going off the meds to hit me, but it hit me. I also learned that I needed to rest all the time, especially when I had a job, and that I should stay away from alcohol. It did not help things at all. As bad as this all was, the experience in Salt Lake City helped me understand how to manage my illness better. First the doctor in Utah and then my doctor back East were able to help me reduce the amount of medication I took to minimize the side effects while still providing me with enough treatment to keep the illness at bay. This way I had a chance of working again.

Back East

So, I spent the Winter of 2006 resting in Salt Lake City. I was feeling better each day back on the medication, and I spent my days in the least stressful way possible... coffee, walks, listening to music, watching the Winter Olympics on TV. This helped a lot, and those few months turned out to be the time period when I felt the best during the entire 2000's.

I would find in future years because of the health problems that I had little or no tolerance for work-related stress; each job I tried would eventually crush me mentally and I would last anywhere from a few weeks to a few months to a year or so. Once off work I would recuperate and then think I was capable of working again. This cycle would go on for the next twelve years.

After a month I was feeling good and started to make plans for returning to the East Coast, and I would go straight to Baltimore. Washington, DC people were starting to relocate to Baltimore in the 2000's as it is a nice, livable city relatively close to DC with much lower rents. Speaking of rents, I had some money saved but not nearly enough to move to Baltimore and spend months looking for a new job. For the move I was able to secure a risky loan, and I was amazed that I was approved and granted the loan, but in later years I realized I was part of the easy credit and excessive borrowing in America that ended with the debt crisis of 2008. I was hopeful that with my recent experience working in procurement in Salt Lake I would find a comparable position in Baltimore or Washington and start chipping away at my debt.

In early March 2006 I packed my six year old Saturn Sedan as full as possible with my possessions and took a southern route across the country. First stop was Moab in southern Utah, a comfortable oasis in the middle of desert wilderness. This is an incredible area of the country, I would recommend driving through if you have the nerve! Driving south from Moab to Arizona is one of those desolate "last gas for 100 miles" drives; every thirty minutes or so I might see some Native Americans drive by in a pickup truck, other than that I was completely alone in the desert. Luckily my car didn't break down.

I finally did fill up the tank in the town of Chinle, on Navajo land, the most populated area of my drive. Other towns had names like "Many Farms" and "Mexican Water." This here gringo had "Much Sweating" until his car made it to the relatively traffic-filled Interstate 40 in Arizona. I kept thinking of the Eagles' song "Take it Easy" with the lyrics "I'm standing on the corner in Winslow, Arizona, such a fine sight to see, a girl my lord in a flatbed Ford slowing down to take a look at me." Well, Winslow, AZ was west of me on Route 40, and I was going east. No girls were slowing down to take a look at me.

I stopped for the night in Albuquerque, a place I had been before as one of my brothers lived and worked there in the late 1990's. I visited him in Albuquerque one Easter, and no girls slowed down to take a look at me in Albuquerque back then, either. I don't know, maybe you have to actually go to Winslow, AZ.

Next morning was a terrifying drive up the Sandia Mountains east of Albuquerque, 70 mph traffic up the winding mountain road with the dawn sunrise to the east directly in my eyes. I don't remember why, but I didn't have sunglasses with me and I couldn't see a thing. After this things calmed down completely, flat brown New Mexico and Texas plains, easy sailing but with enough traffic to make me feel comfortable. I was interested to see what Amarillo, TX was like, but from what I saw it looked just like Salt Lake City, Los Angeles, Fairfax, VA and every other place with a long stretch of McDonalds, TGI Friday's, Wendy's etc. Given, I didn't venture far from the interstate on this drive but I was amazed at how similar every place looked across the country in 2006. The landscapes were different, but the towns and cities along the main highway were all the same.

That is until I stopped for the night in West Ireland! Otherwise known as Shamrock, TX, this place was awesome. Yeah it had the standard hotels and fast food places, but to attract tourists everything had an Irish theme. In the middle of Texas. The bars were Irish-themed, there was lots of green everywhere, and the Pizza Hut where I had dinner had green shamrocks plastered all over the walls. Also the hotel's indoor pool had a very dark green color, not kelly green, but a very dirty green color, which was probably because it had a lot of dirt in it. No one was swimming there, in fact I was one of the few guests in the entire hotel. Still, I like Shamrock, TX a lot. It was one of the highlights of my trip.

Another highlight was the next night's hotel in Arkansas. I can't remember the town this was in (I made a practice of staying at small town hotels along the interstate because they were cheaper and more interesting than the big city ones), but the young woman at the front desk was brilliant. The embodiment of all the Arkansas stereotypes, her curves were busting out of her work outfit, which consisted of cut-off jeans, sneakers, and a t-shirt with cartoon rabbits on it that said "Kiss My Bunnies." She had a cool, thick accent like "Flo" from "Mel's Diner" of the 1970's sitcom *Alice*. Remember "Kiss My Grits!" I think "Kiss My Bunnies" is even better. I also loved Arkansas because I noticed it was where the landscape turned from brown to green. Utah, Arizona, New Mexico, Texas, Oklahoma had a lot of brown, but Arkansas had lush green grass and trees, just like the East Coast, and this felt more familiar to me. I was getting closer to home.

A big music fan, I was so pumped to be in Nashville the next night that I had to call one of my best friends and his wife who were by coincidence crisscrossing the USA on vacation for a few weeks. He stopped to visit me in Salt Lake weeks before, and I had no idea where he might be, but I had to tell him (also a big music fan) that I was in Nashville. I said, "Guess what, I'm in Nashville!" He laughed and said, "We are too!" They stopped there for a week and had been going out every night to see different acts, so they knew the best place to take me.

The bar was filled with guys in cowboy hats, and the movie "Brokeback Mountain" (a love story about two gay cowboys) had been in the theaters that last year. One of the cowpokes in the bar kept shouting "Hey Brokeback! Come here boy!" and "You broke my back and then you broke my heart!" The music at the club was great, all unsigned but talented artists hoping to get their big break.

I stayed out much later than I had any other night of my cross country drive, so I was tired the next day. Still, when I crossed into Virginia the adrenaline kept me going. I didn't dislike the West, but Virginia, Maryland, and DC were home to me, where I knew I belonged. Despite being unemployed and in debt, I was ecstatic to be back.

Procuring a New Job

I arrived in Baltimore one afternoon, a week after leaving Salt Lake. The plan was to go straight to a high rise apartment building near Johns Hopkins University where I knew they had vacant apartments, because there was an advertisement for this building in my Johns Hopkins alumni magazine. Time was money – every day without an apartment was another expensive night at a hotel, I wanted to take care of things myself and not just show up at the door of my brother's place in Virginia looking to stay. I tried calling ahead the day before but no one answered the phone at the apartment building's rental office (what was up with that?), so I parked the car out front and walked right in.

It turns out the woman at the rental office missed work the day before and was all backed up on her duties so that she hadn't had time to check her voice messages. She was a bit taken aback at my urgency, I had my gear all in the car and could have moved in right then and there. This was not possible but she did have an empty one bedroom and she totally hooked me up – the apartment needed a paint job which was done in a day and she even let me leave my belongings in the place that day away from the walls that were being painted. Just one night in a hotel then I could move in for good!

Starting a job search was a pleasure as usual… I applied for one budget analyst job in Baltimore where I spoke with a headhunter. This person asked for my references, then turned right around, called and asked one of my references if *he* wanted to apply for the position! Headhunters are swell people. Luckily on my own I soon found a temp assignment working for an investment firm in Baltimore that was rolling out a new version of its website for customers to use for the customers' investment portfolios. Sounded good.

The idea was for the temps to test all the features of the site and see if we could "break it" (find problems now before the rollout and the firm would fix the bugs before any customers used the site). Unfortunately there was no chance at a permanent position at the firm but it kept some money coming in for me while I searched for a permanent slot somewhere else. I liked the temp job a lot – it wasn't difficult or stressful, also my coworkers were cool, and I got a kick out of riding the elevator each day. At age 41 I was balding and sporting some grey hair, so when permanently employed twenty-somethings entered the elevator they nervously said hello to me and lowered their eyes in respect – I eventually realized that because of my age and appearance these employees thought I was a high ranking permanent executive at the firm to whom they had not yet been introduced. Ha! Little did they know I was a 41 year old sucker temp with massive debts who probably made 1/3 the money they did. I didn't let on, it was rare for me to be treated with such respect in the workplace in those days.

A higher power must have been looking out for me as well, because just when the temp assignment was about to end I secured an interview for a well-paying budget analyst position at a nonprofit in Washington, DC. Older and wiser than in my twenties when I botched the negotiation for the Imports R Us Russia position, I nailed the interview without exposing what a desperate situation I was in. The clock was ticking, my money was running out, and I did not even have the temp assignment anymore. The kicker was that the Chief Financial Officer (CFO) of what I'll call "DC Charity Organization" already had hired a budget analyst, what he really needed was someone with procurement experience (like what I had from the Salt Lake City job) willing to work at his nonprofit and he said he could not find anyone. Like a shark sensing blood in the water, I accepted *if* the CFO could pay me 10% more than what he was paying the new budget analyst since that is the job I actually wanted to do. What balls I had! I was months away from bankruptcy/homelessness, with no other job prospects in sight, and the CFO immediately caved. The job was mine! Bien fait (well done) monsieur McGill MBA! Whew.

On my first day of work at DC Charity Organization I got to know the *real* CFO. Before I start criticizing let me say as I got to know him I realized that he was a very good man, smart (Ivy League MBA) and extremely hard working (he arrived at the office at 6am (!) every day and left around 6 or 7pm). Also, he was very generous with his time and money, not so many Ivy League MBA's work for charities and he made donations to the cause too.

Still, as calm and polite to me as he was in our interview, he was off the charts stressed and angry most of the time at work. His people management skills and ability to control his temper were nonexistent. I shadowed the CFO my first day and when we met with another manager who gave the CFO some bad news about this manager's department (the department needed more money) my boss flipped out, veins bulging on his forehead, first clenched and yelling. I thought I might have to make a quick call to the paramedics at the time but it turns out this was a normal day for him.

The CFO took a planned month long trip to Europe – going home to visit family I assume since he was originally from Europe – and I had a new problem. The CFO hadn't given me anything to do. For a month! I spent a few days arranging my office, reading the old files, configuring my computer of course, but by week two I was climbing the walls. So I went to the Controller and told her about my situation and she laughed at me. "You're asking for more work?" she said, very amused. I was later to learn that the Controller and CFO were always so crazy and busy in a very disorganized way that she couldn't conceive of the fact that I had no work to do. I asked her several times over the course of the month but she never really gave me anything.

The CFO was a master of micromanagement who tried to do all of the finance department's work himself, so as soon as he came back from overseas the shit got crazy of course. I composed lots of memoranda about procurement issues at DC Charity Organization which he would proceed to mark up with a red pen. Often I would revise these 3 and 4 times, each time waiting for long periods outside his office to see him, and often I noticed that he would change things I had already changed at his request that he had apparently forgotten were his own corrections of my writing.

Once I had a Power Point presentation prepared, with nice brief bullet points stating my ideas. When he was done with that thing it looked like *War and Peace*, each bullet point had paragraphs full of his language inserted. Was this the cutting edge Power Point technique that they taught you at Ivy League business schools? I was just a hoser Canadian MBA, what did I know, eh?

I quickly learned from reading the "sign in" and "sign out" sheet he had in the office to track employee attendance that he started work each day at 6am! Not rolling out of bed at 6am like me before driving from Baltimore to arrive by nine in the morning, but at his desk at 6am! Actually 5:58am, or 5:56am, or 6:07am (When he was late! I understood, everyone has a slow morning now and then!). He logged his "in" and "out" times to the minute, not rounding to the nearest quarter hour like a sane person might do. And he walked around the office in the mornings with a two-fisted drinking technique… in one hand a gigantic mug of coffee and in the other a gigantic bottle of Gatorade. Yikes! In 2018, with all the new technology these days, I worry about him. I suspect he might be at his current job strapped to an intravenous tube containing equal parts Red Bull and Oxycontin! I don't want to know.

I also learned *never* to walk past the CFO's open office door upon my arrival to work in the morning. If I did he would see me and start shouting at me, from behind mountains of paper on his desk, lists of tasks to do immediately (can I take my jacket off first, sir?). This meant that I had to walk an almost complete circle around and through the building and other departments to get to my office, but it was well worth it to avoid him first thing each day. Once I had the misfortune of hitting the men's room when the CFO was already in there. Immediately the stream of consciousness delegation of tasks began! Within a minute or two however, after noticing the pained expression on my face, he relented and said sheepishly, "oh… ok… do your business." My bladder thanked him.

The best was the time he appeared at my office door first thing in the morning very upset and began to explain a project to me. I asked calmly, "So what's the timetable for this, when does it have to be finished?" His body writhing and twitching in stress-filled agony he replied, "Well…..*NOW!!!*" For a second I thought he was having a seizure.

The DC Charity Organization was a majority African-American nonprofit in DC, and my boss the CFO and I were two of only a handful of white employees who worked there. Now I understood! Back when I was hired the CFO could not find anybody with procurement experience in DC *willing to work at a majority African-American charitable organization* (he did not mention the part in italics) – that is why he was so desperate to hire me. I mean it is not like Washington, DC, the mecca of government and military procurement, did not have anyone with procurement experience!

Like any workplace, most of the people were super nice, while a few did not like the fact that we were white people working there. Especially the security guard at the front desk, to whom I would say hello every day, and who would scowl at me every day. I understood though, you never know what experiences these people may have had with whites in the past – their trust level of white people was low in many cases.

Our African-American CEO gave a speech at a company-wide meeting once where he discussed some problems we were having. He said that while we work and are professional in the building, and "street" activities go on outside our doors, sometimes "the street comes in here." Given the charity work we did in the city sometimes this was tough as people could show up unannounced looking for help or whatever else at our headquarters, which was an administrative building with no facilities to help anyone. One very sad fact was that an employee of our nonprofit had as one of her responsibilities the task of typing up, copying, and distributing funeral arrangements for relatives of our staff. These seemed to come out every week or so, and most often they were for funerals of young black men in their teens and twenties: grandchildren, sons, and nephews of people who worked at DC Charity Organization.

On a lighter note, during this time I had some adventures in my social life back in Baltimore. I had no girlfriend upon my arrival in Baltimore, and I did not date anyone during my time in Salt Lake City. When I kept bumping into a cool single woman a few years older than me who lived on my floor of the apartment building, it was on! After one elevator ride together we talked at length and I said, "See you later, I'm sure I'll bump into you again," and I decided next time I saw her I'd ask her out for coffee. Each trip to the elevator became thrilling (would she be there this time?), but she was never around. Finally I could not stand the suspense any longer, and decided to write her a note. It listed my phone number and my apartment number, and asked her to have some coffee with me.

The problem was, I did not know her phone number of course, and I did not know her apartment number either! I did, however, know which hallway she walked down to her place, so

I took a chance. I folded the paper over so no one could read it, wrote on the outside of the note in big letters "NOTE FOR (HER NAME) WHO LIVES DOWN THIS HALLWAY," and I taped it to the hallway wall. The following week was exciting – like a John Cusack romantic comedy! Would the maintenance man rip the note down? Would some nosy apartment dweller read it instead? Would she get the note at all and if she did would she respond? Well, a week afterwards she still hadn't called me, but when I came home from work that day there was a piece of paper under the door. It was my original note with a response written on it, something along the lines of "I'm going away this week but when I get back I'd love to have coffee with you." That was a great day.

This was a bright spot in some rough times; with the stress of the office and the daily drive to work which took 1 ½ hours each way, I was not in the best health as time went on. In hindsight I should have moved somewhere closer along my commute like College Park, MD which was near the office, but I loved living in Baltimore. Hindsight, especially twelve years later, is 20/20, and it was a moot point anyway. DC Charity Organization was taking its toll on me and I did not know how much longer I would last there. After a year or so I could see I was in trouble.

In my office there was an annoying, very squeaky ceiling fan, and on a number of occasions I asked the facilities manager if it could be fixed. He said sure, called one of his direct reports who did not answer. So, as usual, he left a voice message asking his subordinate to please look at and fix the ceiling fan in Mike Pollard's office. That would be the last I would hear about it. Never got fixed the entire time I worked there. This was symptomatic of the environment at DC Charity Organization, the people were very nice and the cause was very good, but the bureaucracy was out of control to the point where it was impossible to get anything done.

Often I would send an email to a coworker with a question and get no response. So I would call their phone and no one would answer. Then I would leave a voice message and never receive a response. Finally I would walk to the person's desk at three o'clock in the afternoon when you would expect they would be around and the person would be gone. None of the people in their department would know where the person was. This went on constantly, to the point where eventually I was tracking fifteen or so tasks and projects that I could not work on. I had fifteen piles of paper on my office floor with notes on each listing what was keeping me from continuing work on them. Usually I could not get an answer to an important question or get some important information, and could not track down the person. Total gridlock.

This shit drove my boss the CFO insane as he was a good hearted but stern and serious person prone to outbursts of anger. Once he and I walked over to another department to consult with the people there in the middle of the afternoon and the department was like a ghost town. Everyone gone. I thought my CFO was going to have a stroke. Imagine how I was doing, struggling to work in the first place, and knowing that leaving this job was not an option due to my debt and dubious job prospects if I quit. I got up every morning and drove to work in despair.

After a year and a half of this, piles of undoable office projects littering the floor of my office, drowning in frustration, I just could not cope. Every now and then I had to call out sick for a mental health day. Later I missed a week. This just made things worse, so I came in on a Saturday to try to get caught up and organized with no one around to stress me. This did not help. I just crashed, had trouble functioning, and had no other choice but to quit. This began an awful period of several months in my life that I spent unemployed, deep in debt, desperately job hunting knowing full well that I would not succeed. I did not know what I was going to do.

No More Debt

At a loss on how to proceed in Fall 2007, I tried to conserve money and to search for new jobs every day, but attempts at both were futile. I knew soon I was going to have to explain the situation to my family and get some sort of help. Summoning up my courage, I finally called my father and tried to explain my situation. He never understood my health problems very well and how it disrupted my ability to work, and he was dumbfounded when I mentioned the amount of debt I had. He was getting older and I hated to come at him with this – he did not get my situation at all, why I had debt and why I did not just work hard and make more money. His lack of understanding was odd to me as his own father (my grandfather) had a similar illness and stopped working in middle age, forcing my grandmother to get a job at Macy's in New York City to support the family.

I was a bit better off than my grandfather as medication and counseling had come a long way since then. The fact was a less creative and less resourceful person than I would have had a mental and financial crash years before given my health situation, but multiple times in previous years I had snatched victory from the jaws of disaster and kept going on my own. I was very good at pretending things were ok for short periods of time, whether at dinners or short phone calls with family members. I did not want to burden anyone but things had gotten so bad I had no choice at this point.

After regaining his composure my father reluctantly agreed to help me pay down the debt and we would talk about the details later. This still was only half the problem – my inability to earn money in the future was an even bigger problem, how would I pay for rent and food in the future? This was the real issue for me all along, an income problem not a spending problem. Rent and food do not get paid on their own, I had next to no possessions, there was no wild spending spree that put me in the hole. Just years of unavoidable expenses without a steady revenue stream to cover them.

Soon I got a call from my older brother in Virginia, my father had informed him of my problems, and he was fantastic. My brother did not judge me, he just helped come up with a plan after discussing things with my family via conference calls to my other brother, my sister, and my father. I would file for bankruptcy and live with him in Virginia until I got back on my feet. I was really sad to leave Baltimore, I still remember the last weekend I spent there. My future was totally uncertain, but there was no doubt in my mind at that time that I would never live in Baltimore again.

The bankruptcy went smoothly as my illness was a valid reason for the accumulation of debt over the course of the 2000's. Job searching was another matter. My brother encouraged me to take my time and apply for well-paying professional jobs but this was fruitless. It was 2008 and the economy was in disastrous shape with the debt crisis coming to a head. The closest I came to a job was in a lengthy process with the TSA – Dulles and Reagan National airports were nearby and the TSA was one of the few places hiring at all. My health problems came up during my background check and TSA decided I was not fit to do what is quite a stressful job. They were exactly right, I would not have lasted a year there, but I did not know what else to do but apply everywhere I could.

Eventually I gave up applying for higher paying professional jobs and took a shot at the big box retailers. In the Fall of 2008 they were hiring seasonal employees for the holiday rush and I got an offer from one store. I expected boring retail work but it was not so boring, more like brutal with difficult physical tasks for hours on end. My new job was on the overnight shift when the store was closed, and it consisted of truck unloads, pulling and back stocking merchandise in the warehouse, stocking shelves, and my personal favorite – scraping dirt and glue off of store shelves with razor blades! We did a lot of measuring and resetting of shelves according to planograms sent to us from headquarters, and we had to do it as fast as possible. Somebody has to clean store shelves, and many other ugly things need to be done in retail stores as well, something shoppers do not really think about much. I got a real education at the "Big Box" retailer, a working man's MBA. It was a humbling experience, but it also gave me some hope – I seemed to be better able to cope mentally with physical work than the mental stress inherent in the white collar jobs I worked previously.

After working through the holidays at Big Box I took stock of my situation. I was no longer a seasonal employee but a permanent employee at Big Box and, I was able to save money as long as I was living at my brother's house. I crunched some numbers and realized that while things were progressing, I would need to earn more to get a place of my own in the expensive suburbs of Northern Virginia. A *second* job was necessary, and I found one fairly quickly. So I began working Sunday through Thursday overnights at Big Box, and Saturday and Sunday overnights at a kennel feeding and caring for dogs and cats. *Seven days a week overnight shifts...* things were getting real.

As bad as it sounds, a person can get used to just about anything. Getting my own apartment after the time at my brother's was magic. With all the hours worked, albeit at low pay, I was earning more than I was spending and debt free as a result of the bankruptcy. After hitting rock bottom I was slowly moving upward again. I tried not to think about the future too much, and just took things one day at a time.

The Big Box Grind

When one first starts working on the overnight shift at Big Box it is tough. There is an almost prison-like atmosphere to the place – they lock the doors of the store overnight and no one can go outside unless it is an emergency! This is hyperbole of course but I just mean that one is thrown in with this mass of people and it is dog-eat-dog. Most coworkers criticize new employees for not knowing what to do and do not help them learn. The loudest and most aggressive type of employee tends to do best there.

There were some terrific managers, but many were bad at dealing with their employees. I remember setting up a planogram adjusting shelves and pegs on an aisle as a group of shelf-stockers were slowly working their way toward my aisle. Their manager stood right next to me for a good half hour, not lifting a finger to help them or me, and kept repeating to me every 60 seconds, "You've got to hurry up. You've got to hurry up." What the hell. Fortunately I spent most of my time working to set up aisles and I had a good supervisor with whom I got along.

The overnight logistics manager was brutal, he cultivated an atmosphere of fear as he shouted instructions to his workers. His assistant was a very conscientious young guy whom he would boss around mercilessly; there was one incident I will never forget when the manager needed his assistant. The overnight manager yelled to his assistant, "Get over here!." The assistant said, "Alright" and began walking toward him. The manager replied "NO, I MEAN RUN!!!" Everyone on the floor heard this as the humiliated assistant ran to his manager like a little child would. One of my coworkers named Andre said to our group with disgust, "All a man's got is his pride." There is a limit to what workers should tolerate from their bosses, and this crossed the line.

My boss was great to me, but he did not care for the overnight logistics manager. I gathered this by the way my boss called him an "ass monkey" all the time (but not to his face of course). My boss did rebel in his own way, mainly by not showing up for work without calling in or coming late on random days. My boss was so good and experienced at his job that he had little fear that he would be fired. I do not condone this but I secretly cheered his passive aggressive pushback against the tyrannical overnight logistics manager. My boss always treated me well, taught me how to do many tasks, and encouraged me in my work.

I dealt with the bad managers by generally keeping silent and never letting on that I had an MBA. I worked hard voicing only an occasional "Ok" when responding to the worst managers. I went a little too far with this as I realized when one manager "complimented" me by telling me that if I ever learned how to print price labels (incredibly simple task which my boss did for our group) I had the potential to someday be a supervisor (!) In fact the sixty-something manager of the entire store liked me but I suspect he thought I had an intellectual disability as he would talk to me slowly and deliberately.

The majority of the overnight crew were Latin Americans and they were very wary of the American overnight logistics manager. They had each other though, and were a tightknit group. The warehouse manager was Hispanic, bilingual, and very experienced. He protected his crew from this abuse pretty well. It was an interesting mix of people overnight, a few whites and some African Americans in addition to the large Latino group, and a Chinese husband and wife who spoke zero English. They could usually be seen sweeping floors or loading cardboard into the bailer. There was not much animosity between the staff, but once Andre had a dust-up with one of the Hispanic workers. My boss amusingly warned him, "Andre, don't mess with them, they'll jump you outside… you'll see Andre laid out in the parking lot, draped in the Spanish flag!"

There were a lot of Latin American immigrants in this area of Northern Virginia, and we clearly had a stellar group at Big Box. They worked their butts off, long hours, and performed amazing and dangerous feats in the warehouse that I refused to perform for safety reasons whenever I was asked. They often climbed around the scaffolding, ignoring all the safety rules, working twice as quickly as I did. Our current American President in 2018 is very critical of these people, but I have nothing but respect for them.

The only hint of gang activity or criminality I saw was in the men's room. A big drawing extolling "18th Street," a Mexican gang and arch enemies of the notorious Salvadoran gang MS-13 prevalent in Northern Virginia, was scratched on the inside of one of the stalls. I do not know who was responsible for the artwork, but I never heard any mention of this stuff during our shifts; the Latino guys were speaking Spanish most of the time though so who knows?

When we had staff meetings, the American overnight manager would select a bilingual Hispanic worker to translate the manager's words to the majority of the crew whose English was weak or nonexistent. Although possible, it was difficult to imagine any of my Latin American coworkers involved in criminal activity, they were just good, tough, hard-working people. Neither were they illegal immigrants as Big Box had strict rules about having your work application papers in order; I do suspect a lot of my neighbors in the majority Latin American apartment complex where I lived were illegals, however.

One day I looked out of my apartment window and saw a church van zoom into our parking lot. An Hispanic woman leaped out, arms full of clothing, and ran into our building. Hmm, that was strange. I kept watching as the church van sped away and within a few minutes what was this I saw? A police car appeared and slowly patrolled our complex's parking lot, as if the driver were looking for someone. A loyal Trump supporter would have ratted her out but I did not; I am a loyal Catholic supporter and we treat immigrants with compassion. 150 years earlier that woman could have been one of my Irish ancestors just trying to make it in the USA.

I lived in an apartment near my brother's house, but other than his family I had no friends in town. I was too busy working every day anyway. I can not even say I had many true friends at work either, though we did have some laughs. One of my coworkers was a twenty-something African American guy who told us grandiose tales of his life. To this day I do not know if he was telling the truth, but it was entertaining in any case. It seems that although he worked the ugly and low paying overnight shift at Big Box, he was actually heir to a fortune. His uncle was a tycoon and owner of a well-known hotel chain and my coworker had access to an almost unlimited amount of funds.

His uncle made him work like a dog so he would not be spoiled, apparently. Amazingly, my coworker said he had: a personal trainer who made him exercise and eat right each day despite the fact that my coworker was always terribly sleep-deprived, a beautiful condo in the area near Big Box, and best of all a six-figure Lamborghini Italian sports car that my coworker would drive at high speeds (but never drove it to work) and often was pulled over by policemen for "driving while black and twenty-something." I think about this guy and can not help but laugh now. I wonder what he's up to in 2018. The stories he told did not seem plausible, but the amount of detail with which he spoke at the time still makes me wonder, could he really have made all that up? I will never know!

I was truly starved for friendships at Big Box, to the point where I would bring the Washington Post sports page to the break room every day just to help foster conversations with people with whom I had nearly nothing in common. That is except for later in my time at Big Box when I got to know a Colombian guy named Juan in his early twenties who was obsessed with punk rock. He flipped when he discovered that I had been a drummer for a punk rock band when I was his age. Juan could not stop asking me questions in broken English and he became like a little brother to me. I laughed once when he asked if I had ever heard of the band "Flag Black." "Actually it is Black Flag," I corrected him, but he liked Black Flag so much that I gave him a book I had on the DC punk rock scene of the 1980's in which he immediately recognized a picture of singer Henry Rollins of Flag Black. I mean Black Flag (!) Juan later told me that his English language teacher was using the book I gave him to help him learn English. This made me feel great. I bet around the mid-1800's there must have been some American in New York City who helped my Irish ancestors get acclimated to their new country too.

7 Nights a Week

Working seven nights a week was tough but I settled into the routine after getting the second job taking care of the dogs. Things slowly got better at Big Box as I caught on. I learned blue collar terms and skills that were new to me, like what a pallet is, and how to pull a heavy pallet with a pallet jack. How to stack merchandise on a pallet and wrap it up in plastic for shipment or storage. There was the standing forklift which I started to use with a minimal amount of training; a worker is not allowed to use one unless he or she is certified, but the certification training process amounts to someone telling you: "This button lifts it up, this button brings it down… ok, got it? Great, see you later!"

I really learned by watching certain employees who were masters of the art, using the forks to nudge a pallet heavy with merchandise on it an inch to the right or left 20 feet above on the warehouse scaffolding. I got the hang of it, same with the cherry picker which lifts you 20 feet in the air so you can take down individual boxes. I learned not to freak out when I was high above and the button to bring me back down would not work for five or ten seconds. The button always worked eventually, as long as the machine was sufficiently plugged in and charged before I used it.

All this was an education for me, one that I doubt many of my MBA friends received in their lives. Blue collar work is at least as hard and as important (if not more important) than white collar jobs, the only difference is that one gets paid less and receives less respect from others for the work the blue collar person does.

I have not mentioned the dog kennel yet. Well, on some weekends there might be ten or fifteen dogs in the cages, and that was easy – just feed them once, keep an eye on them, exercise them a bit and clean up any mess they make. No problem on an eight hour shift. It was a different story on holiday weekends when dog owners went on vacation and we had 100+ dogs to deal with. There were only two of us working overnight (and no vet available to us, very stupid on the cheapskate kennel's part, that would have actually cost them money!), sometimes even just one person working if my coworker called out sick, meaning I was on my own.

All in all, working at the kennel was a trip. Not because of crazy dogs, but because of crazy coworkers. As much if not more so than Big Box, this job was a magnet for dysfunctional people. I know, then what about me? I worked there too. I had health reasons to blame for being there as part of my train wreck of a career, but I was reasonably responsible and had good social skills. This is more than I can say for some of my compatriots at the kennel.

Let us start with my original coworker on the weekend shift. He seemed normal enough to start, and we had plenty of time to talk as the kennel was new and had relatively few customers (dogs) to take care of at first. My new friend soon detailed to me his alcoholic past. In college he was an engineering student at a quality university in Virginia with a promising future, but then came the alcohol. Things came to a head once when my coworker got so drunk that he went to a grocery store and started yelling, taking product off the shelves and throwing it around the store. When he threw one package he realized (oops!) there was a man walking toward him in a blue uniform. Next thing he knew his parents were picking him up from jail.

But hey, that was all over now, my coworker was on the straight and narrow. He had a son with his girlfriend (he detailed another story of being out with her and after a few drinks deciding to drive drunk for hours to drink more at the bars in their old college town, I forget how that story turned out). His thing now was to work a lot, make money, take care of his son, which is great, except he still wanted time to have fun like in college so he just decided not to sleep anymore. My coworker would show up to work in a sleep-deprived stupor, and insist the need for sleep was all mental. Sometimes he would stand motionless facing a wall for close to a minute at a time, his eyelids closed and his body screaming for sleep. A good way to be at work. But that is ok, I think his reason for not sleeping once I remember was that he had to take his grandmother to Charles Town casino in West Virginia for a day of fun. He drove all the way back just in time for his overnight shift, which he began looking like he was going to pass out. He did not last too long at the kennel.

Next up... a big white guy who was so cool he tried to dress like Biggie Smalls. This guy I will call "Biggie Smalls" and he had life all figured out, and despite the fact that I had worked at the kennel longer, my new coworker always tried to talk to me like he was *my* boss. My real boss, a twenty-something woman who was reasonable and nice, was the object of his affection. So, Biggie Smalls would show up to work an hour before our shift to flirt with her, and to learn what special work needed to be done on our shift. When I arrived he would stand before me, clipboard in hand, and go over the tasks he was assigning me that evening. Ba ha. Week after week I would let Biggie know that I was doing none of this, then he would be offended, and protest that these were tasks for me to do *"only if I choose to do them."* I let him know week after week that I would be doing only those things my official boss directed me to do. He was so tiresome to deal with.

At least my new coworker Biggie really had it together in his personal life, though. He talked real big, but always seemed to be living in these dodgy situations with a revolving door of roommates who shared one car, which was often his excuse for being late. He liked to explain his cost-saving techniques for recipes with Ramen noodles which he ate every day. Biggie Smalls came up with another great money-saving technique too! In Virginia there is what is known as the "Toll Road" to Dulles Airport. It was meant as a fast, direct highway to Dulles, so if you took it to the airport it was free of charge. But, if you used it for local drives and got off the highway at one of the exits along the way, you had to pay a toll. Fair enough. But no, my coworker was too smart for that. Biggie liked to drive all the way to the airport, then pull a U-turn, and drive back to his local exit on the Dulles Toll Road, which made it a free trip. Hey, 50 cents is 50 cents! What about the extra miles and the cost of gas (probably more than 50 cents), you ask? I am not sure if he was aware of this expense, but if he was I am sure he tricked his roommates into filling up the gas tank at their expense. He was crafty that way.

But what about his affection for our boss? How did that turn out? Oh… she rejected him when he asked her out, despite the fact that he wore his best gold chain with medallion around his neck that night to impress her. Soon enough Biggie fell by the wayside and became another ex-coworker of mine. This shit to me was the most difficult aspect of these minimum wage jobs, not doing the work but coping with moronic coworkers. Just let me do my work in peace, please!

My life did have some nice, simple pleasures in those days. Working the two jobs allowed me to save up enough to buy a net book with an internet connection which was fantastic to have. Previous to this I used the county library computers for internet job hunting and the like. Also, Big Box only allowed time and a half overtime work in certain cases, like during the holidays. In most instances I worked extra time early in the week and then would get sent home early during the Thursday overnight shift upon reaching the weekly 40 hour limit. This made Friday like a day off! I would get to bed at maybe one or two in the morning, wake up around 8 or 9am and the whole Friday was free for me before doing the kennel overnight late Friday.

Fridays were party time! Eat some Chinese food for lunch, cruise by the local Town Center cigar shop and have a good smoke outside if the weather was nice. I did enjoy these times, I would look forward to Friday afternoons all week, and I did feel a lot of satisfaction in being able to save money and be debt free as a result of working so hard. As brutal as the seven-night workweek was, I am very proud of how I handled my affairs during this period. Talk about pulling yourself up by your own bootstraps! And, except in some rare cases, my health was holding up ok through this as well. Things could always be worse.

Hot for Teaching

All told, the 2000's was the worst decade of my life personally and professionally. Still, not every aspect of the decade was bad, and I am tremendously proud of how I came through all of it. I made it through the decade intact, and there was some light at the end of the tunnel as 2010 began.

I heard about a program called "Teach for America" that fast-tracked people from other fields into public school teaching positions. I always thought I might like teaching later in life, so I did some research and found that "Teach for America" was really more for recent college graduates to make a difference in the public school system. I was too old for that. But, I did see this other program specifically in Baltimore that fast-tracked professionals from various other careers into public school teaching positions. What the program wanted most was math and science teachers of course, but it also needed social studies teachers. I considered myself a social studies expert with a good knowledge of history and politics, I had an International Relations degree from Johns Hopkins, and an MBA to boot, so I was well qualified.

Not expecting much, I decided to take a shot at it and apply online. The application was similar to university applications with essays to write, university transcripts to request and the rest, so I went and knocked it out in my spare time. I also had to take Praxis standardized teaching exams, one general exam on English and math, and a second in social studies. True to form I smashed the social studies test, scoring in the top 15% of all prospective social studies teachers who took the exam. I still have the special certificate they sent to congratulate me, it looks like a cheesy version of a diploma, but I treasure it. I passed the first hurdle of the application process and was invited up to Baltimore one Saturday in Winter 2010 for personal interviews. There were a lot of smart, outgoing people in the pool of applicants, most of whom were younger than me. I was age 45 at the time, and I really had no idea how I did in the personal interviews. I tried not to get my hopes up, and went back to the Big Box grind.

I was told to check the organization's website over the following few weeks to see if I were accepted. It turns out I was!!! This changed everything for me, my whole mindset was different suddenly. I had been plugging along at Big Box and the kennel, doing fine but with no real hopes or dreams for the future. If I could pass the challenging summer bootcamp for teachers I would be offered a teaching position, for much more money than I was pulling down at the time. Not only that, I could move back to Baltimore, the place I most wanted to live! Wow, I always try to remind myself of this time period, because no matter how bad things get it is important to hang in there. Life can surprise you, even when you think all hope is lost.

I was so fired up to be a teacher after all my past career disappointments and problems, that I became temporarily superhuman in my endurance and ability to work. This was good because the process was going to be very challenging. It involved days like working the overnight shift at Big Box, then immediately driving up from Virginia to a Baltimore hospital for a physical exam. Or one day when I finished my overnight shift at the kennel and drove straight to an Arlington, VA testing sight to crush that Social Studies exam I mentioned.

I had no illusions about all this, though. Given my past health issues, I knew there was a distinct possibility I would crash out somewhere along the way and have to give up this dream. I was so careful in this regard that when it came time to start the Summer 2010 teacher bootcamp in June I hedged my bets by not leaving my Virginia apartment to move to Baltimore right away like most of my fellow prospective teachers did. I quit Big Box and the kennel of course, but got up at the crack of dawn each day and drove to Baltimore for the bootcamp. Then, tired from a days' worth of practice teaching and lectures, I would make the long drive back to Virginia and do my night time bootcamp assignments before going to bed and repeating it all the next day. At the time I felt like I could not risk moving to Baltimore before knowing if I were going to complete the strenuous bootcamp. Still, I wanted this so badly I never wavered in my determination to complete the program.

Prospective teachers were all given a large textbook on teaching methods to read, which I did, and I began all day coursework with homework assignments most nights. Within several weeks we were assigned real schools where we taught summer school each morning then continued with our own coursework each afternoon back at the training center. Though all this was challenging and difficult I was surprised at my progress, I did well for the most part!

My only stumble was when an instructor who "observed" my summer school teaching was critical of me on her first two observations. I certainly had a lot to learn and improve in my teaching method, but I think part of this was due to my age. I was just starting out teaching and needed practice like everyone else in the program. The observers were much less critical of my younger teaching partner at my assigned school, who was really no better than me. I tried not to be bitter about this, I implemented the observer's feedback and later came through with flying colors. If I had not turned it around, I would have been kicked out of the program.

In the midst of this we had several "job fairs" where various Baltimore standard public and charter schools sent recruiters to interview us. This was where the real age discrimination came into play. Clearly the mid-twenties to mid-thirties candidates were favored over those of us in our forties and fifties. In some ways I could understand the recruiters' reasoning – there were advantages to hiring younger prospects, I just did my best in the interviews. As the interview process wound down it was clear to me what was happening. The only two social studies teacher candidates who still had not been hired were me at age 45 and a woman who was

58. Our resumes were spectacular in terms of education and work experience outside of teaching, but that did not matter. The younger social studies candidates were consistently hired over us in head to head competition, and this did not upset me that much. What did upset me was the attitude of the teacher training organization, staffed by twenty and thirty-somethings, who disrespected the two of us and blamed us for not being hired quickly. We weren't trying hard enough, apparently.

Anyway, this was a moot point as the two of us were eventually hired. I was not too bitter about anything really, more than anything I was truly impressed by my fellow teaching candidates as well as many of the experienced teachers who trained us. I still have yet to meet so many smart, honest, hardworking, and dedicated people in one group in my life. One drawback of being hired later was that the two of us did not get the school assignments for which we were hoping. Mainly I really wanted to teach high school, but ended up at a middle school. My hope was to try to work with disadvantaged 16-18 year old young men to help them transition to adult life and jobs.

Instead I had hyperactive, screaming sixth graders, a nightmare for me and my stress issues. I liked them, they were funny and clever kids, unruly as they were. Teaching sixth graders will dispel any idea a forty-something person has that he or she is young and cool. Once when I called for order and quiet in my class, a student yelled out, "Y'all better calm down or that old man (me) is going to have a heart attack!" I had a class of eighth graders as well, and even they were somewhat more mature and easier to deal with compared to the twelve year old kids.

After I completed the training program and received my school assignment I made the move to Baltimore settling into a fantastic neighborhood where I once lived as a sophomore at

Johns Hopkins University. Years before, facing bankruptcy and moving to my brother's place in Virginia, I remembered mourning the fact that I would never be able to live in Baltimore again, but here I was! As I said, life can certainly surprise you, in great ways as well as bad ways.

Quickly, however, I discovered how different real teaching was going to be in comparison to the practice summer school class I taught. That had gone pretty well, but the actual September classes were a reality check for me. My summer school class actually gave me an ovation on my last day teaching there, I was stunned and keep this as my happiest and most rewarding moment of my short-lived teaching career. That was a distant memory come September. First of all, my commute was about as long as it could have been for someone within city limits. Rather than walking to my first choice school which was a high school with small class sizes, I drove to a remote southern section of the city to a middle school. In addition to the difficulties dealing with the sixth graders, it was difficult in that I also was not given my own classroom or office in which to work and keep my belongings. At this school the students stayed in one room for the most part and teachers walked the halls to teach in different rooms for each class. I was like a confused homeless person with bags on my back trying to learn the hallways and class locations.

And, like is common for public school teachers these days, I spent a lot of my own money on supplies for my classes. The worst was the copier situation – only one copier available to all the teachers in the one school. It was always in use by someone, and after waiting in line when I finally used it there were frequent paper jams and other problems. Soon I gave up and stopped by FedEx Office everyday after school to pay my own money for reliable copying services.

The hours were a surprise to me as well. I envisioned teaching maybe 9am to 3pm each day then going home to work on lesson plans for an hour or two each night (and only 10 months out of the year, time recover each summer from my health woes during the school year!). Yeah right. More like 7am until 4pm, then trips through rush hour traffic for copying and supplies. And, there just were not enough hours in the night to do all the lesson planning, grading, and other duties at home. I was exhausted physically and mentally. As much as I struggled and fought, a mental crash came soon enough. I had done well in the bootcamp, which we were led to believe was going to be super difficult, but it was laughable compared to the demands I faced in the real classroom.

Inner city public school teaching is incredibly challenging, there is pressure on the teacher from all sides. There was the teacher training organization monitoring you, school administrators (often telling you to do the opposite of what the teacher training organization tells you to do), parents to deal with (if they are able to be active in their children's education at all), and all the obstacles I mentioned previously. I was basically passing out each night from exhaustion while trying to complete lesson plans. Finally one day I showed up to school without finished lesson plans and had to wing it. If I had been caught doing this by a school administrator I would have been in big trouble.

Soon I realized I could not hack it and the kids deserved better than what I could give. One trainer at bootcamp told us that if we needed to quit, we should do it early in the school year otherwise we might ruin a year of the students' education because the school will not be able to find a good replacement later in the year. What really shocked me was that my experience was fairly typical for the participants of the teacher training program. Many of the social studies teacher prospects in my bootcamp group left teaching within a year or two of our time together.

I thought when I quit that I was the aberration, I felt so guilty and stupid at the time. I do not feel so bad anymore, I gave it my best shot and I have to leave it at that. Still, this was an incredible disappointment to me, with all the effort I put into teaching and the idealism I once felt was all gone. I had been dreaming of finishing off my career for ten to fifteen years as a teacher, but it was not to be.

Back to Big Box

I took a week or so to rest and decompress after leaving teaching, and then I had to figure out what I was going to do. To start from scratch job hunting seemed daunting, and it would be time consuming. Also, I now lived in Baltimore, the city where I often looked for jobs over the years and never succeeded. Oh man.

The obvious thing to do in the short term was to go back to Big Box. Actually there were Big Boxes in the Baltimore area, why not apply to these? So I drove out to one, where they have little computer stations in the store for job applicants to apply. I submitted my information, certain that my previous Big Box experience would easily get me a job in a Baltimore store, and then waited. And waited. And waited. Oh no, no response, it seemed I could not even get a job at Big Box now. I started grasping at straws, including giving my resume to a friend of mine from Johns Hopkins who was now a doctor in Baltimore. Maybe he could hook me up with a loading dock job at his hospital ha ha ha. Yes, I was really grasping! The longer one is unemployed, the less pride one has. Just desperation.

Speaking of pride, it was tough but I gave a call to the Human Resources woman at Big Box in Virginia, explained everything and asked if she could help me. She was always super nice and liked me, and it turns out she said I could come back to Big Box if I wanted… back to the store in Virginia where I worked before! Doh! I had just moved from Virginia to Baltimore months before. I accepted, since I had no other options, figuring I would move back to Virginia maybe. This was becoming a mess but I there was no choice, I just had to take the job and worry about the rest later.

Yes, I began to commute for the overnight shift at Big Box every day from Baltimore to Northern Virginia, costing crazy gas money and giving me little time for anything but eating and sleeping. I did this for months, and since I was experienced at Big Box my old boss was glad to see me back. During one month of the holiday season I worked so much overtime that I doubled my normal income for four weeks. That was good because I needed the money, but I was so tired driving back to Baltimore every morning that I would stop halfway at a rest stop on Route 95 in Maryland and sleep for an hour in my car. It was either that or fall asleep at the wheel!

So, I had ended the short-term crisis, now it was time to "worry about the rest later." I went to work early one day and used a Big Box Virginia office computer to apply for a transfer. It seemed like I waited forever, but eventually I got a call from a Big Box store in the Baltimore suburbs and they interviewed me. Good news, they wanted to hire me, bad news was they only wanted me if I would do the same overnight shift job for them that I had done for years in Virginia. Fine, whatever, I'll take it! Successfully gaming the system and getting a Big Box job in Baltimore after all, I said my goodbyes to everyone in Virginia, leaving their store for the second time in a year.

Girls Against Boys

The grass is always greener, they say. Who are they? Anyway, I was much better off at Big Box Baltimore of course. Yes, I had to drive from my apartment in the city to the outer suburbs for work, but it beat the commute to and from Virginia by a longshot. Also, I was looking forward to a new store with new people. Maybe I could even make a few friends at this new Big Box. I know that is a lot to ask, but I am a dreamer at heart. Hope springs eternal, and all that stuff. Eventually I did make some friends, since there was a bigger pool of coworkers to choose from because everyone at this Big Box was fluent in English! But Big Box Baltimore was bad in a very special way I had not experienced before.

There was a group of women at this Big Box who considered themselves tough and strong leaders. Problem was, no one had given them any authority, they operated whenever there was a vacuum of power at the store, which was quite often the case. Like watching a huge kindergarten class at Big Box, supervisors could not supervise everyone all the time, although some tried.

My new overnight group that set up aisles consisted of eight or so people and there were three of us guys – the guys were happy to see me added to their group and we became fast friends, watching ESPN SportsCenter on our breaks and talking football all night. The remainder of our group was made up of middle aged white women who seemingly had had no other jobs in their lives but setting aisles at Big Box Baltimore. It seemed unlikely they would ever work anywhere else at any other jobs (I laugh when I imagine them in an actual job interview). They fiercely defended their territory and jobs at the Big Box Baltimore, using their years of store-specific knowledge to terrorize their coworkers. I remember one of women saying

"I have this job and I know how to do it, why would I ever do something else?" Now that is what I call ambitious!

During my time at Big Box Baltimore the women burned through multiple supervisors. Of course, I mean who could manage these people? The first supervisor I had in Baltimore was a good young guy in his mid-twenties. As someone who started as a cart attendant at this store as a teenager when he was old enough to work, he had a lot of store-specific knowledge himself. He also knew the women well enough to take any opportunity he could to escape them. Most nights he would set us up with our assignment, then say "I'm going to work back in the warehouse by myself pulling merchandise for the aisles you're setting tonight. You guys don't need me anyway, you know what to do (!)" No, he knew what to do... run!!! This essentially left the women in charge, and they took every opportunity to tell us guys what to do.

Thankfully I had my Big Box Virginia experience so I understood the whole situation. My two male friends were tough guys outside the store I'm sure, but they wilted when confronted by the women. This is because it was all about control of information and store-specific knowledge, not physical prowess. The most the two guys could muster was an occasional "oh Mike, you know how they do," then reluctantly my two friends would comply with the women's orders. The women quickly gathered all the information on our assignments each night, then doled this information out piecemeal, so that they were the de facto bosses and in control. No one stopped the women – our supervisor was back in the warehouse hiding from them. So, very early on in my time at Big Box Baltimore I clashed with the worst of the women, essentially the queen.

In any job there are rules, and there are instances where you break rules in minor ways to work faster and more efficiently. Everyone in our group was taking shelves down and leaning them against the aisles; it is ok if one is careful, if not people can bump into them and fall with a loud crash. When I rested my shelves against my aisle the queen came over, ready to attack the new guy (me). She said "You know that's a violation of safety rules, you can't rest shelves against the aisle like that!" As an experienced Big Box grunt, I replied, "I know, but everyone else is doing it too," and went about my work. I guess I was supposed to cower in fear but I did not, and she went ballistic! All night long I could hear her gossiping with the other women, "Did you hear what he said to me!?!"

Later one of the other women came over to me and caught me looking disgusted and rolling my eyes. Knowing full well the answer to her question, she asked me anyway, "what's the matter Mike, are you mad?" Oh man. This shit would go on most nights. Two of us guys worked on one set putting a certain size of pegs into an aisle for a good hour or so in full view of the women. When we finished one of the women said, "you were supposed to use different sized pegs for this set." So I asked, "You saw us doing this all along and didn't say anything?!" Two of the women then looked at each other and just started laughing.

Soon our supervisor transferred to another store (not because of the women, of course not!). A guy from another store was hired as the new supervisor of our group and was fired as he was inexperienced and clueless about the work we did. The main thing I remember from his tenure was his favorite catch phrase… "Teamwork makes the dream work." This still makes me chuckle when I think of it. This manager's firing only emboldened the women. I think the store management became desperate (promoting one of the women within our group to be our new supervisor was out of the question). So the store moved in a middle aged woman from our store, who had supervised our group years before my arrival, to be our new supervisor. An experienced woman to supervise the women, and it was a great move on the store's part.

The women had no knowledge advantage over this woman and luckily for me she was a tremendous supervisor. Very fair, knowledgeable, and not harsh at all. Our new supervisor saw the politics of our group very clearly, it was the girls vs. the boys, and she did her best to keep us busy working apart from each other. When the boys and the girls had to work together, our new supervisor was right there to snuff out any disputes. One time when our group was meeting to go over the assignments for the night, our new supervisor paid me a great compliment. She said to everyone, "Do you notice, Mike *never* complains." The women just grumbled under their breath in response to this; they made a career out of complaining.

This fact dawned on my supervisor, and it might surprise the reader now because half of this book is devoted to me complaining about and mocking previous jobs, managers, and coworkers. That is true. And that is the point, actually. I was taught early in life not to complain at work and I rarely do. One thing this book is for is to get my complaints off my chest. I always keep things bottled up and often feel miserable at the end of each shift, but I do not know what else you do. One has to try to be professional in the workplace.

Hey Mike, Get a Life

Now that I was settled in to Big Box Baltimore I had to think about a second job. It needed to be part time and on the weekends, and I did find something that sounded interesting and doable. There was a valet parking company which had contracts with buildings around the city, and this company made the job sound good. Work at a downtown hotel, make big tips on the weekends etc. etc. I was skeptical as always but decided to give it a shot. The interview was fine (on the second try!). The first time I went to a scheduled meeting no one showed up, no one contacted me to apologize later, and when I called the company they were baffled as to what happened too. This should have told me something, but I had to try anyway.

I got a call or email, I cannot remember which, with my work assignment, great! Wait a minute, I was supposed to go to a big mall far outside Baltimore city. When I got there it was just a mall, no luxury hotel in sight, what was this? Well, it turns out the company was testing a valet parking service at the mall. What? You see, there was a big new fancy casino being built there and the valet company was in on the ground floor. Within a year or so the casino would open and valets who worked at the mall would have first dibs on the *lucrative* valet positions for the casino high rollers. Weren't we lucky!

This was ridiculous… instead of working at a downtown hotel I would have to drive way outside the city and for the foreseeable future valet cars in a huge parking lot at a mall. I just agreed to do it anyway, adjusting my sleep pattern each week… overnight work at Big Box during the week, daytime work Saturdays and Sundays parking cars. The tips were next to nothing, the conditions were awful (a long hot summer) and I was bald by 2011 so I wore a hat. Wait, the hat is not part of your official uniform, you can't wear that while working! A supervisor bought me a tube of sunscreen to put on my bald head. What a nice guy! I plugged away that summer in spite of all this, and when fall was near I got lucky – a hurricane came up the East Coast – yes! This meant I would not get sunburn on my bald head!

The news was projecting the hurricane to hit on the weekend, surely the valet company would not make us work in a hurricane, but just in case I reserved a room in a hotel next to the mall just in case. I am glad I did, because the hurricane arrived during my shift! People still came to the mall as the hurricane was hitting us (?) and guess what, more people than usual wanted valet service because it was pouring rain! Running back and forth through a torrential rain and huge puddles in the parking lot, the insides of the cars of these dummies became soaked because my coworker and I were drenched when we parked them. Oh man. We waited and waited for a manager to call a short end to our shift, visibility was low, it was insane. Finally the word came with the hurricane hitting full force. It was a damn good thing I had the hotel room, it would have been a difficult and dangerous drive back to the city. All is well that ends well right? Yeah… except the hotel room costed more than I earned on my shift. Hurray!!!!

During this summer I got some bad news about my father. He was retired on the coast of North Carolina and had become ill. I got conflicting reports on his health during that week, first it was bad and he was in the hospital, so I packed my bags ready to drive down there. Next our family was told he was sick but might be ok, so I was advised not to go to North Carolina right away. Finally though, my sister called me towards the end of one of my shifts at Big Box and told me it did not look good. I should go down there as soon as possible.

I caught a few hours sleep after my overnight shift then hopped in the car. I was in the car near Richmond when my sister called and left a message on my cell phone. I stopped off at McDonalds to listen to the voice message, which said my father had just passed away. Sad and exhausted, I crashed at a hotel in central North Carolina, deciding to go meet my family on the coast early the next day. It was very sad, but my father was older and had lived a full and interesting life.

In spite of the women at Big Box I was getting by ok at work. Things were settling into a routine. My father left most of his possessions to my stepmother of course, but he was very thoughtful in leaving part of his life insurance money to each of his four children. This final gift was a godsend to me, it took the pressure off me financially so I could stop working a second job for a while. I even used part of the money to take a Quickbooks course and passed the certification exam, since Quickbooks seemed to be in great demand at the time for bookkeeping jobs around the city. I hoped to secure one of these positions which were better and higher paying than Big Box, but in the end I had no luck. No responses, no interviews. I was getting older, and work options were fewer and farther between for me.

My life evolved into a routine similar to when I was at Big Box Virginia before the teaching bootcamp. It was ok, a good commute, friends at work, I got to live in Baltimore which I loved. But, nothing out of the ordinary was happening until by chance I became aware of a reunion show at the nearby "Ottobar" by the band Grey March. Grey March was one of the most popular bands in the Baltimore punk scene of the 1980's, along with Reptile House, Slug Log 3, Friends of Enemies, and my band 21 Deaf Men. I just had to go, yes to see Grey March but mainly to see if I recognized anyone in the crowd; although I lived in Baltimore I really had had no contact with any of the people from the 80's punk scene in 25 years.

I went to the Grey March show with a college friend and his wife and unfortunately I did not see anyone I recognized until wait a minute, a man and woman looked vaguely familiar. It hit me, it looked like Katie and "Toad" Brennan, brother and sister! My band 21 Deaf Men used to practice in their basement thanks to the kindness of Katie and Toad's mother, nicknamed

"Mama Toad," who was like a den mother to all the Baltimore punk rockers. I walked across the Ottobar and said hello, asking "are you the Brennan's, Katie and Toad?" They answered yes! "And who are you?" they asked. I replied that I was the former drummer of 21 Deaf Men who used to practice in the basement of their house! I spoke to Katie for a good ten minutes getting caught up on everything, and the next week contacted her by email.

Katie and I met first for coffee, after that dinner and a movie, realizing on the phone that we lived a block away from each other in Baltimore. Things went very well from there as we started dating, and over the course of 2012 it dawned on me. I had a job, I was not in crisis mode, I liked where I lived, I had a great girlfriend with whom I went out all the time. Holy shit, for the first time in ten years or so I actually had a life!

Best Wedding Ever

Life with Katie Brennan was just great... smooth and easy all the time. By Summer 2013 I moved out of my apartment and moved into her row house across the street. Six months later we were engaged. It all came very naturally and did not require much thought, things were fantastic and getting engaged was the obvious thing to do. In July 2014 we had what we like to call "The Best Wedding Ever." With our friends and family all there the wedding was a tremendous celebration and full of joy. It all went very quickly and I did not feel like I had time to talk to everyone at the reception as much as I wanted to; I almost forgot to eat something there because I was talking so much. This was a tipping point in my life, everything was much better after reconnecting with and marrying Katie.

Changes were happening at Big Box as well. I managed to make it through several years at the store in Baltimore but now the shift hours were adjusting. Instead of 10pm to 6am for the overnight shift, the new hours became 4am to noon. In theory I welcomed this, I thought it would put me on a more reasonable schedule during my time away from work. Once I started this, however, I realized how difficult it would be for me. There is no time more difficult at which to wake up for work than 2 or 3 in the morning. This change took its toll on me mentally and I soon found myself struggling more with my health. I started to have to call out a day here and there, and soon after I took a leave of absence for a few weeks. When I felt a little better I returned to Big Box but I could feel the clock ticking, I was not going to last much longer there.

The job market got better as the 2010's went on, and I was surprised to find another job quickly. I left Big Box for a job at a fast casual restaurant which had several advantages over my previous job. First and foremost a free meal every shift (!) and the hours were much more reliable – Big Box varied depending on the time of year. Also "Fast Casual" was walking distance from where I lived, so I sold the car saving a ton of money in the process. I was excited about something new to do.

The excitement did not last long. At jobs like this, just like at the kennel years before, there always seems to be someone who fancies himself in charge when he has no actual authority. This "Biggie Smalls, the Sequel" would always watch the work I was doing instead of doing his own, and kept yelling "Hey Mike!" I would drone in reply "What, Sequel?" The Sequel would always say "don't do it that way... do it this way, I'll show you." More often than not he would tell me a method that conflicted with what the real assistant manager told me.

The real assistant manager was a piece of work at times as well... "Mike, I need to see more urgency from you," then fifteen minutes later, "Mike, calm down, don't rush around." Or, "Mike, sweep from this part of the room to this other part of the room." Then, five minutes later after I was halfway done the room he would take me back to where I started originally, "No Mike, sweep from *here* all the way across the room." I would end up sweeping the same area over and over. I became fed up when The Sequel asked the assistant manager, "Do you think Mike should come in early tomorrow to watch some instructional videos on the computer?" Amazingly, the assistant manager would do what The Sequel told him, and the assistant manager agreed about the videos. When I got to work early the next day they did not even know which videos they wanted me to watch, it was a bit ridiculous.

These situations were annoying but the real problem was the pace and lack of breaks in this job. I went in thinking the tasks would be simple and straightforward, but they had me cooking food and washing dishes simultaneously. I would have been happy to only wash dishes all day just to have the job like at a normal restaurant. No, the orders to cook items almost never stopped. On the rare occasions when the orders did stop, I would get set up over at the sink, wash the first few dishes, then the call would come to cook more food! Dirty dishes would be piling up in the sink and on the floor, and the assistant manager acted as if I were not doing my work. The hours of the job were killing me as well, many times I would stay to close until 1am then report back to work to open at 7am. It was not long before I had to leave "Fast Casual."

With support and encouragement from my doctor I applied for Social Security Disability benefits; he said with certainty that my application would be granted, given my condition and the extreme lengths I had gone through to try to work in the past. He was right, and I took some time to decompress.

The Best Years Ever

After a long break during which I received disability payments, I managed to go back to work at a local Baltimore pet supply store under the Social Security Disability's "Trial Work Program." It serves as a safety net, one receives disability while one tries to work; if one earns more than a certain amount in a given month, the disability payment is returned to Social Security. This kept me relatively flush with money for a while, at least more so than in the recent past, but somehow I knew it could not last like this forever. Sensing this, I lived life to the hilt like there was some sort of timer set, and the buzzer was going to sound at any time to bring things to an end.

I took the train to Brooklyn, NY and saw my favorite singer Tracy Tracy of the Primitives perform. As I sat waiting outside the club on a city bench hours before the show, a woman came out and started walking directly towards me. It was Tracy! Apparently taking a break from her soundcheck, she sat next to me on the bench very preoccupied, fished through her bag in search of something for about fifteen seconds, then got up and was on her way. She has been my favorite singer for 30 years (!) and I always wanted to meet her. Still, I made a split second decision to just leave her be, and not say anything. New York can be a scary place and a small woman from England might be frightened by some random big guy loitering on a sidewalk bench.

Later I regretted this of course, and thought of a million clever things to say to her hours after the fact. Still, if she had been in a bad mood and snapped at me it would have killed me and my decades of being a Primitives fan. I will never know if I did the right thing. A year later another favorite English band of mine, St. Etienne, came to Washington, DC and I hopped a train to see them at a club on U Street. Once again, this time walking down U Street hours before the show, I spotted the entire band in the distance. I jogged in their direction but before I made it to them, they ducked into a restaurant for a pre-show dinner. To hell with it, I thought, remembering the lost opportunity with the Primitives, and I followed them to their table at the restaurant. St. Etienne was a bit surprised but very pleasant when I said hello, and I was able to take their picture before quickly allowing them to return to their menus.

Other trips during this period included visiting family at the beach in North Carolina, a weekend at Monticello in Virginia, and a road trip to the Finger Lakes in NY to see my best man and his wife. Finally, thinking that I might never again have the opportunity, I took a week off work and went to Ireland, the achievement of a lifelong dream. First Dublin, then a train to Belfast where I took a taxicab tour of the Shankill and Falls Road neighborhoods with a Belfast native describing his experiences during "The Troubles."

I was right to do these things while I could. There was to be no topping 2016-17 as I ran out of mental gas at the small local pet store. I am not going to recount all the difficult situations at work, I have done enough of that in this book. Well, ok, maybe one more to get off my chest. An older female customer asked me, "Can you assure me that the dog food isn't roadkill?" This was top of the line gourmet dry dog food at $70 a bag. "No, believe me, it is very good food." I replied. She responded, "But really, are you sure, can you be sure the food isn't roadkill?" What planet do these people come from?

My "career" cycle continued in the usual way, I hit the mental wall working at the pet supply store, had to quit and took a rest. In months I had the answer. Feeling better, I would try my hand at a well-known shipping and logistics company, and I might be ok because it would be all physical work. I was not ok, not at all. I greatly overestimated my physical abilities. At age 53 I was not able to handle the demands of this most physical job, it was really suited to twenty-somethings. Mentally too, it crushed me, as it was no leisurely physical activity. Working full-speed by myself for hours at a time in an area that really required two workers instead of one, I wilted under the mental pressure. It was a shame, as this was a great company, good coworkers, great managers, and plenty of opportunity for advancement given the exponential increase in online ordering and package shipping in the late 2010's.

I am in my mid-fifties now and I cannot cope with this revolving door of jobs any longer. Maybe I will change my mind in the future but I have a feeling this is the end of the line for me as far as work is concerned, so I better get used to being on disability and drop any ideas of advancing in a new career. I have made payroll deduction contributions to Social Security for 35 years. Now I need to take Social Security to keep me going.

The End of the Book?

So is this the end of the book? Who knows? Maybe in another twelve years I will write more. Maybe not. My career certainly did not turn out the way I hoped or expected early in life, but I had my moments. I worked in international finance, used my French and Russian, traveled for work to places like London, Moscow, and Kiev, and even taught social studies at a public school. These are all things I dreamed of doing when I was younger. Given everything that has happened to me it is a bit miraculous that I ended up in this good place. Living in Baltimore, married to my old friend Katie Brennan. I never accumulated a financial fortune after doing an MBA, but I've got things pretty good now nonetheless. My career is really over at age 53 it seems, but that is ok. The Ravens (Katie's team) and the Redskins (my team) each have televised preseason games on tonight. I am going to have some ice cream and enjoy the games with my excellent wife, and not worry anymore about my career.

Made in the USA
Columbia, SC
28 October 2018